A Short, but Foamy, History of Beer

The Drink that Invented Itself

A Short, but Foamy, History of Beer

The Drink that Invented Itself

by

William Paul Haiber

&

Robert Haiber

A Short, but Foamy, History of Beer
The Drink that Invented Itself

© 1993 by the Info Devel Press

Information in this book was developed by William and Robert Haiber for the Info Devels Inc, and its subsidiary, The Info Devel Press.

Book design by William and Robert Haiber

ISBN: 0–944089–09–7

LIBRARY OF CONGRESS CATALOG CARD NUMBER: 93–078823

First edition: December 1993

Printed in the United States of America

1) World—History—Brewing—Beer—Style guide

The Info Devel Press
La Grangeville, New York 12540
Telephone: 914.223.3269
Fax: 914.227.5520

Other Info Devel Press titles

The First Minnesota Regiment at Gettysburg
Manfred von Richthofen, the Red Baron
The Vanity Plate Spotter's Logbook
The Great Beer Safari
The Beer Drinker's Logbook

Titles distributed for CAMRA Books (UK)

The Real Ale Drinker's Almanac
The European Beer Almanac
The Great British Beer Book
The CAMRA Guide to Home Brewing
Brew Your Own Real Ale at Home
The Good Beer Guide 1994

"…I am in the process of becoming very serious here, almost

German; I believe this is caused by the beer. I am homesick

for Berlin. If I stay in good health I shall see whether I can

move there. In Bavaria, I have become a Prussian."

by

Heinrich Heine, the Rheinlander poet, in 1822, in a letter to
Varnhagen von Ense, his friend.

Table of Contents

Acknowledgements xiii
Preface xiv
Introduction xv
Clarifying notes xvi
Production notes xvii
Chapter 1:
What is Beer? 1
    Beer components 1
        Grains used in brewing 1
        Specialty grains 3
        Hops used in brewing 4
        Yeasts used in brewing..8
            Flavour imparted to beer by yeast 9
        Water used in brewing 10
        Adjuncts used in brewing 12
    Filtration & clarification 12
    Packaging beer 15
        Bottling 15
        Canning 16
        Casking 17
        Kegging 18
Chapter 2:
A History of Beer 19
    Brewing's Distant Past 19
        Back to the beginning 25
        The beverage stream 26
    A Babylonian vignette 27
    Early Christian Era 30
        The slow spread of brewing & hop cultivation in Europe 30
        The role of Christian clerics and monastic orders 31
        Brewing guilds 33
        Development of local styles...34
    Europe: The Middle Ages..34
        The Beer Line 35
    17th–19th Centuries 37
        Improved production techniques 37
        Spread of Euro brewing to the rest of the world 38
        Beer and European settlement of North America 38
        Hops become the predominant bittering agent 39
        British and Dutch brewing techniques, American ingredients ...39
        Lager is born and quickly supplants Ale..................................40
        Refrigeration aids beer's growth..40
        Railroad transport enlarges the market for beer 41
        German immigrants bring Lager to North America 42

Chapter 3:
Once around the Beer World **43**

Country reviews 43
    Canada 44
    USA 45
Latin America 47
    Mexico 47
    Argentina 47
    Brazil 48
    Belize 48
    Bolivia 49
    Chile 49
    Columbia 50
    Costa Rica 50
    Ecuador 50
    El Salvador 51
    Guatemala 51
    Honduras 52
    Peru 52
    Uruguay 53
    Venezuela 54
Asia 55
    Japan 55
    Hong Kong 57
    Korea (South) 57
    India 58
    Indonesia 58
    Malaysia & Singapore 58
    Sri Lanka (Ceylon) 59
    Taiwan 60
    Thailand (Siam) 60
    The Philippines 60
Africa 61
    Algeria 62
    Burundi 63
    Cameroun 64
    Central African Republic 64
    Chad (Republic of) 65
    Congo (Brazza) 65
    Cote d'Ivoire 65
    Egypt 66
    Ethiopia 66
    Gabon 66
    Ghana 67
    Kenya 68
    Liberia 68
    Malawi 69
    Mauritius 70

Table of Contents

Reunion Island 70
Morocco 70
Namibia (ex-Southwest Africa) 70
Nigeria 71
Rwanda 72
Senegal 72
Seychelle Islands 73
South Africa 73
Sudan 74
Tanzania 74
Uganda 75
Zaire 76
Zambia 76
Zimbabwe (ex-Rhodesia) 76

Europe 78
Albania (Republic of) 79
Austria 79
Belgium (Kingdom of) 80
Czech Republic & Slovakia 82
Denmark (Kingdom of) 83
Finland (Suomi) 84
France (Republic of) 86
Germany (Deutschland) 87
Greece (Ellas) 89
Hungary 89
Iceland (Republic of) 90
Italy 91
Malta 92
Norway (Kingdom of) 92
Poland (Republic of) 93
Portugal (Portugese Republic) 94
Romania (Republic of) 94
Russia (Russian Federation) 94
Spain (Kingdom of) 95
Sweden (Kingdom of) 95
Swiss Confederation 97
The Grand Duchy of Luxembourg 98
The Netherlands (Holland) 98
United Kingdom 100
Scotland 101
Wales 102
Isle of Mann 102
Channel Islands 102
Northern Ireland 102

The Middle East 103
Cyprus 103
Iran 104
Iraq 104
Israel 105

Jordan 105
Lebanon 105
Syria 106
Turkey 106
Oceana 107
Australia 107
New Zealand 108
Beer's future 109
Growth or shrinkage? 110
Anti-alcohol forces 111

Chapter 4
Beer Styles **113**

Ales: Top-fermented beer 114
Aged Beers 114
Old Brown/Belgian Brown Ales 114
Old Red 115
Holy Beers 116
Trappiste, Abbey & Belgian Strong Beer 116
Trappiste: 116
Abbey Beer 117
Dubbel and Trippel 117
Pale Beers 117
Special 117
Altbier 117
Kölsch 118
Pils Ale 118
Bitter 118
Best or Special Bitter 119
Extra Special Bitter 119
Pale Ale 120
India Pale Ale (ipa) 120
A story about a unique IPA 121
Strong Pale Ales 122
Strong Golden 122
Strong Pale Ale 122
Extra-strong Pale Ale 122
Dark Ale 123
Mild Ale 123
Brown Ales-British 123
Porter/Entire 123
Scotch Ale 125
Stouts 125
Bière de Garde 126
Old Ale 127
Strong Mild 127
Barleywine 128
Seasonal Beers 128
Bok Ales 128

Table of Contents

Christmas Ale/Winter Warmers 129
Saison 129
Other Seasonal Beers 130
North American Real Ales 130
Fruit Beer 130
Frambozen, Kriek & Peche 130
Other Fruit Beers 131
Spiced (&c) Beers 131
Wheat beers 132
Berliner Weisse 132
North German Weisse 133
Graetzerbier 133
Weizen 133
Dunkelweizenbier 133
Steinweizen 134
Weizenbock 134
Weizen-Doppelbock 134
Witbier 134
North American Witbier 135
North American wheat 135
Wild Beers/Lambic 136
Faro (also called Faro-Lambic) 136
Gueuze 137
Mars 137
Other Beers 138
Tafelbier-Bière de Table 138
Grand Cru and Cuvée 138
Dampfbier 139
Steinbier 139
Lager 139
California Common Beer 140
North American Lager 141
North American Light (low calorie beer) 141
North American NABLABS 141
Economy Beer 141
Standard & Premium American Lager 141
Japanese-style Dry Lager 142
North American Malt Liquors 142
North American Bock & Double Bock 143
North American Dark Lager 143
Real North American Lager 144
Continental Lagers 144
Oud Bruin (The Netherlands) 145
German NABLABS 145
Bière de Paris 145
Pilsner, Pilsener, Pils 146
Dortmunder-Export 147
Münchener (Munich) Bayerisches 147
Dunkles (Darks) & Schwarzbier 147

Table of Contents

         Hell (Light-coloured Lager) 148
         Märzenbier...148
         Wiener (Viennese) 149
     Bock Beers 149
         Doppelbocks (Double Bocks) 150
         Eisbock 150
         Maibock 150
         Bokbier 150
         Dubbelbok 151
         Meibok 151
         Real North American Bock 151
         Real North American Double Bock 151
         Strong Pils 152
         Rauchbier 152
         Liquor-flavoured Lager 153
         Stout Lager 153
   Belgium, a special place for beer 153

Appendices I
   Brewing organisations I
   Brewing schools I
   Brewing publications II
   Brewing statistics II
   Beer contents IV
Bibliography V
Definitions   VI
Charts XXII

Acknowledgements

In any undertaking of this scope and size, there are many behind-the-scenes people, without whose help, encouragement and constructive suggestions this work would surely be poorer and, thus, of less value to you, the reader. To them, we say, "Thank you very much". We hope to be able to return the favours.

So, without further yammering, here are the people who helped us in various ways, great and small:

Steve Cox and Roger Protz, writers *extraordinaire*, and all the others at the Campaign for Real Ale (CAMRA) for the hard work they've done over the years to promote Real Ale and quality beer;

Mein bruder, Matthias Fräbel, u Nicole, his lovely Frau, our main contacts in Germany who have done so much over the years to help our research;

Frau Martha Ott, of La Grangeville, for assisting us with translating German texts (and for cooking fantastic meals);

Ian McAlister at Merchant du Vin, the excellent beer importer, who organized much of the clip art used herein;

Mark Dorber of the White Horse pub, Parsons Green, for schooling me (however briefly) in cellarmanship, and for organizing that excellent special Bass IPA;

Bill Woodring for doing his very informative beer tastings, and helping me conduct beer judge certification study groups;

John (JC) Calen, Wendell (Cyberbrew) Choinsky, Nat (Ese) Collins, Jack (Zappa) Colon, George (Maibock) Martin, Steve (Studs) Williams, Bob (I'll bring over some beer) Delio, and all the others of the Hudson Valley HomeBrewers for the countless hours we've spent discussing beer and all its related subjects, and brewing togetherness (we've drunk quite a few, too);

Mike Bosak, ex-publisher of All About Beer, for giving me a start as a professional beer writer, and to Dan Bradford, the new publisher, who kept asking "when will the book be done?";

writers such as Michael Jackson, Fred Eckhardt, Alan Eames, and on and on, whose work have been a source and an inspiration;

Mission Bay Liquors and Ingrids Delicatessen, both of Pacific Beach, California, for stocking over 500 imported beers (combined), which started me down the inquisitive beer-path I've been on since 1976;

and finally, to my father and co-writer, William Paul whose decision, in 1970, to take the family to Germany on holiday first exposed us to high-quality beer like none we had ever had before; and to my mother, Florence (aka Merry Mutti, Mona, Laurie, Flo, Aiti, Ipo Wahini, et al), whose not-so-subtle hints that I should brew special batches for her, and "Where's the book?" comments which kept us chugging along.

REH—La Grangeville—2 November 1993

Preface

We have striven to give the reader a clear look back down the long road of brewing history. Many are unaware that brewing dates from Mesopotamia, ~4000 years BC. Even most home-brewers don't know they are engaged in one of man's oldest traditions. In fact, they carry the tradition forward.

We've broken the information down into four chapters, plus appendices. Chapter 1 describes the individual components of beer, and the brewing and packaging process. There is much work and skill that goes into making any beer. Chapter 2 is a purely historical look at beer, from brewing's beginnings up to present. Chapter 3 is a country-by-country review of beer and brewing. Population, production and consumption figures are given, as well as a look at past and current brewing happenings. We ask readers, especially those living outside North America and Western Europe, who have additional information pertaining to breweries and brewing histories in their particular countries, to send their information to us for use in future editions of this book. We want to make it even better by closing some holes left open due to lack of information. We plan to upgrade this book at intervals, as we gather more information (which is on-going. All reader help will be appreciate. Chapter 4 is a complete style guide with profiles of commercial beers used as examples. Finally, there are appendices of brewing statistics, charts and a list of beer and brewing definitions.

Introduction

Beer is back. For decades the juice of the barley has been held in low esteem—aided by the growth of "international brands" largely devoid of taste—while wine has been treated as the only alcoholic drink made with skill and rich in heritage. But now we know that it takes as much skill to make good beer as wine. And we know, too, that in such diverse countries as Belgium, Britain, the Czech Republic, Germany the Netherlands, and the United States there are beers, both ales and lagers, that offer a stunning cornucopia of aromas and flavours.

I have just drunk a fine Pilsener-style lager brewed on the island of Mauritius, a thousand miles from nowhere in the Indian Ocean. The message is spreading…

Americans are rediscovering the joys of ale as well as lager. My fellow beer writer, Michael Jackson, believes that the best India Pale Ales bare brewed, somewhat incongruously, in the United States. Having just drunk an IPA, in the Manhattan Brewing Co's brewpub, of enormous complexity, and with a shattering hop bitterness, I would not disagree with him.

Bill and Rob Haiber's brisk canter through the art and the mystery of beer is a timely tome. It unravels the history, the heritage, and the noble culture of beer, and will help you distinguish a Lambic from a Lager, and an Ale from an Alt. I heartily commend it to you, and wish you good drinking and many a foaming glass.

Cheers!

Roger Protz

☛ Roger Protz edits *What's Brewing,* national paper of the Campaign for Real Ale in Great Britain. His many books include the Real Ale Drinker's Almanac, The European Beer Almanac, The Great British Beer Book and The Village Pub.

Clarifying Notes

☞ In this book, the alcohol content of beer is indicated as either ABV 5.8%, or OG 1058, or possibly both, if they diverge. By this we mean, a beer normally attenuated by its yeast should typically have an ABV mark equal to the final two digits in its OG mark, divided by ten, as in the figures above. This isn't always the case. A beer, for example might have an OG of 1058, but an ABV of 5.4% (if it isn't fully attenuated). If it is highly attenuated, on the other hand, it might have an ABV of 6.0%. ABV stands for Alcohol by Volume, as opposed to alcohol by weight, another common unit of measure, which the Germans use. OG stands for Original Gravity, the specific gravity of the wort before it is fermented, measured at 60°F (15.56°C). OG (also called Starting Gravity, Starting Specific Gravity, and Original Wort Gravity) is a measure of the total amount of solid dissolved in the wort. Water is 1000. Any reading less than 1000, ie 0.995, indicates the liquid is less-dense than water. Often there is a decimal point in the figure, ie 1.000 or 1.058. We've omitted it, since most brewers speak the figure as "one thousand" or "ten-fifty-eight" (to use the two examples above).

We have recently been told that the OG indicator is on the way out in Great Britain, the victim of the excise man. Excise duty will be calculated on alcohol content and not on original gravity, as had previously been the case. We are sure it will continue to be used by home-brewers throughout the world because it is one of the scales on the necessary hydrometers most use.

☞ Temperature readings: we try to give in both Fahrenheit and Celsius.

☞ Hop bitterness readings are given as IBUS, International Bitterness Units.

☞ Throughout the text of this book, when referring to Huge Commercial Brewers, we use the letters HCBs to ease readability.

☞ CAMRA stands for the Campaign for Real Ale, a British-based consumer and pub preservation organization. It was founded in 1971.

☞ We have often maintained the spelling of foreign proper nouns (names and places) in their original language, whether it be Dutch, Flemish, French, German, or whatever. First, it is ed-ucational. It never hurts to have some foreign-language skills, especially on a topic that interests you. Many foreign beer labels are printed in native language, so knowing some brewing terms and ingredient names in other languages helps one comprehend what's written on the label (or other printed matter such as beer mats). Second, many brewers in English-speaking countries are now starting to brand their beers with non-English names. Sam Adams Weizenbock im-mediately comes to mind. There are many others.

Many English brewing-related words are very similar in other languages. Brewery is *brouwerij* in Dutch, *brauerei* in German and *brasserie* in French. City and place names, too, are easy to figure out. Bavaria is *Bayern* in German; Munich is *München*, &c. Other similarities are indicated in the text.

☞ Units of measure abbreviations immediately follow the figure with no space between them, or punctuation, ie $3m is three million dollars; 28gm is twenty-eight grams; 18lb is eighteen pounds; 128mi is one hundred and twenty-eight miles, and so on.

Production of this book

(Technical stuff)

This book was produced on an Apple Macintosh IIci computer.

Page layout and all editing was done using NISUS, an excellent text processing application published by NISUS Software Inc of Solana Beach, CA. We chose NISUS because of its superior text-handling, spell-checker, editing, and contents- and index-making capabilities.

The front and back covers were laid out in Quark XPress 3.1.

Body copy type is set 11/13 in Palatino, and some of its various faces. The headline font is Optima set, variously, at 24pt, 16p and 14pt. These Postscript fonts are published by Adobe.Systems Inc.

Output was done using an NEC Silentwriter 95fx Postscript laser printer.

Artwork was done, diversely, in Aldus Freehand, Adobe Photoshop 2.5, Fractal Design Sketcher and Color Studio 1.5. Image management was greatly helped by Aldus Fetch 1.0.

Scanning was done using Ofoto 2.0 by Light Source Computer Images Inc.

Typeset by R Haiber using *The Economist's Style Guide* as reference.

Much thanks to all in the Macintosh companies mentioned. Without their hard work to bring these products to market, desktop publishing would not have developed to the extent that it allows us to publish this book.

Chapter 1: What is Beer?

BEER IS A generic name for an alcoholic beverage produced by fermenting grains (cereals), usually barley malt, or a mixture of grains such as malted barley and wheat. Beer is flavoured with hops, and sometimes with other herbs or spices. Alcohol strength varies from near nil in the No alcohol/low alcohol beers (NABLABS) to about 14% by volume (Samiclaus Bier from Switzerland, and Guinness Book of Records entry as the strongest beer).

That's the short of it. Good morning.

The etymology of the word English word beer is from the Latin verb *bibere,* to drink. In other languages beer is spelt *bier* (German, Flemish and Dutch), *bière* (French), *olut* (Finnish), *cerveza* (Spanish), *cerveja* (Portugese), *cervoise* (French, again), *cerevisia* (Latin) and *cervogia* (Italian).

We have become aware that while most people know of beer, they do not know its components, or only one or two of them. People will usually say grain, and the obvious water, when asked what is in beer. In researching this book, we found another author who commented similarly, except that it was his observation that most people guessed hops, as the main ingredient. No one ever says yeast. It is the forgotten third (fourth, counting water) ingredient without which fermentation would not occur.

There are many ways to brew beer. Some ways are very traditional, even ancient. Others are high-tech. The processes are multi-stepped and require great care in execution. Bacterial infection can occur at any stage after the wort is boiled, so the risks can be high, but they also can be overcome with strict sanitary controls.

Brewing is as much a science as it is an art. In fact, science runs through it, from biology to chemical reactions to the physics of heating, cooling and liquid dynamics.

Indeed, to do something so simple as to change the shape and the size of the fermenting vessel alters the profile of the beer. Why? A reason is: yeast live differently in tall, thin and conical fermenters than they do in long, wide and flat fermenters. Drastically restyling the profile of a brand of beer (accidentally or not) can promptly destroy its drinkers' loyalties (people being the habitual creatures they are).

Beer components

Grains used in brewing

THE PRIMARY GRAIN used in brewing is barley, which is malted to varying degrees, and sometimes roasted and even smoked (like ham, not tobacco). Wheat is used with barley to brew certain styles. The most famous wheat styles are the Berliner Weisse, Bavarian Weizenbier and Belgian Wit (white) Bier from the town of Lueven, a few miles from Brussels. Wheat is also used in making many of the Belgian fruit beers and Lambics.

To a much less extent, millet, corn, rice (the last two heavily used by huge commercial brewers (HCBS) in the USA), rye and oats are also used to brew.

Four ingredients, excluding adjuncts such as Irish moss, a clarifier, and a list (too long to go into here) of chemicals most major brewers use as short-cuts from the traditional brewing process, go into beer brewing. They are: water (a natch); yeast, the agent of fermentation; hops, to preserve and to give taste balance and aroma to beer; and grains, which contain the "sugars" yeast convert into alcohol. Grain also figures prominently in the taste and the aroma characteristics of beer. It is the different grains of the grass family of plants (Gramineae), barley, wheat, maize (corn), rice, millet, rye and sorghum used in beer brewing that we will examine here.

German brewers are restricted by the original *Reinheitsgebot*, their beer purity law, to using only malted barley grain (and hops and water) when brewing. Later, malted wheat (and yeast, when it was discovered) was encompassed in the law. The European Union, formerly the European Community, only recently, passed regulations that forced Germany to open its door to beer that did not conform to the *Reinheitsgebot*. German brewers, Becks drinkers take note, are allowed to brew non-*Reinheitsgebot*-conforming beer on export-basis only.

Brewers in other countries, not faced with the strict prohibitions their German colleagues faced, stayed, in the main, with barley, but used other grains too. Their motivation might have been from simple desires to experiment: "John, what say we toss a sacka these here oats into that there Stout mash and we'll see wot we get, eh?" Or it could have been driven by an accountant's sharp pencil: "Mr Buschmann, you can increase company profits 39% if you substitute more rice and corn for the barley. Beer drinkers are stupid. They won't notice the difference. The Board will surely give you a rise with profits going up." Sometimes it was a matter of brewers being forced to use whatever fermentables were at hand. African brewers use cassava flour, millet and plantains, for example.

Now we'll examine each grain.

Barley: Barley are not all the same. The name is a catch-all noun (like cats and dogs and horses), as there are many varieties. There are two main branches of the Barley family: six-rowed and two-rowed. Six-rowed barley (winter barley) has three rows of spikelets at each node. Upon each spikelet six rows of grain grow. It has less well-developed kernels, and has thicker husks than two-rowed barley. Consequently it yields less. On two-rowed barley, also known as spring barley and Chevalier barley, only the central spikelet (of each three-spikeleted cluster) is fertile, forming two rows of kernels. It is the best barley for brewing because its kernels are better developed and the husks are thinner.

Spring barley is mostly used for lager brewing and winter barley for brewing ales. Probably the best winter barley variety is named Maris Otter, though it is coming under pressure from the Halcyon and the Pipkin varieties because they have higher yields, which brewery accountants and farmers love. They earn grain merchants more commission.

Barley malt must be low in nitrogen content. If it is too high, brewers will have problems with the head retention of their finished beers, and force them to resort to less-suitable cereal adjuncts to correct this predicament. Finding barleys with the proper nitrogen content is increasingly difficult, what with modern intensive-farming techniques that call for the use of chemical fertilizers.

Barley is malted at different temperatures, thus producing different characteristics brewers want. It is also roasted, particularly for use in Stout. Roasted barley, as opposed to roasted barley malt, may not be used by German brewers because it has not been malted.

Wheat: There are thousands of varieties of wheat, divided into two classes, soft wheat *(Triticum vulgare)* and hard wheat *(Triticum durum)*. Wheat is used both in malted and unmalted form. The first form is used in beer produced in Germany, Belgium and increasingly so in the United States. When used in malted form it is considered a positive. When used in unmalted form, except in Belgian *Wit* beers, it is called an adjunct (usually with negative connotation). Adjuncts are used to correct the composition of the extract, to produce cheaper beer, or to put out lighter-bodied, less-malty beer. All proper wheat beers are top (ale) fermented, and many are bottle-conditioned. *Weizenbier* contains 50% or more wheat malt. Belgian wheat beers are in the 30–50% range and *Weisse* 25–30%.

Corn/maize: Corn, in flaked form, is used as an adjunct to produce light-bodied beer. Corn produces alcohol, but virtually no colour or flavour when fermented. It is cheaper than barley. Large American brewers use up to 40% corn in their beer. The corn is first cooked (the same applies to the other grains except barley) until it gelatinizes. Without this process, the starch molecules cannot be reached to be broken down by malt enzymes.

Then it is added to the mash.

Rice: This grain *(Oryza sativa)*, too, is used to brew light-coloured beer. Rice, being white, has no colour that can be extracted during brewing. It does produce alcohol, which Sake-drinking Japanese have known for centuries. Rice has more starch (70%) than any other cereal, but less protein (7–9%). In the United States, it is not uncommon for brewers to use 40–50% rice. In Europe, the ratio is 10–20%.

☛ A tip when buying beer. Read the ingredients label, short though it might be. If the label has words to the effect: "Brewed using the choicest select grains" you can be sure the beer was brewed using adjuncts. Such a beer could only be considered premium in the brewer's (and his advertising agency's collective) mind. Don't be fooled by propaganda. Much of this ignorance stems from the propaganda (we prefer the Spanish word for advertising) of the Huge Commercial Brewers (HCBS). There is never a reference to ingredients, except possibly "Mountain water", &c, as if that makes much of a difference.

Oats: These are cereals from any plant in the *Avena* genus of the *Gramineae* family. The most famous beer brewed with oats (flaked) is Samuel Smiths Oatmeal Stout, a fine beer.

Rye: This grain, from the plant *Secale cereale*, isn't much used in brewing commercially, though some home-brewers experiment with it. In Finland, *Sahti*, a beer, is brewed using barley and rye malts.

Norwegians, in the 19th and 20th centuries, home-brewed using oats and rye, but the results were too-bitter beers.

☛ In conclusion, all grains can be used to brew beer, but barley is absolutely the best of the lot.

Specialty grains

Now WE WILL discuss speciality grains made from Barley, but are processed differently.

Caramel malt: malt prepared from fully—modified sugar-rich barley that is lightly steeped, kiln-dried, re-steeped, and heat-dried again at temperatures of 150–175°F for one to two hours, thus converting the soluble starches within the grain to sugar (as in mashing). The temperature is then increased to around 250°F (121.11°C) with frequent colour checks. Caramel malt is available in pale (cara-pils) to dark colours, and is used in small amounts (12–15%) to impart sweetness, aroma and a coppery colour to beer. Synonyms are Caramelized malt and crystal malt.

Black malt: Partly-malted barley of moderate nitrogen content, germinated four to six days and kiln-dried down to 2–5% moisture. It is then roasted at high temperature (±250°F) for 2–2.5hr. It is used in small amounts in Stouts and dark beers to impart its colour and a burnt or carbonized flavour. It has no fermentable sugars. Therefore, all the solids extracted from it remain in the finished beer. Synonyms are Black patent malt, patent malt, carbonized malt, chocolate malt.

Chocolate malt: is similar to patent malt, but it is less-roasted, giving it a "chocolate" colour and lovely aroma.

Roasted barley: is unmalted barley that has been kilned to a dark brown colour similar to chocolate or patent malt, but it has a different flavour.

Roasted malt: is made from barley heated in sequential stages. The malt acquires a brilliant appearance whilst the endosperm turns black. Roasted malt is used to flavour stout and dark beers. **Synonym:** Vienna Malt.

☞ **Note:** Some of these items, and others, are discussed in the section on adjuncts.

Hops in brewing

THE USE OF hops in brewing first became common around 1000AD in what is now the Czech Republic. The practice spread westward and reached the Netherlands in the late 1300s. From there, hoped beer spread to Belgium, but the change from using herbs to hops was a slow and gradual process taking several hundred years. The use of hops in Britain didn't become accepted (meaning widespread) until the early 1800s.

Hops are now universally used in beer brewing. The main reasons for using hops in beer are: as a preservative; to impart some bitterness to the beer to counter-balance the sweetness of malt; and to give the beer a particular aroma. They are raised commercially around the world in such diverse places as England, Europe, North America, especially in the Pacific Northwest, Australia and New Zealand. Some home-brewers in this area of New York are re-introducing hops, where they are doing quite well.

Hops are one of four essential ingredients in beer, the other three being malted grain (usually barley and sometimes wheat), water and yeast. Indeed, the *Reinheitsgebot* strictly forbids the use of anything else in commercial brewing. No other country has such a strict law, though Norway and Finland have similar regulations. They allow their brewers to use whatever they wish (but, obviously, within their food and drug regulations). Without hops beer would be a very sweet drink. Therefore hops are the "balancing" agent in beer. There is, in Europe, a product called malt beer that is a nutritious drink. It contains very little alcohol, and was originally brewed for children and nursing mothers, and is now consumed by sportsmen and the health-conscious also. Captain Bligh, of HMS Bounty fame, tried a similar concoction with his sailors as a scurvy inhibitor (the preventative powers of citrus fruit had not yet been discovered).

Hops are a climbing perennial vine with the Latin name *Humulus lupulus*. They can grow to 30 feet tall or more. It is a member of the *Cannabinaceae* family, thus making it a close relative of *Cannabis sativa*, the oft-dreaded/much-loved weed. As with pot growers, it is the female of the specie that has the desirable qualities needed for brewing. Male hop plants are up-rooted so as to not fertilize the female, which produces unwanted seeds. Fertilized hop cones, the part of the plant used to brew, have less bitterness than do their virginal sisters, quite the opposite of human behaviour. The British practise is to use, more often than not, seeded hops. Continental brewers avoid seeded hops.

A new dwarf variety of hops is being developed at Horticulture Research International. They have hop breeding grounds, run by Dr Peter Darby at Wye, Kent. These dwarf hops grow to only about eight feet tall. The advantage is that labour costs involved with harvesting traditional-height hop plants is greatly reduced. The costly systems of tall poles and wires can be eliminated, and automated harvesting equipment can be brought into the field instead of the cut-down hop bines brought by trailer to a central harvesting machine. The last change may, alone, halve hop farmers labour costs. These innovations will be quite a change from the days when London's Eastenders used to take their holidays working at hop farms during harvest at the end of August (they were often too poor to take a proper holiday. In this way they at least got out into the clean country).

The dwarf strain was first identified around 1911 by Professor Ernst Salmon, who began the hop research programme at Wye. He chose to ignore it, figuring it had "no direct promise", but times have changed. By 1997 all the brewing trials on the new varieties should be complete. Then the commercial hop growers of England's South-east and West Midlands will can begin raising the new types. So far, results of the trials have been encouraging.

Dr Darby said, "Dwarf varieties produce a hop with exactly the same brewing quality as from a conventional plant."

Returning to pre-mechanized days of hop harvesting, here is a description of how hops were harvested. This is an extract from an article written by Clem Huzzey, published in The Guardian Weekend, 23 October 1993. Mr Huzzey recalls an activity that he was a part of from practically his birth in Worcester and, sadly for some, is no more.

"*The soothing aroma seemed to permeate my entire childhood. My first 18 months were spent in the old hop warehouse in Sansome Street, Worcester; and even when I knew the building later as a solicitor's office the usual stationery smells could never completely mask the lovely, lingering presence of dried hops.*

"*...Over the years, the hop pockets had been stored on wooden floors and the pollen had trickled between the joists.*

"*...my parents moved to a pair of knocked-together labourer's cottages about four miles north of Worcester. These lay on the western slope of the Severn Valley, with acres of hopyards on the level land below.*

"*In the hopyards, the system of poles and wires supported two rows of hop vines rising from ridges of soil, with a cart's width between the ridges. The young shoots were trained up the newly-strung twine in the spring, the mass of cords giving a brown tinge to the whole field before the plants clad them in pale green. Training the plants was seasonal work for the labourers's wives, who boosted the farm workforce of the Fifties. ...*

"*Then the pickers came: some were Gypsies...pitching tents and caravans in or around the coppice in the middle of the plantation would be country families, arriving on foot to earn some much-needed extra cash; the majority were collected from Worcester city, often being transported to the countryside in a hosed-out cattle lorry provided by the farmer; and, finally, there were the fringe pickers—such as my sister and I, and the farmer's family.*

"*Most of the picking—close repetitive work—was done by women, and the common denominator was prams, pushchairs and children. So long as the weather stayed fair the hopyards had a holiday look and atmosphere. But if heavy rain came, the red Worcestershire clay soil turned into a dismal quagmire—and then the pay was really earned, as the prams and pushchairs which carried so much became a liability.*

"*Tools were few and simple. A hand knife cut the vines near the ground, and a blade lashed to a pole cut them free of the wires at the top, A good tug then brought the whole plant falling down.*

"*The hop crib was shaped just as the name suggests Stout beams, bolted together, formed a St Andrew's cross at each end; then a sacking pocket for holding the picked hops was stretched between the two crosses.*

"*Picking from the cut vine into the crib was constant labour. Nimble fingers were needed to pull the yellow-green flowers gently from the stems into the sacking without any leaves or woody pieces. As you picked, your fingers changed colour: first, they were merely yellow, and aromatic with pollen; then they turned true green; and any prolonged work at the crib made them black, deep into every wrinkle. The pollen only washed off with time and effort, but the aroma from your hands was heady.*

"*Cribs were covered at night and in bad weather. Regularly, during the day, the pickers bounced the sacking upwards to fluff up the hops. Pay was by the wicker bushel basket, so crushed hops were money lost. Horse and cart or tractor and trailer carried the harvest to the farm where there were hop kilns."*

This brief recollection illustrates how hops used to be harvested in England, but it could as easily have been in Belgium, Germany, Bohemia or America. Mr Huzzey describes, with local variations, a process that was repeated yearly for centuries, if not millennia, until modern machinery changed it, and consigned the previous practices to history.

Hops are used in four forms: loose leaf, pellets, extract (syrup) and a "pre-isomerized" extract, used in clear-glass bottle beers as a preservative. The latter also acts to prevent "skunky" aromas that result from bottled beer being exposed to light.

There are three categories of hops from which brewers can choose. The choice is dictated by the use (and tradition) to which they are intended. The three categories are Copper Hops, Late Hops and Dry hops.

Copper hops are used in the boiler, ie the Copper (the boilers of old were made of copper). Copper hops are usually high in alpha acid, the bittering agent. When used in the boiling stage, less high-alpha acid hops than low-alpha acid hops are needed per brew volume, making them more economical.

Late hops are used just at the end of the boil, usually within the last 5–15 minutes, to restore much of the aromatic and flavour-giving elements that are driven off during the boil. These elements evaporate very quickly when heated. They are also called volatile.

Dry hops are inserted either in primary, secondary or in the cask directly after filling. The purpose of dry hops is to add additional aromatic properties to the beer.

To avoid imparting harsh hop bite to beer, high-alpha acid hops should not be used as Dry hops. Goldings and Fuggles are traditionally the most popular dry hops in Ales.

What of the history of hops? The use of hops in beer dates from somewhere between the 10th and 7th centuries BC. Egyptians, at least from 600 years BC, are known to have flavoured beer with hops. Germans cultivated hops as early as the 3rd century AD. French and German monasteries, prime brewing centres in the medieval period, extensively cultivated hops. From there, their use was extended to Belgium, the Netherlands, Ireland and Britain, most often by monks spreading the Christian word. Jean Sans Peur founded, in Flanders, the *Ordre du Houblon* in 1409 to encourage the use of hops in brewing.

Before their introduction in to brewing, hops were preceded by herbs and spices such as absinth, camomile, cloves, cockle, coriander, cumin, gentian, guassia, lime blossoms, nutmeg, oak leaves, romarin, rosemary, et al. Fruit was also used, as it still is today in several Belgian brands such as Crombé's *Oud Kriekenbier*, Liefmans *Frambozen* and Vander Linden's *Frambozen*.

Presently there are over one hundred varieties of hops grown around the world. The most well-known hop-growing regions are Germany, ex-Czechoslovakia, ex-Jugoslavia, England, the Pacific Northwest of the United States and Tasmania. New York was, at one time, a hop-growing region during its brewing haydays of the 1800s, but a blight forced eradication of the crop. They are gradually being re-introduced by home-brewers in their gardens. The best-known hops are Brewer's Gold, Bullion, Cascade, Challenger (Wye), Cluster,

Comet, Eroica, Fuggles, Galena, Hallertauer, Kent Goldings, Nugget, Northern Brewer, Northdown (Wye), Perle, Saaz, Styrian Goldings, which isn't a Goldings but, rather, a Fuggles variety, Tettnanger, Willamette (another Fuggles variety, Target (Wye), Yeoman (Wye), and Zenith (Wye). Hop varieties with (Wye) following their names were developed at Horticulture Research International's hop breeding programme at Wye College, England. Fuggles, Goldings, Hallertauer and Tettnanger are often called "noble hops" because they are so associated with excellent ales and lagers.

Some hops are most-prized for their bittering flavours, others for their aromatic qualities. They are commonly called bittering hops and aromatic hops. Two of the most bitter hops are Galena, grown in Washington and Idaho with an alpha acid content of 12.5–13.5%, and Northern Brewer, grown in Kent, England with an alpha acid content of 8.5–11%. It is also grown in Washington and Oregon where it has an alpha acid content of 9.5–10.5%. Kent Goldings, an aromatic hop, has an alpha acid content of about 4.0–5.0%. Another aromatic hop is Hallertauer, which has an alpha acid content of 7.0–8.0%, but we've recently bought some with a listed alpha content of 2.9%. Go figure. Actually, the biochemical make-up of hops varies from crop to crop. If for some reason the alpha acid content of a particular crop decreases, so does its price. Brewers won't pay the same for a hop that they need to use more of to attain a specific bittering rate.

Besides the bittering hops imparts to beer, it also adds to beer's aroma and flavour, it reduces surface tension during the boiling stage of brewing, assits in the forming of the yeast head during ale fermentation and, very importantly, inhibits the growth of bacteria in wort and in beer, in effect acting as a natural preservative.

Let's talk about the brewing process and the different hop-additions. Brewers usually boil the wort for one to three hours. The fullest utilization rate is about 28–30%. Boiling hops for, say, less than 15 minutes has a utilization rate of about 5%. German brewers typically have two-hour boils; some Belgian beers are kept on the heat "over night". The bitterness hops imparts is caused by its alpha acids (stated as a percentage, which varies from crop to crop and variety to variety). Boils of under one hour, as just mentioned, do not extract the full amount of alpha acids and hop oils, the latter mostly driven off by steam evaporation. Hop oils are extremely volatile. They are responsible for hop aroma of beer. The hops selected as bittering hops are added at the beginning of the wort boil (usually at a rate of 200 to 700gm per hectolitre of wort). This causes "hop break", the precipitation of unwanted proteins and tannic materials. Each time hops are added they cause another hop break in the boiling wort.

Near the end of the boil there is an other addition of hops. This addition imparts the bouquet one smells (even in a malt-dominant beer). Remember the hop oils are mostly driven off during the long boil. This late addition does virtually nothing to increase the amount of bitterness the brewer has calculated he wants in his beer, but it does release the hop oils necessary for bouquet. There is another addition of loose dry hops, called "dry hopping" that takes place either in the primary fermenter, the secondary fermenter (more often), or the cask (as in the case of cask-conditioned ale). Hop extracts (resins and oils) are not normally used, except as a short-cut, to dry hop beer because they contain traces of the organic solvents used to remove them from the hop cones. Cask-conditioned ales sometimes have some hop oil added to improve hop bouquet.

Hopping beer has more to it than buying a type of hops that, at the moment, strikes the brewers fancy, and then chucking a handful (or shovelful) of it into the boiling vessel at appropriate times. Over time, certain hops have become inextricably linked with particular styles of beer: Kent Goldings and/or Fuggles in English ales; Hallertauer in most German lagers; Galena, Nugget and Target hops with Guinness Extra Stout, Saaz hops with Pilsener Urquell. One is not a substitute for another, because doing so would alter the taste and character of each beer. Remember, once a beer has gained commercial acceptance, it cannot easily be tampered with, or else its loyalists might very well desert to some other brand. Most American HCBS have pulled this off, though, by slowly decreasing, over time, their brands' flavour profiles. Typical HCB-brewed American Lagers have a hopping rate of 2–4ppm over the taste threshold. Some simply introduce a "Lite" version (Good God, they can't even spell. Worse still is their atrocious habit of labelling as "draught/draft", canned and bottled beer. Draught beer, by its very definition, can only be kegged or casked).

Perhaps now that you know more about the role hops plays in the make up of beer, you will take time to savour it whenever you drink beer. Seek it out, both in the bouquet and in the taste of beer. There are only a cent or two worth of it in each pint, but it is as valuable to beer as is malt. As the old song about marriage goes, "You can't have one without the other."

Lieutenant Colonel Harold E Hartney, DSC, had an unusual encounter with hops during the first world war:

"And with a slithering crash we landed in a nice, muddy Belgian field, containing several hundred fifteen-foot hop poles, a familiar farming sight in that district."

Yeasts in brewing

BEFORE WE TALK about what yeast does, and its place in brewing, it is necessary to explain what it is, but first a word of warning. Like everything biological, discourse on the subject is difficult because scientists, in their great wisdom and desire to seem mysterious and more learned than the average person, adapted a Latin and Greek nomenclature. In this instance, because yeast belong to the plant family, they are named according to the International Code of Botanical Nomenclature (ICBN). Each yeast has two names. The first

indicates its family (genus), the second, its species. There has been some name changes as the icbn has been accepted. Old habits take a while to die. Actually, it is not a bad scheme because it simplified matters by improving communications between scientists speaking different languages. Whilst it's not important for lay people to know scientific nomenclature (mankind, no matter what language they speak use local words for whatever it is they are describing. People don't sing, "When the red, red Turdus Migratorius comes bob-bob-bobbin' along."), it is important scientists speak the same language. We will endeavour to keep scientist-speak to a minimum.

Yeast are microscopic, single-celled vegetal organisms of the fungus family. They are differentiated from bacteria because yeast have a true nucleus. They can resolve sugar into alcohol and carbonic acid.

There are two main classifications of yeast used in brewing, ale yeast (top-fermenting) and lager yeast (bottom-fermenting), plus a third, air-borne or wild yeast (top-fermenting) that are used by Belgian Lambic beer brewers. I've separated wild yeast from the others because they are not procured or pitched in to sweet wort in the same way.

Saccharomyces cerevisiæ is the scientific name for ale yeast. A brief etymology of the name. *Ceres* was the Roman Goddess of Agriculture (and therefore, grains). *Cervesa*, the Spanish name for beer, which, of course, is made from grain(s). When scientists first identified yeast in beer, it was a natural for them to give the yeast a name associated with beer since that is where they found it. The first half of the name derives from the Latin word *saccharum* (sugar), and the Greek word *mykes* (mushroom). Voilá!

Lager yeast used to be called *Saccharomyces carlbergensis* (it was first isolated to a single cell in 1846 by Emil Hanses, a micro-biologist working at the Carlsberg Brewery at Copenhagen, Denmark, hence the name), but has been renamed *Saccharomyces uvarum*. It is thought that lager yeast was first isolated early in the 1800s by Benno Scharl, a German monk. He ran a München-area brewery around 1810.

Saccharomyces candida is just one name amongst the many wild yeast names.

There have been over 500 different types of yeast identified. Not counted in that number are the wild yeast strains.

Antoine van Leuwenhoek, a Dutch scientist, was the first to view yeast through a microscope. This was in *1680*. It was nearly two hundred years later when Louis Pasteur discovered during his research into wine, that yeast lack chlorophyll. As a result, to develop they need an environment containing both carbon and nitrogen.

Commercial brewers normally either maintain their own yeast culture(s) in a laboratory, or they purchase it from commercial yeasts banks, which also operate under laboratory conditions. The strains brewers use are often pure single-strain cultures or, perhaps two *cultures used together. Lambic brewers, on the other hand, get their yeast cultures from nature: whatever comes in on the wind through the brewery, plus any residual yeast that has settled throughout the brewery. Wild yeasts belong, by nature, to the ale yeast classification, but rates a separate listing because of its uniqueness.

Ale yeasts, also called Top-fermenting or Top-acting yeasts, do their main work in the upper reaches of the fermenting tank. They ferment optimally between 59–77°F (15–25°C). Most stop fermenting below 55°F (13°C). One way brewers can clear their beer at the end of secondary fermentation is to cool the beer below 55°F (12.75°C). This causes most, but not all, of the yeast to precipitate to the bottom of the vessel. The now-clear beer is then separated from the trub at the bottom. This is a valuable technique homebrewers should use more frequently. The highest temperatures ale yeasts work at are in the 99–107°F range. It is a good idea for the temperature of the yeast slurry to

be very closely matched to that of the wort so the yeast are not shocked by sudden temperature change. This ensures a rapid start to fermentation, which in turn helps keep bacterial infections to a minimum.

Lager yeast, also called bottom-fermenting yeast, works toward the bottom of the fermenting vessel after initial fermentation commences. They work best at temperatures 41–50°F (5–10°C), but their maximum growth rate temperature range is 88–94°F (31–34°C). They can work at temperatures as low as 33–35°F (1–2°C).

From the above, one can see that lager yeast can be pitched at a fairly warm temperature, then as the yeast population reaches a peak of growth (in a matter of hours), the wort is then chilled to 41–50°F range. When primary fermentation is completed, the beer is racked to a secondary fermenting tank where the temperature is again lowered to near 0°F, for several weeks or months of conditioning. This period also clears the beer of most suspended particles.

Lager yeasts ferments slower than do ale yeasts. Too, they generally have less tolerance for alcohol than do ale yeast, but the two strongest beers, EKU 28 and Samiclaus, are lagers. Lager yeasts do convert dextrins much better, making for a drier beer.

Flavour imparted to beer by yeast

MOST PEOPLE THINK first of beer as being made of malt or, simply, grains. They think grains impart beer's taste and aroma. Perhaps the more knowledgeable understand hops and the role they play in the overall taste profile. Rarely, though, has it been our experience, when we have talked to people, other than (home)-brewers, who understand the critical part yeast play in defining beer's characteristics. Has any one ever seen a yeast depicted in a brewers logo? Of course not. There are plenty of representations of barley (either as stalks or as bulging bags crammed full of it), and of hops (either as climbing plants or as beautiful hop cones). What graphic designer/artists would depict a container full of frothing, vile-looking yeast in amongst the barely and hops on the label or advertisement they were creating for a brewery? One glance and the artist would be out on the streets again.

What we know is often limited by what we see (or what is shown to us). A picture may be worth a thousand words but, without descriptive words, the picture may very well be incomplete, or we may misinterpret it.

So, our ugly, unpraised, unrecognised yeast continues to be kept in the dark (where, incidentally, it likes to be) by brewers and their admen. Yet without it we would not have beer (and wine) or fermentation-derived alcohol. Isn't nature wonderful? (Hey, hey! Yeah, yeah, yeah, yeah!)

We will not go in to the biological and chemical processes caused by fermentation. It is extremely complex, and beyond the scope of this book. If you want to find out more, any home-brew book worth its salt will have a section devoted to yeast. Too, the American Homebrewers Association sells many books on brewing and can help you buy exactly what you need.

Returning to our discussion, what does yeast impart to beer other than alcohol? There are so many hundreds of aromas and tastes (and combinations thereof) we won't even attempt to begin describing them individually. Rather, take it for granted that, excluding the effects of oxidation, being light-struck and bacterial contamination (we are talking about commercial beers that should never have any of the previously stated maladies), any scent and taste that is not directly and clearly identifiable as either malt or hops (or their blends) comes from the yeast.

One could take and exactly follow a recipe for a beer, say, a Lager, duplicate it ten times, the only variable being ten different lager yeast strains, and you would have ten different smelling and tasting beers. Each yeast would ferment at a different rate, and to different degrees of attenuation, leading to greater or lesser amounts of alcohol production. Every one would convert dextrins at differing rates and degrees. In addition, each would produce different amounts of diacetyl and dimethyl sulphide at varying amounts and at different temperatures.

Think of yeast as being made up of two races, each consisting of many different tribes. Within each race, some tribes may be strikingly similar, yet different enough for them to distinguish between each other. Others tribes are clearly dissimilar, yet they do still all belong to the same race because they possess the same defining racial characteristics.

Many home-brewers know a technique for propagating yeast from commercial beer to use in their own batches. They do this because of the very few yeast strains available to them from home-brew suppliers. Often these yeast strains do not match the type beer they wish to brew. By preparing a malt solution, and then adding several ounces of beer from the bottom of a bottle of, say, Lindeman's Framboise Lambic. Within a week one could, with a good recipe and proper ingredients, be making a reasonably similar beer. Sane home-brewers don't try to duplicate HCB's domestic lagers, for example. Why bother when they can be bought inexpensively.

Water used in brewing

ALL WATER IS not alike. Yes, all water is made up of two hydrogen atoms and one oxygen atom. It is the suspended chemicals, salts, minerals and other elements that alter the characteristics of beer. Too, there is a difference between well-water and surface water that is prone to contamination from farm-use chemicals and other air-borne matter. Well-water is preferred because it is most likely to contain desired salts, especially calcium because it stimulates yeast growth and fermentation and aid yeast precipitation. Change the water, change the beer. Again, as with yeast, we won't go into detail about chemistry, &c. Instead we will detail two cities, Burton upon Trent, England and Dortmund, Germany, their water and how brewers in these two cities adapted to local conditions to produce unique beer styles.

Bear in mind that water was not the only reason these two cities prospered as brewing centres. Location and easy transport access actually had more to do with it than the waters, but the unique waters certainly defined the styles of beers that are classics. Water's impact on the taste of any beer is subtle, but minerals in water do enhance the sensation of bitterness.

It should be pointed out that water treatment is a traditional operation and should not be considered as an adulteration of the beer.

Before we get to the two cities, we want to point out that breweries are often, by far, the largest commercial users of water wherever they are located. What is obvious is that brewers consume vast quantities of water to make beer, since beer is mostly water. (Nature does recycle it all, in time.)

There has been a movement amongst brewers in North America and elsewhere to examine and implement ways to decrease the amount of water they use that gets turned into wastewater via their sanitation processes, waste-yeast and trub disposal. Every gallon saved reduces brewery operating costs at both ends. On the front end is their water bill, if hooked to a municipal system, or their electric bill if they are pumping water from their own wells. On the back end are sewerage disposal/treatment charges. Water conservation makes good sense environmentally and is good business practise.

Burton upon Trent

BURTON UPON TRENT is famous for its Bitter Beer and Pale Ale, the bottled version. Compared to London deep-well water, which has a total-salts concentration of 463ppm, Burton upon Trent has a concentration of 1,226ppm (265% higher).

The beers brewed there are world-famous, not because they are heavily marketed ala Budweiser, but because they are excellent examples of their style. They are virtually unmatchable without undertaking the very costly steps of altering local water to duplicate that of Burton upon Trent's. Brewers there have a competitive advantage simply because other brewers must make extra efforts to brew beer like ones brewers have been making there for a very long time. In fact, brewing has been going on at Burton upon Trent since 1004AD, most likely, at first, at Burton Abbey, founded by Benedictine monks two years earlier.

The first commercial brewery was founded at Burton upon Trent by William Bass in 1776, the year of America's Declaration of Independence. The brewery also holds England's first registered trademark on their logo, with its distinctive red triangle.

There were times when there were 40 operating breweries at Burton upon Trent, an incredible number. Another of the big surviving breweries at Burton upon Trent is Ind Coope, part of Tetley-Carlsberg, brewers of Double Diamond. Both Bass Ale and Double Diamond hold the prestigious "By Appointment to Her Majesty the Queen" designation.

Dortmunder wasser

EXPORT BEER IS Dortmund's contribution to fine brewing. The style is usually placed between the very hoppy Pilsener and the malty Münchener.

Only brewers actually in Dortmund may call their beers Dortmunder (under German law). Beers brewed elsewhere can be labelled Dortmunder-type beers. There is a subtle difference. Outside Germany, brewers will often tag their lagers as Dort or Dortmund beers, much as more and more brewers in North America are labelling their ales as British or Burton-style. The Dortmund Export name is a mark of distinction.

The water at Dortmund, again compared to London's 463ppm, has 1011ppm. Though it has lightly less salts than does Burton upon Trent, Dortmund does have more Sodium, Chloride and Carbonate. It has less Magnesium, Nitrate and Sulphate, and about the same amounts of Calcium.

When compared to München, 273ppm, or Plzen (Pilsen), 30.8ppm, the water at both Burton upon Trent and Dortmund seems hard as granite.

Adjuncts used in brewing

ADJUNCTS CAN BE defined as any ingredient other than malted barley, malted wheat (essentially all malted grain), hops, yeast and water used to make beer. Therefore, any use of adjuncts is illegal in Germany because they violate the *Reinheitsgebot*.

Unmalted wheat and barley, brown sugar, caramel (for colouring), corn, glucose (pure and as corn syrup), lactose (a sugar from milk), millet, molasses, oats, rice, rye, invert sugar, cane sugar, tapioca flour, wheat flour, flaked grains, and torrefied grains (popped, like corn) are typical adjuncts. Grain is flaked by steaming it, then running it through heated rollers.

Some are used to cut the cost of production, especially corn, rice and invert sugar. Belgian brewers typically use between 10–20% unmalted cereals to make their distinctive beers. This is an acceptable practise to all but the most die-hard beer purist.

Have you ever wondered how North American and Australian national brewers are able to brew beer so light-coloured that the only colour lighter is clear? Here's your answer. Inexpensive corn and rice produce alcohol, just like malted barley does, but they impart no colour. Used with the palest of malted barley, they are able to produce their inferior products. The power of propaganda (advertising) is so great they have been able to convince nearly everyone that the beer they brew is the best in the world. Nothing could be farther from the truth, except political campaign promises.

North American national brewers have created a unique style of bland, nearly colourless, fizzy alcohol-water, while they tout its "Old World" or European heritage. Bull chips. Their "Lites" and "Drys" are even worse. We do, though want to commend Miller Brewing Company for introducing their Miller Reserve Lager and their Miller Reserve Ale, which are all-malt.

We are not saying North American national brewers can't brew excellent beer. What we are saying is that they choose not to do so, with the above mentioned exception. The breweries of the nationals are some of the most technically excellent in the world. Too, we feel that the situation will probably change for the better as the growing avalanche of superb micro- and contract-brewed natural beers picks up steam and increases their market share, which has been happening.

North American national brewers and many French brewers use 30–40% adjuncts of the wrong type.

Filtration & clarification

HOME-BREWERS HAVE few options when it comes to filtration and, but a few more for clarification. Filtration systems are costly (most homebrewers strive to keep costs down— that's one of the reasons they homebrew). They can filter the hot wort as it is poured from the boiler to the primary fermenting vessel to remove the hops and coagulated proteins. To clarify beer they can resort to some simple techniques. After primary fermentation is complete, homebrewers can rack the beer off the sediment of settled trub, by syphoning into a secondary fermenter (also called a maturation tank). A further period, a week to several months, in secondary will result in more precipitation, especially if the secondary fermenter is placed in a cool place or refrigerator. The beer is then syphoned off the remaining sediment one more time, primed and bottled.

Fining agents also can be added to aid in clarifying the beer. Many home-brewers, though, follow the German practise of not adding any thing to their beer except what is permitted by the *Reinheitsgebot*.

What, though, of commercial brewers? What choices do they have, and what reasoning determines their decision to filter out yeast or not to? The dilemma is really multifaceted. The pros and cons of filtering are much more complex than simply determining what taste characteristics they want to impart to their beers.

The first decision commercial brewers must take is whether or not the brands they market are going to be bottled or kegged. This is often determined by finance. Bottling lines are very expensive, label design is likewise, and label approval is time consuming. It is much simpler to keg. Too, kegged (draught) beer is consumed much quicker than bottled beer, therefore eliminating a main concern of brewers—shelf life of their product. Normally, draught beer is consumed within 30 or 40 days. Brewers view this as short-term. Should a brewer determine to take a long-view, 120-plus days, he invariable will choose to bottle his beer, seeking stability and consistency. To achieve this he must, then, filter it to some degree.

There are exceptions.

The exceptions exit because there are so many styles of beer (beyond the broad ale and lager categories), several different means of production and delivery, method of dispense, and varying historical and localized consumption habits and tastes. The alcohol content of beer is, also, a factor. The stronger the beer, the longer it will keep in bottle. Eldridge Pope's Thomas Hardy's Ale, for instance, with an original gravity (OG to brewers) of 1125 (ABV 12%) will keep for twenty to twenty-five years. In fact, it is not very good the first few years until the yeast has had a chance do its magic. These factors play important roles, influencing a brewer long before he unveils his first brand to the drinking public and the media.

It's a given that A new micro-brewer, without sufficient finance no instal a bottling line must, instead, keg. He determines how many different styles of beer he has capacity to offer (and market): say, three; an American Pilsener (think Budweiser), a Burton-style ale and a Stout. The most likely of the three to be filtered would be the lager, which to be marketable, should be crystal clear—like all good-looking Pilseners. The Ale and the Stout will drop bright during a proper-length stay in secondary fermentation tanks.

If, on the other hand, our make-believe micro-brewer had chosen to brew a weizenbier mit hefe (a top-fermented Wheat Beer with yeast [in the bottle]), a very popular style in Germany presently, especially amongst young people, filtration would obviously be out of the question.

Consider, now, a larger brewer, a regional, with both a bottling line and kegging equipment. He needs to decide whether or not to offer the same beer in bottle and in draught. If he does, he will more than likely filter both. If not, he won't filter the draught beer, and market it as a fuller, more robust-tasting version of its bottled twin. By the way, "genuine draft" in a bottle or can is ludicrous. If it were so, then the draught version is as dead as the bottled. The expression Dead is used by beer judges, and those who know, to refer to beer that has all its yeast removed by filtration and pasteurization, and is artificially carbonated before it is bottled or kegged. Now, dear reader, you know.

What does filtration gain the brewer, especially his bottled beer? Time and taste consistency, or as Bill Newman, brewer of Newman's Albany Amber and Saratoga (a Dortmunder-style) Lager told me, "stability". Knowing that much of his bottled beer will sit at point-of-sale locations for months before being bought and consumed (how many of us are guilty of buying beer and then leaving it in the fridge for God knows how long before drinking it, or attempting to? Tastes bloody awful, dunnit?). This a brewer tries very hard to avoid because of the bad-mouthing his beer will get from consumers. One or two bad batches have been known to ruin a brewer. Cautious brewers will yank their product from store shelves by expiry date to ensure, as best they can, that consumers get the freshest beer possible. Small-capacity breweries have the worst of it because uncaring distributors give them short shrift, preferring, instead, to promote the monster brewers' products.

Then again, a small brewer with a bottling-line, serving a small geographical area, with demand so great that everything he brews is immediately bought and consumed can dispense with filtration. This is a common situation in many countries. Think of Germany with its 1,100–plus breweries. Belgium too (though with not nearly so many breweries). The beer drinking traditions there, and in many other countries are to drink their beer fresh, unfiltered, but often clarified, and dispensed out of hand-pumps drawing from wooden casks. This is a tradition CAMRA has been fighting twenty-one years to maintain. In the United States, such Anglo-Saxon and Germanic traditions died, sadly, with Prohibition. Thankfully a revival, of sorts, has been underway here. Micro-brewers are the new standard-bearers of this rebirth.

So, what does all this mean, and how does it affect beer? I've left the explanation of the effects filtration has on the taste and appearance of beer towards the end because it is actually very short. Nat Collins, owner of the newly established Woodstock Brewery at Kingston, NY told me: "By passing beer through a very fine filter, made of either of diatomaceous earth (6–8 microns fine), which is a primary filter placed between secondary and finish tanks, and/or a membrane of sterile cellulose, placed between the finish tank and the kegging or the bottling apparatus, solid matter in suspension is removed. Particles as small as 0.50 microns (a micron is one thousandth of a millimetre) are removed. This eliminates yeast, bacteria, solids produced during fermentation such as protein fractions and polyphenolic compounds." The latter two cause chill haze, a condition brought about by chilling beer too quickly, too cold or for too long. It appears at about 32°F and disappears at about 68°F. The removal of these particles, called colloidals, makes a beer thinner tasting, less malty, and more neutral tasting than its unfiltered version.

If one's sole goal of drinking beer is to get drunk, this all means nothing. We hardly suspect those people of reading anyway. To those who are into seeking and enjoying beer in all its styles, knowing the pros and cons of filtration can influence several things: your understanding of why beer can taste so differently within its style, the choice you make when selecting beer, and give you a little better insight in to why brewers might take the decisions they do.

The health conscious, too, should be aware of the nutritional value (real beer is full of vitamins), and lack of chemicals, of unfiltered, naturally-carbonated beers.

Most home-brewers would chose an unfiltered fresh beer, given the choice. Unfortunately that is not often the case, but given the ever-growing number of micro-breweries throughout America, more and more people are getting the opportunity to experience the pleasures of tasting fresh beer at its best.

Packaging beer

THERE ARE FOUR ways to package beer: bottling, canning, casking and kegging. The first two are for "individual serving" sizes, and the latter for bulk packaging. Of the four, casking is probably the least-known in North America.

☛ **Note:** refer to the section Filtration and Clarification, to read more on this subject. There we discuss the processes brewers go through deciding how to package their beer.

Bottling

BOTTLING CAN BE done by hand, as homebrewers and very small micros do, or on very expensive, automated bottling lines. These are often, initially, out of the reach (financially) of micro-brewers. There is a saying: "The bottling line is at the bank."

Like just about everything connected with a brewery, the room a bottling line takes up can be enormous—sometimes even complete buildings. The HCBS have many bottling sites. In a country the size of the United States, operating this way is essential. Other brewers might resort to shipping their beer in bulk to regional bottling sites. It is cheaper to ship a train-load of beer in bulk than it is once it has been bottled—glass is heavy, after all.

Label design and bottle design are areas where breweries can really strut their stuff to the public. An awful lot of thought goes in to both. Indeed, the bottle Carlsberg Brewery uses was so well-designed that it has a permanent place in a prestigious art museum. Too, most beer drinkers can identify Budweiser's long-neck bottle from across a pub. Other brewers have adopted it as well. Refer to Grolsch beer and some one will immediately mention their distinctive ceramic-capped 16oz bottle. The bottle is a favourite of home-brewers. Not only do they have to fill fewer bottles, they don't have to manually cap them with an awkward implement either.

Brewers are also innovative when it comes to bottle labels, &c. Some place front, back and neck labels on the bottles. Others paint the glass directly. Japanese brewers use beautiful label art. Others wrap the crown with different coloured foil. Sometimes this signifies something, other times not. In 1970, while touring the Carlsberg and the Tuborg breweries, we were "clued" to grab all the gold foil-crowned bottles as fast as we could once we reached the tasting room. They were quicker to identify that way rather than reading each label!

We would be remiss if we didn't mention that bottle colour is important to the preservation of beer. There are three colours used, brown, green and clear. Green glass is as useless as clear glass, in preventing light-struck beer. Beer can quickly become light-struck if bottled in other than brown glass. Light-coloured beer is particularly prone to this because light passes through it more easily than it does through dark beer. Light-struck beer has a skunky odour —not a pleasant thought to a brewer trying to present a delicately-scented beer.

What to do? Brewers using green or clear glass try to completely encase the bottles in thick paper-products, ensuring no sunlight will reach the glass. The Miller Brewing Company resorts to adding chemicals, which impede the process, to their clear-bottled beer. We did notice they used brown bottles in their two new all-malt beers. Samuel Smith, The Old Brewery, takes a unique approach to using their clear bottles. They had a substance added to the clear glass which blocks or deflects the harmful ultra-violet light.

The argument for using clear glass, one could suppose, is that it allows the consumer to see the beer's colour, a particularly important point to breweries marketing light beers, where light colour is associated in propaganda with hipness, and dark colour with calories and alcohol strength.

☞ The following is the Bass Brewery's instructions for bottling beer circa 1880.

1. Ale should not be bottled during summer, or in warm weather. Home bottling should be completed by the end of June at the latest. Summer-brewed ale should, however, be bottled as soon as it gets into condition.

2. When ale is received, it should be at once placed, bung upwards, on a scantling in the cellar, so as to allow the porous spiles to work; when thus placed it must be left undisturbed.

3. Each cask is usually provided with one or more porous pegs in the bung, which will carry of the gas generated by fermentation. It will only be necessary to make any alteration with regard to these pegs in the case of their having become so much clogged that the cask would burst if the requisite vent were not given; or in the opposite case of a tendency in the beer to become flat, when hard spiles must be substituted.

4. The cellar ought to be well-ventilated, kept perfectly clean, and as cool as possible. Underground cellars are usually the best.

5. Immediately the beer is bright and sparkling, and in a quiet state, not fermenting, it is in the proper condition to be bottled.

6. If, from any cause, the ale should not become fit for bottling in the usual time, it will generally be sufficient to pass it through the grounds again, ie, roll it over and put it up again on the scantling.

7. Ordinary bottling taps, with long tubes reaching almost to the bottom of the bottle, are recommended. All taps, pipes, and vessels used for ale should be kept scrupulously clean.

8. The bottles, when filled, should be corked without delay.

9. The bottles should be piled standing upright. Should the ale be sluggish in ripening, the bottles may be laid down; but this is seldom necessary.

10. Bottled ale is never fit to be sent out under a month. It takes at least that time to acquire the bottled flavour.

11. As the ale ripens in bottle, a sediment is thrown dawn. In uncorking a bottle, therefore, be very careful to avoid disturbing this.

12. In decanting, pour out the ale in a jug, carefully keeping back the sediment within the bottle.

NB: With respect to ale consumed on draught, remarks Nos. 2 to 6 inclusive are equally applicable, always taking care to give as little vent as possible.

Have you ever wondered why classic beer botttles have long necks? As the preceeding Bass instructions indicate, bottling was often done at the pub. Before brewery pasteurization and filtration became common practise, all bottled beer was bottle-conditioned. Anyone who has ever had a home-brewed beer or a commercial one that is bottle conditioned could not help but notice the buildup of yeast that settles at the bottom of the bottle. When pouring care has to be taken not to pour out the yeast sediment with the beer. A long neck allows the pourer to quickly halt the pour when he sees the yeast trails begin to enter the long neck. This keeps the beer looking bright in the glass. Of course, for those keen on drinking beer with the yeast (as is done certain wheat beers), this is no impediment. A benefit of ingesting yeast with beer: constipation is never a health problem.

Canning

What can be said about canned beer, except that it's probably here to stay. It is often said that canned beer tastes metallic, which is, of course, dictated by the sensitivity of each individual's tastebuds.

Actually, canning appeals to brewers who are run by their accounting department, whose job it is to shave every thousandth of a penny of the cost of production of each beer they sell. Nothing beats aluminium for its lightness and strength. Think of the money saved each year in transport costs alone when compared to glass. As an added bonus, it is completely impervious to light.

The first can satisfactory for packaging beer was introduced in 1934–35 by the American Can Company for the Gottfried Krueger Brewing Company located at Richmond, Virginia. Pabst Brewing Company and the Joseph Schlitz Brewing Company both introduced canned beer the following year, after observing the success Krueger Brewing was enjoying.

Casking

 CASKS ARE THE oldest form of packaging beers still in commercial use, unless there is a brewer we don't know about in Tibet or the Andes who is using gourds or earthenware for that purpose. Casks are made of either wood or of metal, usually aluminium or stainless steel. The term "from the wood" refers to beer that has been conditioned in and dispensed from wood casks. This is now very rare.

Cask-conditioned beer is allowed to settle (in the cellars of pubs), carbonate and clear (drop bright) for three days before it is dispensed. This also allows it to cool to about 56°F (13°C). This is hardly the "room temperature" at which most people think British beer is served, but is well above the near-freezing temperatures at which North American Lagers are frequently served. Cask-conditioned beer is traditionally dispensed by beer engines, the most obvious part of which is the hand-pump.

Beer is naturally carbonated. Therefore, there is no need to pressurize the cask with carbon dioxide to force the beer out and to carbonate it. As long as the cask is consumed fairly quickly, there is little danger of the beer going flat or stale or becoming infected by bacteria.

Managing casks is a much more complicated process than installing and dispensing from pressurized kegs. In England there are programs run by breweries to train "cellarmen" in proper cask handling.

Several things led to the demise of cask-conditioned beer in the United States. They are all inter-related. The switch to lager-drinking by the public, and the growth of HCBS, with their all-consuming desire to ensure a stable, consistent product that could withstand transport across long distances led to the HCBS packaging their product in kegs. This desire, at the expense of taste and variety, led to the creation of bland products, which barely qualify as beers. In a traditional sense, they don't, so that is why separate categories has been created for them. When HCBS pasteurize and force-filter their beer to remove yeast, they are selling a dead product with no means to carbonate itself (remember, yeast does this naturally). To overcome this fatal handicap, the beer is injected with carbon dioxide, which the beer absorbs. Now that the beer is pressurized, the need for hand-pumps was obsolete. As hard-pumps were replaced with the now standard taps, pub owners, &c had no cause to order cask-conditioned beer. This was, also, the direction Great Britain was heading, but, thankfully, camra was launched, and they have managed, through a lot of hard, sustained work to stop and reverse the decline in cask-conditioned ale.

There has been a rebirth, led by brew-pubs who instal British equipment, in cask beer in the United States, but it is still a rarity to find hand-pumps in pubs. One place that springs to mind is the Commonwealth Brewery at Boston, Massachusetts.

Kegging

KEGGED BEER IS near-universal at breweries, pubs and restaurants. It is often the only way they sell beer because it is the least expensive system to instal at both the brewery and at drinking establishments. Most pubs, &c are set up to dispense beer from kegs.

Since the enactment of Bottle Return laws in many states, some high-volume establishments have discontinued selling bottled beer and switched to keg beer. One owner told us the cost of hiring (or designating) an employee to solely handle empty bottles for return was too costly to justify. Instead, he discontinued bottled beer and installed 16 more taps.

Keg beer is served chilled whilst cask beer is served at cellar temperature. Keg beer is forced out by pressurized, say 10–12psi, carbon dioxide (or by a mixture of carbon dioxide and nitrogen). Temperature has an effect on how much carbon dioxide is absorbed in to the beer. Therefore, cool temperatures must be kept fairly constant or problems with the carbonation rate occur. Either the head will be too big (or gush) or the beer will quickly go flat—both costly and embarrassing.

It is a safe bet to say metal-kegged beer will be with us for a long time to come.

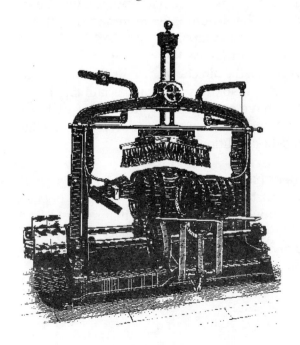

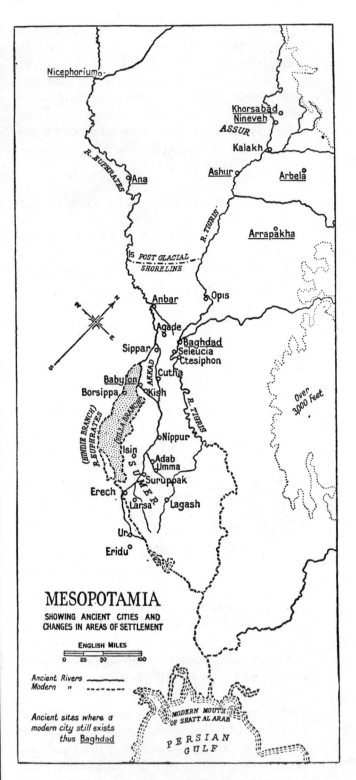

Mesopotamian Cities of Yore, Closeup

Chapter 2:
A History of Beer

Brewing's Distant Past

Beer brewing is an art first developed in Mesopotamia (present-day Iraq) more than 5,000 years ago. Evidence of this is in the form of clay tablets with cuneiform (wedge-shaped) inscriptions on them. These tablets were discovered around 1840 at Nineveh and Nimrud by Austen Henry Layard, an Englishman who chanced upon Assyrian ruins while journeying overland to Ceylon. He had hoped to find some sort of inscriptions in stone, but what he discovered was a buried library of over 25,000 broken tablets he removed to the British Museum for translation. The translations were begun by Henry Rawlinson, a British officer who had discovered the key to deciphering cuneiform—the "Record of Darius" on the Behistun rock near the city of Kermanshah in Iran. The writings were in Old Persian, Elamite and Babylonian the 'Rosetta stone' which helped him unlock the mysteries of cuneiform.

Many of the cuneiform tablets were commercial ledgers, which show us how beer, or kash was used as currency or an instrument of barter, if it was not consumed. Records describe how the stonemasons who built the great structures of the Pharaohs were paid with vessels of beer. Too, beer was used as a staple of man's diet before bread-baking was discovered.

According to Shin T Kang, translator of cuneiform tablets:

"Together with bread, onions, fish, and seed-seasoning, beer was one of the more important items in the Ancient Mesopotamian diet. The Sumerians seemed to have made a fermented beer by combining barley and water, and adding flavourings such as malt. Beer was used as part of the rations of government officials, and messengers, and was widely expended in offerings to gods and goddesses, such as for the goddess Angina, at the field-offering (for deceased persons), and much was consumed at the palace. For all these purposes, beer was collected from the people, either as a form of taxation or as a religious gift".

From the following translations of cuneiform tablets by Mr Kang, one can see that beer was an important commodity.

Nr 191

1 ordinary beer, royal (quality)

—inspected by the constable of the king: for the sheep-shearing.

Receipted by the governor.

The year when the city Simurum was destroyed for the 9th time. [!!!!]

Nr 293

550 sila of fine beer

31 gu, 190 sila of ordinary beer for the meal offering: from Lú

Receipted by Ur-sa

The month of the goddess Lisin

The year when the city of Sassurum was destroyed.

Nr 300

18 sira of fine beer,

70 ordinary beer,

60 weaker beer, 15 sila,

for the offering of prayer to the goddess Inanna at Uruk,

on the 28th day.

From Ur-mes.

Receipted by the governor.

The month of the divider.

Year that in which the city Simanum was destroyed.

Nr 307

5 sila of fine beer, 3 sila of loaves,

2 gin of oil, 2 gin of seed-seasoning,

1 fish, 1 braid of union

to Adalal;

3 weaker beer: 20 sila

30 ordinary beer, 1 loaf, royal (quality)

for the rations of the messenger.

Via Adalal.

1 weaker beer, 3 sila of ordinary beer,

10 sila of loaves, 2 gin of oil, 2 gin of seed-seasoning,

3 fishes, 3 braid of onions

to Arsiah.

On the 7th day. The month of laying the bricks from the brick moulds.

And a final beery entry:

Nr 313

15 sila of fine beer,

55 sila of ordinary beer,

on the 16th day;

15 sila of fine beer,

50 sila of ordinary beer,

on the 17th day;

10 sila of fine beer,

40 sila of ordinary beer,

on the 18th day;

40 sila of beer,

on the 19th day;

15 sila of fine beer, 40 sila of ordinary beer

for queens and priestesses.

From A'alli.

Receipted by the governor.

The month of the 6-month temple.

It must have been one hell of a party.

Translations also reveal laws and religious prayers and hymns. Amongst the former:

"The waitress, who gives free beer or barley, can not ask for anything in return."

" When certain criminals and political dissidents gather at the tavern, and the waitress will not turn them over to the Palace (authorities)—she will be killed."

Life was tough for nuns, too:

"Should a nun open a beer-house, or even so much as step into a tavern (beer bar) for a beer—this citizen will be burned."

The allure of beer must have been strong, even for the religious, though nothing is said of the priests.

Adultery, even when one party was in the dark as to the other's marital status, was severely punished.

"When a citizen sleeps with another citizens wife (not knowing that she is another citizen's wife) in the tavern, or outside of the city's walls, the same

punishment should be applied to him, as the husband applies to his wife."

We doubt the cuckolds gave their wayward wives roses and forgave them.

We wonder what the old dear did to induce this beseeching request on her behalf:

"Oh, Sir, do not step into the beer house, do not kill the Old Lady by the beer bar."

They were a cheery lot. Cheery, but violent.

Here is a prayer to (or about) Nimkassa, the great goddess:

"Nimkassa, the smart gem of her mother,

Her mash tun is of greenish Lapislazuli,

Her beer stein is made of hammered silver and gold.

Her presence by the beer makes it seem magnificent,

She brings joy when she sits by the beer.

With a special mug she pours the beer, and goes about untireing, having the mug tied around her waist.

May the wine I serve be especially good.

The bird who drank the beer is sitting here and is happy,

He is supposed to help me find the troops of Uruk."

Another prayer:

"The gods cried over the land.

She was not hungry because of her distress, but was thirsty (longing) for a beer."

Evidently, water was meant for evil-doers, and other assorted nasties, while beer was reserved for the good:

"This is what it is: I should drink water with the masses of the underworld—instead of bread, I should eat clay."

Here is a little something from King Schulgi:

"In her brewery, she produced the best drink for the bronze container.

With her beer I sprinkled the earth.

Have dark and red-brown beer, brewed with excellence,

For the large dining hall (of the Gods),

Served for the evening meal."

And another:

"On the 20th day you will exult with joy and pleasure,

You eat and drink her pure Kurunnu beer, beer of the 'Safe-haven Giver'.

The beer is offered by the tavern owner,

And you accept it."

Do you get the idea that beer was more important to these people than to us? Here's another:

"To let beer be poured in the pitcher, and wine in the jug,

So that Ennubeer, in the Brewery of the Temples,

The pure house of power,

Hike the water of the Pasira Canals.

Gudea lets the man do Gods work by the sparkling workstation [brewery?]

By Ningirsu, his godly official ruler."

Here is a hymn, not of the sort any Westerner has ever heard in his place of worship since the days of the Vikings.

"Sweet beer is in the Buninu barrel.

Cup-bearer, waiter-waitress, servants and brewer gather around.

When I have abundance of beer,

I feel great. I feel wonderful.

By the beer, I am happy.

My heart is full of joy, my liver is full of luck.

When I am full of gladness, my liver wears the dress befitting a queen.

The heart of Inanna is again happy.

The heart of the queen of heaven is again happy."

Rough times, hot country, but beer seemed to keep both the people and the gods happy., and their livers clothed and in luck.

It is time to move on, but not before passing along a Sumerian triplet. In some respects it shows how little people have changed during the past several thousand years.

"He who does not know beer,

Does not know what good is.

Beer makes a comfortable home."

In 1933, the ancient city of Mari, on the Middle Euphrates in eastern Syria was excavated by French archaeologists. Some 13,000 tablets were discovered, as well as the ruins of a palace and an administrative centre whichcovered about six acres. Mari was pillaged by Hammurabi of Babylon round 1760BC. The important point is that the tablets shed light not only on international relations (before the sack), but also on the public and the private lives of the inhabitants.

The people at court lived well and ate well. The tablets reveal that the people ate beef, mutton, wild game, and fish, as well as vegetables such as peas, beans and cucumbers. Garlic was available. Dates, figs and grapes were commonly mentioned in the tablets.along with herbs and spices. Bread was made in several forms. One was thin crisp disks made from barley flour (for baking bread, wheat flour is vastly superior to barley flour). There was also leavened bread. So, quickly we come to see that the basic ingredients for making beer were at hand—barley, and yeast in leavened bread. Indeed, beer was locally produced, but wines had to be imported from other countries.

In Babylon, under Nebuchadnezzar, beer was the main drink. It was brewed in many different styles which determined which herbs and spices were used to flavour it.

So, before we had the Great Pyramids, and the Sphinx, and Cleopatra's needles; before the mighty Greek and Roman empires there was beer.

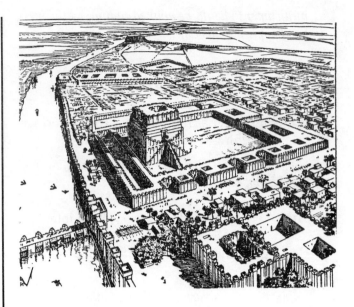

Babylon as it Once Was

Sadly, brewing and the culture in Mesopotamia, were wiped out by the Mohammedan conquests of the Middle East in the 8th century AD. The Koran, their holy book, forbids the consumption of alcohol. (Some secular Middle Eastern states do, now, brew beer: Iraq, Iran, Israel, Lebanon, Syria and Turkey. Most of the breweries are state owned.)

It is easier to understand the spread of ideas and products if we take a brief look at this land. Phoenicia was the ancient Greek name for the long and narrow coastal strip of Palestine-Syria extending from Mount Carmel north to the Eleutherus River in Syria. Phoenicia developed into a manufacturing and trading center early in the history of the Near East. By the second millennium BC, a number of Phoenician and Syrian cities—including Arvad, Berytus, Byblos, Sidon, Tyre and Ugarit—achieved pre-eminence as seaports. They vigorously traded in purple dyes and dyestuffs, glass, grain, cedar wood, wine, weapons, and metal and ivory artifacts. Since the beer culture passed from Mesopotamia into Egypt, it is conceivable that Phoenician ships made beer runs along the North African coasts.

Phoenicia had no central government. It was a series of coastal city states which may have experienced brief periods of independence, individually and collectively; but payed tribute to whatever army was passing through, as they had no standing armies. Initially under Egyptian cultural domination, and then under imperial control (c 1200BC), Phoenicia was autonomous for about 350 years before it fell successively to the Assyrians (860BC), the Neo-Babylonians (612BC), the Achaemenid Persians (539BC), Alexander the Great (333BC) and his Seleucid successors and, finally, to Rome (64BC).

Early in the first millennium BC, Phoenicians explored the Mediterranean as far as Spain and into the Atlantic, establishing colonies on the Tunisian coast at Carthage (c 800BC), beyond the Strait of Gibraltar at Cadiz, and elsewhere along the Atlantic coast. Phoenician enterprise turned the Mediterranean, from the Levant to Gibraltar, into a great maritime trading arena. The Phoenicians were merchants and sailorsThey did no brewing but domestic home brewing; if they made a contribution to the beer culture, it was local.

It is the thesis of this book that the European beer culture developed independently to produce a beverage stream of its own. The Romans were a wine culture; and they were not over anxious to promote beer., although archaeologists have found the remains of a regimental brewery in Germany. But if we remember that the Roman legions recruited locally from a Romanized population that kept its identity in beer. This does not contradict our theory that brewing in Europe was done from the top down, as evidence the beer jugs discoo-

vered at Kulmbach, Germany, which were dated to 800BC, long before the Romans came to Germany.

Pliny, the Roman orator and writer (c 62–144AD), wrote:

"The nations of the west have their own intoxicant from grain soaked in water; there are many ways of making it in Gaul and Spain, and under different names, though the principle is the same. The Spanish have taught us that these liquors keep well."

Pliny's statement confirms our theory: nowhere does he say that the Romans introduced beer or brewing to the West. The inference is that the locals had the grain, and they had prior experience.

Looked at this way, the Romans were sandwiched between the German Beer line and the Babylonian-Egyptian Beer line. They had eliminated the Phoenicians in The Punic Wars, the last of which ended in 202BC with Hannibal's defeat at Zama. Carthage, the last dominant Poenician city was put to the torch, its inhabitants massacred, and the site of the city, and its surrounding acriculturaly lands furrowed over and salted.

The Empire continued to grow but with any large military corporation it got tougher and tougher to administrate; the return on investment hardly matched the cost of doing business. Any reader of Livy's *Early Hitsory of Rome* should come away with the notion that the Romans under the repubican form of government had its ups and downs, with more ups than downs. When this system was replaced by the imperial system of the Cæsars, widespread corruption hastened the end. When the old gods were swept away by the Christian religion, the break with the past was complete.

Then about 400AD the Romans withdrew from England, and by 476AD, the Empire had dissolved into two parts, and the political cell division that led to the conception of national states began.

Europe was on its own.

With the growth of cities and towns in midieval Europe, the homebrewing declined, as each village and town constructed breweries to service the thirst of the people. Monasteries built breweries on Church lands and so did the nobility. Brewing became a regulated industry and provided a large tax base for the rising nations of Europe. It is only necessary to mention the famous *Reinheitsgebot* of the Bavarian prince, Ludwig IV, a law the germans still honor, a law which controlled how beer was made, what ingredients went into its production, and what was to be charged for it. Beer supported the Holy Roman Empire; it was, with wine, one of the first products scrutinized by the new methods of scientific enquiry; even the calculus was designed to measure the exact contents of the huge beer barrels inr which beer was lagered.

To complete our thesis that brewing developed independently there is evidence that Iron Age (C 1000BC to 100AD) Celts in Britain brewed beer called curmi. In 21AD, it was noted that the people of the north, the Celts included, were excellent coopers, who made wooden barrels of curved wooden staves to store their curmi and even dry goods.,while the ancient peoples of the Mediterranean kept their beverages in pots. Many traditional craft breweries in Europe still employ coopers to maintain their wood barrels, although there is a large shift to make and use metal and plastic barrelage that maintans the rounded shape of the prototypes.

Beer was a vital constituent of the diets of the people of Britain, Northern Europe and Scandinavia. Diseases such as cholera and typhoid were widespread, and surface and well waterwater was often spoiled and dangerous to drink. With the growth of towns and population water purity and supply became a problem.Beer and wine were safe beverages and for all normal purposes germ-free, as beer was boiled in the makings and the alcohol did the rest. The Vitamin B in beer and bread helped stave off disease. Beer was drunk, on a daily basis, by all levels of society from babies to kings. and queens.

During this time the practice of using spent grain for second and third runnings were used to make lower-alcohol beer. This beer has been variously called Small Beer or Table Beer. It is still produced in Belgium, France and The Netherlands.

As the Roman Empire contracted, they pulled out of Britain and were quickly replaced by the Saxons, Angles, Danes and the Vikings of Scandinavia. These wild tribes were very fond of their beer, which they called Öl or *ealu*. From these words, the English word *Ale* evolved. Another Anglo-Saxon word is *woet*, which becamethe English word Wort, still used in the brewing industry. Ale quickly became the dominant beverage, replacing mead and cider.

Before commercial breweries existed,.all brewing was done in-home by women, called alewives when they later ran ale houses. Alreck, the king of Hordoland, married Geirhild because she brewed good Ale. Those homebrewers amongst us are following an ancient tradition.

Valhalla means *Hall of the Fallen,* or *heaven* for to these combative northern tribes. Beer and mead played a large role in these warrior societies. Unlike the other European tribes that farmed the land or dwelt in towns, these people were seaborne plunderers for several hundred years They were fearless in battle . To die and go to *Valhalla* was their greatest honor; where one of the primary activities is drinking vast quantities of mead beer. To quote Roger Protz, "The Anglo-Saxon religion was heavy with ale drinking."

Beginning in the third century, monks promoted brewing throughout northern Europe.: monks debouchedfrom Ireland preached and established monasteries in what is now Belgium,Germany and Switzerland These monks continued Celtic brewing traditions. on the continent.

Summarizing our argument: beer and bread were the first consumer products of the civilization that transformed agricultural societies into world powers. Bread and the beer that was initially made from it may rightly be called the father and mother of all civilization. As long as there is beer there will be civilization.

Back to the beginning

IT IS MANDATORY to go back to the origins of beer, to give you some small notion that beer was something more than a common drink like water, but was, indeed, derived from the grasses that made civilization possible. Civilization is but human behavior that is different from behavior of all other animals; behaviour that animals cannot duplicate, remember, or pass on by education, and record in memory or media. To be civilized means that you can change the world and what is in it by your own hand when pushed by a brain that knows what it is doing, so that you do not have to live at the animal level.

To visualize what civilization is not, you have only to burn your clothes, close the factories that make them; shut down the supermarkets, and the farms that supply you with food; then destroy all means of transportation, and demolish all housing; burn all that you read, and the equipment that prints words and pictures. Here's more: shut down the sources of power, smash your TVs and radios, disband the soldiery, fire the farmers, release your teachers, padlock the schools, quit your jobs, turn your cats, dogs, cows and chickens loose, fire your politicians and tax collectors (they'd cling to power the longest!); exile the lawyers and abandon your religions; finally, you can stop talking to one another, and stop living in families. Oh, and one thing more: stop drinking beer.

When you have done all that, walk into the wilds to get the full feel of uncivilized or animal life, when we were all each other's dinner—in the time before fire and short fingernails—before love was invented.

To get that first cool quenching beer, man had to do some evolutionary walking in deserts, in jungles and on ice. When the Great Ice Cap finally melted, foot by watery foot, (10000BC), things that had been captured by the ice began to grow to form the forests and grasslands of the great Danube River Basin—as Nature literally laid the groundwork for life styles for civilizations yet unknown.

With the melting of the ice, something thawed out in the human brain, which had expanded to 1600cc, to give Homo Sapiens (us) more thinking and memory power, the better to modify the new environments opening to the tribes of man. From about 75000BC, one invention at a time, man modified his environment in the grasslands via farming, with such sufficiency that he had time to build nations of people in artificial dwellings called cities.

The men with the hoes and wooden plows did not migrate into civilization, but multiplied into or infiltrated the spaces open to his sowing, until he came into lands between the Tigris and the Euphrates rivers in what is now Iraq (or Mesopotamia, "land between rivers"). Mesopotamia was then the most fertile area in the world, where grain returned itself 200 times, and there were two cuttings a year.

The naked ape, about the time beer invented itself, had 10 thousand years to await the arrival of Christ: it had taken him 90,000 years to separate himself from, and dominate, the animal world from which he had sprung a million years before. In that time he, using a brain that was four times larger than that of the other apes; using a body that supported itself on hind-quarters; and using his forefeet as hands that could fashion the substances of the earth to his needs, man, that heroic coward, observed an experiment of nature that led to the refinement of manufacturing beer—a gift from the Gods, indeed!

No one will argue that the invention of farming was not an act of civilization, which may be defined as the total of all the things we humans have been doing since we lost most of our body hair, stopped walking on our knuckles, and used words. Acts of civilization are human actions, inventions, thoughts and ideas that cannot be duplicated by our animal relatives: acts that must be taught to succeeding generations for the continuance of the culture. It has also been proved that the making of beer was an agricultural activity that preceded the baking of bread. So, it, too, was an act of civilization.

No life form except man can make beer: mosquitos cannot make beer; cats cannot make beer; and monkeys certainly cannot make beer. Only Homo Sapiens can make beer by duplicating an accidental process (and phenomenon) of Nature.

To understand what happened, let us talk about beer, and what it really is, by the process of definition. *The Encyclopedia Brittanica* defines beer as "the beverage obtained by the alcoholic fermentation of malted cereal, usually barley malt, with or without other starchy material".

Although the chemistry of beer is complex, it is only necessary for you to understand the fundamental process involved (unless you are a brewer, in which case you should already have other books and experience devoted specifically to brewing). Cereal seeds are steeped in water; the seeds sprout; the sprouted seeds are dried to form a malt; the malt is mashed in water; the starches in the malt are worked on by the enzyme diastase when the malt is cooked in water at a temperature (approximately 168°F). The resulting fluid, called wort, is first boiled, hops are added, it is strained and cooled, after which it is fermented by yeast in a process that changes the bitter-sweet, harsh-tasting solution into an effervescent beverage with a mildly bitter taste and a delicate aromatic flavour. Always remember that yeast cells are living organisms, and constitute what we call the 'soul of beer'.

This beverage is aged for a time (at 55–77°F for ales and 41–50°F for lagers [lagers can be aged as low as 34°F]) to clear it, and age (mel-

low) it before being allowed in the beverage stream.

The beverage stream

EXPERTS SAY THE average person can go without food much longer than he can go without water before the body calls it quits. Recall now, that the human body is about 90% water, and that bad things happen such as dehydration, loss of consciousness, hallucination, madness and death if that level is not maintained. So, having an adequate beverage supply has always been a main concern since the day we were weaned from mother's milk. Early man satisfied his thirst, mainly from water supplies contained in rivers and lakes and melted snows; secondarily by water in his foods; then by animal milks.

Man's inventive mind delivered the well, the cistern and the reservoir: storage devices to see him through dry spells. Terraced and diked land was designed to lock in the water for farming. Large waterways like the Tigris and Euphrates Rivers were tapped by complex irrigation canals to augment the 10 to 15 inch annual rainfalls.

An old desert proverb says: "Allah made all things of water." People and plants: but man, through ignorance, and neglect, and war came to ruin the lands that flowed with milk and honey.

Here's how:

1. Too many people; not enough water.

2. Polluting his own water supplies by bad sanitary habits.

3. Contaminating enemy water supplies in time of war.

4. Destroying enemy irrigation systems in time of war.

In short, everything we 'scientific' moderns have done to ruin our water was done in the primary civilizations by ignorance and malice.

To overcome ignorance and malice, man supplemented water supplies with animal milk, the juices of various fruit, and with beer, wine and distilled spirits-potables that could be stored in portable containers against future thirst. Of all, beer was nature's gift to man. From the reading and research done, it could have happened this way:

A Babylonian vignette

BAH-LI-PAL, THE FARMER, looked over the stubble of a field he and his family had just reaped of its barley. This was the second cutting of the year, and he had to inspect the in-ground storage pits to see if there was room enough to store the fat brown kernels his people, during the week past, had stripped from the long stems.

The storage pits were centuries-old waist-high hollowings that had been lined with wet clay and straw, and were sealed with clay lids against rain or flood waters. Just as banks in Babylon stared shekels and other forms of currency, Bah-li-pal's pits stored his wealth-the real wealth of his family, guaranteed by Enki, the River God and his consort Damkina, and the Grain Goddess Ashnan (they prayed a lot). The storage pits formed the perimeter and marked the boundary of his holdings; they were set almost flush with the earth, and the lid was covered with earth and straw-nearly invisible at eye level, and immune from the imaginations of thieves and raiders.

Bah-li-pal was able to top off the storage pits with 80% of his crop, and was forced to dig additional pits for his surpluses; but he was conquered by the Gods of Night before he could glean all the remainders.

During the night a storm from the North blew down on the harvest fields; a storm that con-tinued throughout the following day, drowning his fields and washing away the grain Bah-li-pal could not redeem.

"Do the Gods think they have given us too much?", he asked his wife.

"I think the Gods are telling us to rest our weary bodies."

When it was dry again, Bah-li-pal saw that many of the barley kernels had been washed into the shallow drainage ditch that bordered his land, and that the kernels had sprouted. Each sent out a pointed spike from its dark husk. He thought nothing of this growth, but simply watched the grain spin slowly in the water that had not yet drained from the ditch.

"What does it all mean," he thought, pulling a hand through his beard.

The sun was up and burning. By the time it reached its height, the land shimmered and miraged before him. In was as though the Gods had put an invisible straw into the earth and sucked it dry of water.

The grain in the ditch turned hot, dry and brittle Bah-li-pal scooped up a handful and rolled the granules between his palms until the hulls separated.

"This looks like fodder", he said aloud, as he rolled the granules into an empty water jug he carried to his work. Returning to his house, he put the jug down on his well before he entered for his evening meal.

Again during the night, a cleansing, cool rain swept through the Sumerian darkness (Sumeria was an ancient region of the lower Euphrates River Valley, probably populated by people of non-Semitic origins). The rain continued to fall the following day. From his window, Bah-li-pal watched the water overflow his jug, still by his well.

After the rain, he went to check the dikes of his irrigation system, and he took his jug with him.

"That may make a fine tasting gruel," he told his wife.

"Or a barley soup, to say the least," she answered. "By noon it should be warm enough to eat."

Once again the Water Goddess was kind to him; his irrigation dikes were intact. He found the shade of a scrub oak to cool himself, and sat down. He set his jug between his legs, and thrust a straw he made from a reed through the thin fibrous layer that floated on top. He drew into his mouth a fluid that was both bitter, yet had a pleasing flavour.

"What had the Gods wrought," he asked, savouring the after-taste.

When he shook the jug, a white pleasant smelling froth bubbled over the lip. He held the jug above his head and let the foam drip into his mouth. Lowering the jug again, he continued to drink and contemplate his life. Ten minutes later he heard the straw suck air, then clog with fibber.

"I have just drowned the god of my body", he said happily, and took a clay cuneiform tablet from his totebag. With a cuneiform stylus, he pressed the wedges that said: "A new god has entered me to cleanse me of the Seven Devils. His name is Marduk, son of the Water God."

Bah-li-pal ran home (or tried to), scooped more of the grain from the ditches and dips in his fields, but instead of waiting for the rains to help him make this god-given potion he seeped the grain in water himself. Following the process the Water God had shown him, he made the first home-brew, which he shared with the village priest, his father. The year was about 6000BC.

By 4000BC some 16 different styles of beer were being brewed.

By 3000BC hops or similar bittering plants were used in the breweries of Babylonia.

In the section past, we took you to the birthplace of beer in ancient Mesopotamia, and asked you to believe that the civilizations that blossomed between the Euphrates and Tigris Rivers could not have flourished without beer; that they could not have existed at all, but for the kernels of barley grass that was more suited to the making of beer than of bread, which fell to wheat and some other grasses (grains). We ended the section with a statement that the old civilizations disappeared, finally, when the Prophet Mohammed, whose holy book, the Koran, proscribed the use of alcohol. The Muslims destroyed the breweries, and forced the people to drink non-alcoholic beverages, change their religions and speak Arabic. Egypt was overcome by the same changes.

To prove that beer was the liquid, but solid foundation of civilization, we have but to remove the manufacture and usage of this sacred beverage, to see a civilization collapse.

Take Mesopotamia, for example. When Islam conquered the country the people had three choices:

1. Accept Islam

2. Pay a poll tax, if one were a Christian or a Jew (People of the Book)

3. Forfeit life

Since the majority were not Christians or Jews, and did not want to die for their gods, they became Moslems, which required abstention from all alcoholic beverages, including beer and wine. For the Mesopotamians, this meant giving up a foodstuff that was more nutritious than bread, and which made up a large part of their diet. Beer was, like rice in Japan, a form of currency for work performed. It was also, an integral part of their old religions, in which the priesthoods operated large breweries in their temples. It was this beer that was distributed to the people for religious festivals.

In the Egypt of the Pharaohs, c 3000BC, four styles of beer were in common use. Beer was an important item in their daily diet. The peasantry and farmers were paid off with a daily ration of four loaves of bread and two jugs of beer. It was customary for mothers to bring beer to school for their sons.

In religious life, beer was attributed to Isis, the Goddess of Nature. Ramses III (1300BC) had a temple inscription to show that he had consecrated 466,303 jugs of beer to the pantheon of gods.

Egyptian beer was usually made from undercooked bread, using coarsely crushed, germinated barley. The bread was cut into small pieces, soaked in water in a large jug and fermented for a day or two with air-borne yeast. The mass was then filtered through fine cloth, although filtering was not necessary. Both the Babylonians and the Egyptians flavoured their beer with various herbs, honey and spices.

In Egypt, there was an annual feast that lasted 47 days, during which the people of Thebes took out the mummies of their Pharaoh-Gods for parades and celebrations. Vast quantities of sacramental beer were dispensed, free, to celebrants.

The tomb-makers in the Valley of the Kings worked solely for rations of beer and grain brought from Thebes across the river Nile. The surpluses were used to hire servants, and to pay for services rendered.

Barley does not make good bread; it does make excellent beer. Wheat made a better bread and a not-so-good beer (compared to barley-based beer) with the brewing processes then used. So, most wheat production went to the manufacture of bread or to barter.

With the brewers forced out of business, the farmers who supplied the barley grain lost the greater part of their markets, and were caught with surpluses they could not sell.

Prohibition probably forced the farmers to plant other crops such as wheat, millet and spelt, as they were forbidden to use the ancient brews.

It does not take much to imagine the effects the Islamic conquest had on world trade: merchant fleets, not having cargoes of beer and grain to ply across the seas, gulfs and waterways of the Near East were reduced to carrying what was not contraband. Many merchant fleet owners turned to piracy.

If we add to this, that the Islamic armies occupied the cities, and used them for military bases with the conquered population forced to support the soldiery with both substance and service, it is not hard to see what happened to the people: the craftsman, the artisans, the engineers and the farmers disappeared, or were so reduced in numbers that the effect was the same.

For a related analogy (and very close to home), we have but to look at Prohibition in America, when the Volstead Act of Congress (1919) triggered the economic collapse that lead to the Great Depression.

By prohibiting the manufacture and sale of alcoholic beverages, the Government took the liquid bread out of the mouths of the people, forcing the breweries and distilleries to close and lay off thousands of workers in a specialized industry; forcing them to learn new trades (as if that were always possible). Farmers who supplied the barley and wheat for the brewing industry lost markets they could ill afford to lose. The transport industry, the auto industry, the restaurant industry (who can afford to eat out when out of work?), the advertising industry, the timber industry, the clothing industry and the support industries that comprised the total brewing industry all suffered serious declines. Finally, the tax industry run by Government suffered revenue losses when it could no longer tax the industry from which it got major support; and it did not have the willpower and strength to suppress the illegal activities that replaced what it had destroyed. Add to this revenue loss, the cost of enforcement coming out of taxes paid by you-know-who.

Never underestimate the power of BEER.

With the beverage stream dried up, the old civilizations crumbled and disappeared. What was then known of the art of brewing was lost and remained hidden in the tomb paintings of the Egyptians and the clay tablets of the Babylonians. This did not mean that beer had disappeared from the experience and enjoyment of mankind, for there was another beverage stream that had developed in Northern Europe among the Nordic, Finnish and Celtic tribesmen. It was not a tributary of the one that dried up in the Islamic advance, but one that became a mighty torrent in places the Romans could never quite conquer.

What the gods of the Babylonians and Egyptians gave with a free hand to their devotees, was taken away by a single god, Allah, when Islam swept away the old gods, their breweries and the civilization they expressed.

Although beer was not their main beverage, the Greeks and the Romans were known to have brewed beer, an art acquired by conquest. It would be easy to think that the North Europeans learned this art from the Romans, but the Northerners had developed brewing skills on their own. These skills turned out to be far superior to any that were possessed before them. We will talk about these farmer-warriors in the next section.

We'll jump now to lands and times with which we are more familiar.

Early Christian Era

The slow spread of brewing & hop cultivation in Europe

TODAY WE HAVE come to expect rapid change, especially in technology and in products. Man travels farther and faster than at any time in history. Computers become smaller yet more powerful. Telecommunications and new advances in video technology have led some to doubt what they see on screen. It may look real, but the images are computer generated.

What of the "old days"? History and invention moved forward at a slow pace. Interesting and useful things were discovered, invented, and often neglected and forgotten, only to be picked up again decades and even centuries later. Man's innate reluctance to change caused a great drag on mankind's scientific advancement. Galileo discover the earth was at the centre of the universe and, for that, he was hounded by the church at Roma.

Tribes learnt brewing through intercourse with other tribes. World and regional trade were actually larger than imagined by many nowadays. Traders searched out across the seas and oceans (the ships hugged the coast line lest they "fall off"), and overland routes. Commerce was, and always will be, a great driving force.

The Roman and Greek kings might have despised the beer-drinking people of the Middle East, but traders sought profit and products.

The Roman Empire started collapsing when it ran out of gold and silver. This happened when the mines in Europe began to run out. Where did all that precious metal go? To India and the Far East. Asians, being no fools, demanded hard currency for their spices, fabrics and other items much sought after by Rome and her people. There was no counterflow of precious metals, and as trade between Rome and Asia increased, so, too, did the outflow of these metals.

Until this time, the Empire had plenty of coin to conduct business, much as we do today. One of her biggest expenditures was pay for its German mercenary soldiers: the Romans themselves long having given up soldering as an occupation. From the reign of Augustus Ceasar onward, Roman Emperors were forced to buy the allegiance of their barbarian troops by paying them ever-increasing amounts of money. When the Julian line of Emperors expired, succession and overthrow of the thrown happened with regularity. A long-time custom of the Empire was that a newly installed Emperor gave "bonuses" to his Legions. The rapid changes of emperors bankrupted Rome.

This bankruptcy of hard currency lead to a return to the barter system. This, in turn led directly to the Dark Ages.

The role of Christian clerics and monastic orders

AS THE RO-MAN Empire split, and then collapsed, the Christian Church stepped into the power vacuum. The Church and the nobility (the state) of the many "nations" comprising the Empire uneasily shared power. Actually, it was more a power struggle.

One of the first states to break the back of the Church was England. The cause was "love", The lover was Henry the Eighth. When the Church at Rome refused him a divorce from Catherine of Arragon so he could remarry, King Henry broke with Rome and assumed the title of leader of the Church of England. Subsequently, he seized Church property and redistributed it to his nobles, thus beholding them to him. King Henry, though, was not a lover of hops. He forbade his court brewer from using them.

Before these events, monasteries controlled the production of beer before the 17th century throughout Europe. This was a fact of the times. It was, indeed, these monastic orders that spread brewing throughout Europe as they fanned out to spread the Word of God.

The religious orders were given land and monies from noblemen anxious to buy their way into heaven. In this way, the Church acquired great wealth and land upon which they planted grain and raised domestic animals inexpensively.

St Benedict, the Italian monk, founded the famous monastery at Monte Cassino (which was bombed flat during a battle during the second

31

world war). He established the rules of monastic life. One of the most important rules he established was that ever monastery was to have, within its walls, everything necessary to maintain life. There were to be shops, gardens, water, &c. This kept the monks inside the walls and away from outside temptation. They made various items, both for themselves and to sell, such as religious items and, of course, beer. This ensured their subsistence.

Their commercial brewing activities brought them into conflict with private brewers because the monasteries could produce better beer less expensively. This conflict only ended in France/Belgium with the Revolution.

Monasteries were also stopping places for travellers. The monks looked after their guests from many lands. Water was often contaminated, and people learnt to avoid it. The monks at these monasteries, therefore, made beer or wine, which they duly served their visitors. One can imagine these travellers spreading the word about this delicious beverage all over the Continent (and beyond).

Monasteries flourished throughout Europe. Over 500 were established. Trappists monasteries trace their history back to the 1600s when Rancé, a monk established a monastery at le Trappe, in Normandie. His observance of monastic life was very strict, but, surprisingly he built a large following, and other "Trappiste" monasteries were founded in the North of France (including present-day Belgium).

In the 17th and 18th centuries, the nobility wrested control of brewing from the religious orders, though when this happened varied from country to country. In France, it was the Revolution of 1796 that crushed the power of the Church. Monasteries were looted and their lands seized and sold off. Monastic life ceased for 40 years. With their enormous land holdings gone, it took many years for the monasteries to re-establish themselves. One, Orval, which had been established in 1132, did not arise again until 1926. Not all of them did. Because the Trappist monasteries had strict

requirements for manual labour, they again took up brewing. Other sects, without such requirements, did not.

The nobles established a monopoly, with all its inherent and concomitant drawbacks. The monopolies extended over the domain of each noble brewer, which solidified the custom of local styles. Public and commercial transport was limited. There was probably no thought given to national or even regional distribution of products, as is so often the case in this century. Most trade was local, but this does not imply there was not a great deal of international commerce as well. Yet today, in most of the world, the human nature of preferring a local product over something imported prevails. In Germany, local brewers predominate, even in the face of some huge brewery groups. camra, in Britain has led the fight and seen the resurgence, in the face of long odds, of local brewers. Similar occurrences are happening in the United States, as more entrepreneurs enter the brewing business via brewpubs and micro-breweries.

The 17th century saw, too, the first hesitant steps of the Industrial Revolution, and with them, the rise of commercial brewing commenced (again, at a local level): businessmen wrested control of brewing from the elite class, and formed powerful local brewers' guilds. They regulated the composition of the wort. Hop producers did the same. The first English hop gardens were established in Kent, a land of excellent soil and climate for growing hops, in 1520. In fact, virtually every profession had its guild where mastery of profession was taught, along with trade protectionism. They simply fixed prices. To keep prices stable, they authorized the addition of water to the beer as the prices of ingredients rose. It was the guilds that controlled all aspects of the profession down to who would be permitted to brew.

Hop farmers become very wealthy:

A nobleman of Cailes,

A Knight of Wales,

A Laird of the North Countree,

A Yeoman of Kent,

With his yearly rent,

Could buy them out all three.

German brewers started shipping their beer to as far abroad as North America from Hanseatic trading centres such as Bremen, Hamburg, Keil and Lubeck. Dutch immigrants to England settled mainly in East Anglia. They introduced their techniques of brewing with hops (as well as weaving), though this was resisted by the English as a foreign demon or worse. Norwich banned the use of hops in beer. The Dutch were looked on with suspicion. Therefore any practise they employed must necessarily be suspect, but hops eventually won out.

The tussle went back and forth for many years. One two-liner from 1524 is:

Hops, Reformation, Bays and Beer,

Came to England in one bad year.

The Austro-Hungarian Empire, with Wien (Vienna) as its heart, emerged as a power in Europe. Within this empire were many different nationalities, including Bohemia (present-day Czech Republic), the site of Plzn (Pilsen), which came to rival München, Dortmund and Wien as a brewing capital. Wien fell on hard times, the result of coming up with the short end of the stick in two world wars. She lost her empire after the first and her ambitions after the second. Thankfully the style of beer that originated there survived.

Dortmund and München were fortunate to end up in the Western zone after the second world war. This enabled Germany to re-industrialize with a penchant for export. Brewing businessmen were not slow to pick up on this either. They marketed their beers in America and elsewhere, and gained a reputation for brewing a pure, quality product.

Pilsen had the unfortunate luck of being in the not-lamented, deceased Peoples Republic of Czechoslovakia, a most paranoid communist state. Travel there was tightly governed and watched, and there wasn't much market in the West for products from the East Block. Thankfully, those regimes are gone, and the new Czech Republic has, again, access to the rest of the world and market economies. One lucky break was the Pilsener beer style was adopted by many brewers elsewhere, especially in Germany, who kept the tradition alive and prosperous whilst Pilsen sat in isolation.

Brewing guilds

OF COURSE, BREWERS guilds of today no longer hove the power to regulate as they did in the past. Government, logically saw that as too powerful an instrument to remain in guildsmens' hands. Alcohol, being a huge source of governmental income (via tax), and, too, a constant target of prohibitionists, fell victim of laws and regulations.

Brewing guilds, more properly called associations now, are limited to lobbying efforts on their own behalf, acting as information centres where brewers can exchange ideas and discuss brewing technology, market trends, and environmental and other matters that affect them.

A beautiful brewing guild building is in the Grand Place/Grote Markt in Brussels. The Confederation of Belgian Brewers (CBB) is the guild's name. In a square rimmed with guild halls, the CBB is the only guild still occupying its original building, erected in the 16th century. All the others are used for other purposes now. Should you ever find yourself in Belgium, be sure to visit Brussels and see the brewers guild building. It is magnificent. Beside the guild is a brewing museum worth visiting. Beside the brewing museum is the Witte Rose/Rose Blanche (The White Rose), an old restaurant with an extensive beer list.

Companions of the associations are the commercial brewing schools, such as the Doemans Schule in Germany. Guilds provided the mechanism for apprenticeship in a chosen craft.

This helped ensure quality and the reputation of the business. This role is now fulfilled by these schools.

Development of local styles

LOCAL BEER STYLES developed in Europe because the guilds specified the composition of the beers. Much had to do with what ingredients were available. Remember, at that time, goods slowly travelled by cart or by ship (or both). Transport was expensive. Therefore, manufacturers, out of necessity, used locally produced goods as much as possible to hold down costs.

This way of life existed to the 20th century when motorised transport developed. Today hops and grains are shipped all round the world in huge container ships or by aeroplane then trundled to their final destination by motor transport travelling several hundred miles per day. Before mechanization, daily transport might have averaged perhaps 12–15mi per day. Market towns, therefore, were naturally spaced about that distance apart.

People were much more apt to stay put in one locale for their entire lives. People knew their neighbours and were leery of "foreigners". This maintained the stability of local enterprises. Breweries were no exception. Since there was so little contact outside ones locale, the introduction of new styles was hampered. Over time, the cultural habits of peoples settled on their "own" style to the exclusion of others.

Much of this diversity was swept away in certain countries, especially the USA, by the HCBS, who narrowed their offerings to a very few nondescript brands. Thankfully, pub-brewers and micro-brewers are re-introducing many of these styles (though distant from their origins) as they move to differentiate themselves from their competitors. Perhaps new styles of beer will develop from these brewers. It has been a very long time, indeed, since the people of North America (and even England) have had such diversity in styles from which to choose, though not nationally. It is conceivable that beer localism will arise anew, even in the face of national brands. This will be good. As Roger Protz noted in his introduction, some beer experts are asserting that the best IPAS are now brewed in the USA, not the UK where they originated.

Europe: The Middle Ages

ALTHOUGH THE GREEKS and the Romans were imminently wine drinkers, beer was known to them and enjoyed, but not universally. Julian, a Roman emperor, was so appalled by Ale he wrote:

On Wine Made from Barley

Who made you and from what

By the true Bacchus, I know you not.

He smells of nectar,

But you smell of goat.

Hardly an endorsement of British Ale.

The Greeks got whatever beer they needed from the lands Alexander conquered (4th Century BC).

The Romans got theirs from the Egyptians during their conquest. When the Romans extended their control to Germany, below the Rhein, Tacitus observed of them:

"Their drink is a liquor made from barley or other grain, which is fermented to produce a certain resemblance to wine. Those who dwell nearest the Rhein or the Danube also buy wine."

Of their farming habits he said, "They do not plant orchards, fence off meadows or irrigate gardens; the only demand they make upon the soil is to produce a corn crop." Corn is used here to mean barley or wheat-not corn in the American usage.

It took the Romans more than two hundred years of fighting the Germans to advance their "Wine Line" to the Rhein, beyond which the greater mass of the Germanic tribes were free to pursue a beer culture that reached to the North Sea, and continued into Scandinavia and Finland/Suomi.

The earliest proof that the Germans brewed beer was the discovery of a beer amphora in Kulmbach that dates to 800BC. Proof that beer was a commercial commodity came in the discovery of a 100AD beer distributor's inscription (*Bierverlegerstein*) in the city of Trier, by the Porta Nigra, where we began this story.

The Beer Line

FERNAND BRAUDEL, IN his superb book, *The Structures of Everyday Life*, mentions a "Wine Line" that runs approximately along the 49th Parallel across EUROpe; a line which geographically separates Wine country from Beer country. This line, which we will call our Beer Line runs across northern France from the mouth of the river Loire, crosses Germany and Russia to end in the Crimea (southern Ukraine).

The Grape Culture above the Beer Line is climactically inhibited, while the Grain Culture of barley and wheat is similarly closed to the brewer's art south of the Line.

You must bear in mind there were no national boundaries (as we know them today) to the tribes that lived and moved north of the Beer Line. There were tribal areas that moved with the tribe: X-amount of area per about one hundred people (called *huns*), which was how the Germanic tribes grouped themselves. We are speaking of a territory that includes Scandinavia/Finland, Germany, The Netherlands and Northern Belgium: the Germanic/Nor-

dic/Finnic peoples; warrior-farmers who worshipped tree and water and sky (Remember the Babylonians?), and made a science out of home-brewing.

Tacitus, in his book *Germania*, gives a thumbnail sketch of these tribes, among which were the Fenni, a name the *Encyclopædia Brittanica* associates with the Finns, whose language is only remotely related to the Indo-European family.

The Fenni did not originally occupy what is now the Finnish Peninsular, but like so many tribes before them, were immigrants out of other lands to the south and east. For whatever reason, they went further and further north to fight and to farm. At any rate, there was contact between the Finns and the German tribes: Robert Claiborne, in his *Our Marvellous Native Tongue*, reports that the Finns picked up some Germanic loan words such as lamb, king, oar, sand and gold; and the Germans picked up the Finnish *sauna*, which Mr Claiborne deduces from the passage in *Germania* that describes the Germans taking hot baths in winter.

Our deduction is that the Finns and the Germans made beer in a manner similar to that described in the *Kalevala*, the Finnish national epic poem of their race. The *Kalevala* devotes a full runo (NR 20) to the making of beer or *olut*, as they call it. That is more space than the epic singers devoted to the creation of the world. The word *olut* is related to the Germanic word aluth, which Mr Claiborne says comes from the Latin root word *hallucinare*.

The *olut* of the Finns was made in a large jug, in the bottom of which were crossed slats covered with grass and juniper needles. Barley malt was mashed with water, brought to a boil by inserting hot rocks, to start fermentation.

In the *Kalevala*, the barley came from Osmo's field, and in was his daughter who made the olut. The legend does say that a song dealing with the origins of beer must be sung while the beer is made.

Here's a short verse:

"From the tree the Hop halooed. Cried the Barley from the field and the water from Kalevala's well: "When will we, three get together, when unite with one another; living singly is so lonely, Two or three together happier."

(From the Eino Friberg translation of 1988, Otavo Publishing Co, Helsinki, Finland.)

Another verse adds more to your knowledge of brewing:

"From the tree a red bird sang, From beneath the eaves a thrush: 'No, the brew is not a bad one, It is really quite a good drink. All it needs is to be barrelled, Aging in a stone built cellar, In a good stout oak-wood barrel, Banded tight with copper hooping.'"

That's the way it was done north of the old 49th.

Where the Roman could not conquer, Christianity swept the fields, although it took almost 1,000 years from 100 to 1100AD to purge the pagan gods. It did not take long before the monastic orders began brewery operations, and tried to gain monopolistic position that almost eliminated the revenues of the princes and private brewers. Emperor Sigismund (1410–1437) came to their relief with a Royal Decree; in 1803 the Secularization Act signed the death warrant for Kloster breweries, of which only 11 survive.

By the 14th century, German beer was exported to The Netherlands, Scandinavia, England and Russia, from the port city of Bremen. Hamburg, the largest port in Germany, became the export centre for Hanseatic beer merchants. By 1500, there were 600 breweries in its domain. Brewing centres were established at Braunschweig and Einbeck, home of *Bockbier*.

In 1615 we come to the famous edict of Duke William IV of Bavaria, the *Reinheitsgebot*, which established the purity code for beer processing in Bayern (Bavaria). Duke William decreed that only water, malted barley, malted wheat and hops could be used to make beer. Yeast was not then known to be the agent of fermentation.

With German unification (1871), it became a trans-German standard. The standards set then are followed to this day by all German breweries. The only exception is beer German breweries export, eg, Becks Lager sold in North America. Happily, Becks Dark is all-malt. That this law is not taken lightly comes from a report in the *What's Brewing*, which recounted how, when it had been uncovered that a German brewer had put chemical additives in his beer, he committed suicide. Until recently, Germany refused to allow imports of any beer that had additives or was what they call *Chemiebier* (chemical beer). The Economic Union (EU) of which Germany is a lead-member, has forced her to open its markets to these chemical beers because the eu court considered it 'restraint of trade'. Million of Germans protested; "You can send us this beer, but we refuse to drink it," said their petitions. It is the EC's (European Commission) attitude that consumers and market forces will decide what is sold within the Community, not internal laws and regulations of each state. They are trying to increase competition and eliminate state ownership and subsidy of business. We only need say that at one time England was the dominant manufacturer of ales in the 18th century. Germany was second and the good old USA third.

We cannot tell you the whole history of beer technology, but we can tell you that beer developed from a seasonal home-brewing operations as described in the *Kalevala* epic to a beautifully automated year-round process that leaves nothing to chance. There are about 1,190 breweries, in the Bundes Republik Deutschland (Federal Republic of Germany) (BRD), of which about 817 have an output under 20,000hl (26.4gal/hl).

The *Kalevala*, needed just two hundred verses to describe the creation of the world but, perhaps not so strangely, devoted 400 to beer's origins. The Finns are notorious drinkers to this day.

King Wencelas of Bohemia prescribed the death penalty to anyone caught exporting that country's hop plants. The region still provides the world with some of the finest hops.

17th–19th Centuries

Improved production techniques

IT WAS FROM the 17th through the 19th centuries that technology and science came to brewing. Such simple instruments as the hydrometer and the thermometer moved brewing ahead immeasurably because they, for the first time, gave brewers quantitative measurements with which they could evaluate and observe their brewing procedures. To this day, those two instruments are essential to the brewing process. Every home-brewers who cares about the beer he makes has them. It was towards the end of this period that many of the HCBs accomplished their biggest growth.

It was as if the entire activity remained in its infancy for several hundreds of years, and then grew to adulthood almost overnight.

Prior to the introduction, how was it determined if the beer was through fermenting and ready for sale? Very crudely. Some beer was poured on a wood bench and a man (called an ale-conner) in leather pants sat upon it for 30 minutes. If, after that time, his pants stuck to the bench it indicated there was still too much residual sugar in the beer and that further fermentation was necessary. These government beer inspectors also used this test to determine if the brewer was cheating his customers. William Shakespeare's father was an ale-conner.

The advent of the starch test, which indicated if all the starch in the malt had been converted to maltose helped the brewer. It informed him when the mashing stage was complete, thereby maximizing the extract. The simple test consists of adding a drop of iodine to a similar amount of cold wort on a clean white dish. If the colour remains iodine-brown, conversion is complete. If it turns blue or purplish, mashing must continue.

The use of the microscope led to the identification of yeast and its separation from ever-present bacteria. This led to pure yeast strains. The discovery of purely bottom-fermenting yeast led to the domination of Lager over Ale.

This period also saw the development of better brewing equipment, packaging, refrigeration and the concept of quality control. Most commercial breweries were run by the new technocrats—engineers and scientists (botanists and chemists). The industry changed from a seat-of-the-pants operation to one where automation, careful execution of well-thought out brewing procedures, awareness of sanitation, and scientific research ruled. Brewing became Big-business. Big-business demands its own methods, and that is what we have today.

Spread of Euro brewing to the rest of the world

WITH THE SPREAD of European (especially English) colonization throughout the world, it was natural that emigrants/settlers took their love of beer with them. To import beer from the motherland was slow, costly, and more often than not, the beer would be spoilt by the time it reached distant shores. What to do? The colonists started their own breweries where it was practical, climatically, and sustained by the necessary agricultural base. The first great wave of settlers arrived at Massachusetts colony between 1629 and 1640. Some 21,000 souls fled England. It was a time when Charles I ruled without a Parliament and Archbishop Laud expelled the Protestants from the Anglican Church. In that same century, dark English ale was already the common table beverage in colonists' homes. Most diaries of colonists made frequent mention of beer, especially at their feasts. From these references it is plain that brewing was almost immediately established. This clearly indicates its great importance to them—beer was thought of as a foodstuff. Tell that to the neo-prohibitionists and the government now and see their response.

The English Empire spread brewing (as we know it) to parts of the world where it previously never existed: North America, Africa, Australia, Asia. There are whole continents involved here, not merely regions or states.

The growth of German industrial might and commerce at the latter part of the 19th century spread Lager brewing around the world. With refrigeration, beer could be brewed in climates normally to hot and humid to support brewing. Most countries of the world adopted German brewing methods and equipment. Most were taught to brew by the Germans.

Taste beers from China, Korea, Japan, Mexico and Argentina. They have a distinctly German character, even if they are not brewed to the *Reinheitsgebot*.

The English have gotten back in to the fray. Some companies have been formed which instal breweries in other countries. They are doing great business in North America, where new micro-brewers and brew-pubs are again taking up English brewing, equipment, procedures and styles. Because Ale can be produced and offered quicker than Lager, from an economic standpoint, it makes sense to brew Ale. Aging Lager ties up storage equipment for a much longer time than for Ales. Everyone should know that Time is Money, especially to commercemen.

Beer and European settlement of North America

THE ECONOMIC, INSTITUTIONAL and political power structures of North America are, in the main, still run by the descendants of European immigrants. This is a good thing. American Indians, even in the best of times, were never economically powerful, as they were mostly hunters and gatherers. Without being tied to the land via permanent settlements and farming their numbers could never increase beyond what the unfarmed land could support. It takes a tribe (be they of any race) settling down: permanent settlement by establishing substantial towns and cities and farms, to begin the process of population growth, resource development and commerce. The Indians were quickly overcome and marginalized.

How does this relate to beer? No other modern culture, except the Euro-American one, had a brewing tradition (as we know it). Yes, other cultures did brew beverages somewhat akin to beer (in that grains are their base, and they are fermented), but if we define beer by its primary ingredients—barley malt, wheat malt, hops and yeast. Perhaps they could be called *Ersatzbier* or *Faux Bière*. Particularistic Germans, in fact, contemptuously consider beer not brewed to *Reinheitgebot* standards to be ersatz.

Hops become the predominant bittering agent

WE KNOW BEER was brewed over 13,000 years ago, but what about hops and their use in beer? The earliest indications of hops being used as beer flavouring dates to between the 10th and the 7th centuries BC. They were used in pharonic Egypt at least 600 years BC. Evidently, their use in ancient times was not remembered or passed along, or the information did not travel to Europe because their use there as a bittering agent, and as a preservative does not begin until around the 7th or 8th centuries. Some place it in the 11th century in the Czech Republic where it became common practise. There are references, in 768, to humlonaria, the name given to hop gardens given to the Abbey St Denis by King Pèpin le Bref. There were hop gardens at the Abbey St Germain des Prés in 800, and at Corvey Abbey sur le Wesser in 822. Too, in 855 and 875, there are references to *humularium* in the records of the Bishopric of Freising in Upper Bavaria. Is it safe to assume that the presence of hop gardens indicates the use of hops in beer? We think so.

Keep in mind that historical change took place only very slowly before the 20th century. It only began to speed up with the spread and increased economic strength of the Industrial Revolution. The time between discovery and implementation is often measured in centuries. Part of this must surely be because Time, and its most efficient use, is at the forefront of man's consciousness. The plant itself is native to northern temperate zones in West-Central Asia, Northern Europe and North America where it grew wild Of course, now hops are under man's care as a cash crop—nurtured and looked after in much the same manner as are grapes.

The use of hops spread out of Central Europe, carried along by the monks who were the brewers then. Their use was late arriving in England, where brewers stuck to other traditional means of spicing beer. As a bittering agent and as a preservative, which is what brewers were searching for all along, hops are superior to all other plants tried to date. Due to its qualities, it became the standard brewers settled on. Upon standardization, the uniformity of beer narrowed somewhat, though there is still plenty because hops themselves are not uniform in their aromas or their bitterness.

British and Dutch brewing techniques, American ingredients

THE USE OF hops dates to Dutch colonial times in North America, especially New York state and, to a lesser degree, in New England. By 1629 the first hops garden was producing on Manhattan Island. In many ways it was fortunate the Dutch settled there first, because they had begun using hops much earlier than had the English. The English foolishly resisted them for over a century. Now they love hops. Concomitant with the growth of hop gardens came the first breweries in the early 1630s. Some lag can be expected because it takes about three growing seasons for hop plants to develop fully into cone-producing maturity. To further clarify, hops may produce cones in their first year or two of growth. There simply are not enough cones produced to be viable at that age. This stage is referred to as the *baby year(s)*.

The Midwest, especially Wisconsin, got into hop growing in a big way in the late 1850s, but two events destroyed business there. First, there was a commodity price crash. The price fell from $0.58 to $0.04 per pound. Many growers went bust. Then, if that weren't enough, the remaining crops were overrun with aphids and plant rust. By 1879 it was all over but the shouting.

New York continued to cultivate hops into this century, but production shifted, meanwhile, to three valleys in the Pacific Northwest; the Boise Valley in Idaho; the Willamette Valley in Oregon; and the Yakima Valley in Washington. About 70% of the nation's current crop is grown in the Yakima Valley.

Lager is born and quickly supplants Ale

CONSIDERING THAT ALE brewing has been going on since ancient times, it is truly remarkable that Lager, in a span of under 75 years, knocked Ale out of the box, as it were. Today, except Great Britain, and perhaps Belgium, Lager is the dominant beer. This is not to say it is the best-tasting beer, only that it is the most-produced style.

In some ways Lager was a beer just waiting around to be born. All it needed was the isolation of a bottom-fermenting yeast that worked at low temperatures. For centuries brewers in Europe that had caves or caverns (most caves are cold) in their area would use them to store their beer. As a reminder, English-speakers borrowed the German word *Lager*, meaning "to store", and applied it to this style of beer.

Yeast, being the highly adaptive little creatures that they are, gradually developed a bottom-fermenting habit. Several events still had to happen before Lager was born. First, yeast had to be identified as the cause of fermentation. Then it had to be isolated, which needed the invention of the microscope, and awaited a scientist to turn his attention to fermentation. Then a bottom-fermenting strain had to be isolated and made pure from the many strains of yeast that existed. Finally the brewing techniques used in Lager brewing had to be refined so consistent-tasting Lagers could be brewed.

Once that was done human nature took over on several fronts. First, here was a product that, though more difficult to brew than Ale, was more stable and travelled long distances much better also. Second, humans seem to favour light over dark: the good guys wear white, &c. In India, for example, light-skinned people are the socially dominant ones. This is repeated in many countries. When it came to beer, darker-coloured Ales lost out to the preference amongst the upper classes (and the trendies of that age) for lighter-coloured beer. Dark beer developed, in the 18th century, a "working-class" stigma in England and elsewhere that continues to this day. In England, Pale Ale was the result. Elsewhere light-coloured Lager bested them all. Advertising propaganda perpetuates this even further with the calorie-conscious. It has been repeated so often that many people now equate all but the lightest coloured of beers with being strong and highly caloric. This is not true, but it is almost impossible to overcome this belief.

Refrigeration aids beer's growth

REFRIGERATION TECHNIQUES, FOR brewing, were developed by two close friends and brewers. They were Anton Dreher of Wien, and Gabriel Sedlmayr of München. The Dreher family had been involved with brewing since the 1630s.

Whilst studying brewing at München, Anton met Gabriel and a life-long friendship and collaboration developed. Both were dissatisfied with their lack of control over temperature that led to their investigation of refrigeration improvements. Remember, temperature is one of the key physical factors in beer production, especially for Lagers. Warm weather sharply curtailed brewing activity.

In the early 1860s, Gabriel Sedlmayr introduced the first refrigeration plant at his München brewery. Anton Dreher, seeing what his friend was accomplishing, installed an entirely new refrigerated brewing plant at a pre-existing brewery, which he bought at Trieste, located at the top of the Adriatic Sea. It had been said that good beer could never be brewed there, but with his new methods, his brewery flourished.

The then-modern refrigeration equipment brought about three enormous changes to brewing. The first was that operations could now be conducted year-round, instead of having to cease in April or May, then to recommence in September or October. By extension, one could easily claim that it extended brewing to equatorial countries where it is seldom, if ever, cool enough to brew. Second, via accurate temperature control, brewers were able to brew a consistently high quality product, especially Lagers, which are much more temperamental to temperature than are Ales. Third, refrigeration permitted, for the first time, long-distance transport via railways, and long-term storage of beer in any season. This was particularly decisive in a continent the size of North America. The last item led to the death, within 50 years, of traditional Ale there: Lager travels well, Ale does not.

Coors Brewery, of Golden, Colorado, used to promote the fact that their beer was always kept cold from the moment it cooled down in the primary tanks until the customer bought it at a store. We would be remiss if we did not state this fact does not, in and of itself, make a good beer.

It is quite illuminating (and chilling) to visit a modern brewery. From the brew-kettle aft, everything is refrigeration-controlled. With incredible sums of money tied up in each batch, nothing is left to chance.

Railroad transport enlarges the market for beer

RAILROADS WERE NATURAL extensions of tramways and wagon-ways, in use from the 16th century on. They were used primarily to haul minerals, &c to rivers and ports. The invention of the steam engine sparked Richard Trevithick (1771–1833) to mount one, with sufficient power to move itself, on wheels. Mr Trevichick's invention was, essentially, a locomotive. It was tested (1802) on a circular track in London. Two years later, it was again tested, this time in Wales, but it did not turn into a commercial success. Horse-pulled traction was not yet threatened.

On 27 September 1825 the world's first public passenger carrying railroad opened between for a length of 38mi. George Stephenson, its initiator, and inventor of his own steam locomotive, drove the first train between Brusselton and Stockton, England. Between 1825 and 1900 the total miles of track increased from 38mi to 21,855mi.

The first railroad charter in the USA went to John Stevens and his associates in New Jersey on 6 February 1815. It was not until 1829 that the first locomotive railroad in the Western Hemisphere was built in Pennsylvania. The first railroad for hauling both freight and passengers began that same year in South Carolina.

In 1840 there was 2,799mi of track laid; by 1860, 30,283 mi; by 1900, 193,346mi, and so on. This growth was necessitated by the tremendous demand for transport for trade, especially West of the Mississippi River, where rivers were few and the area was enormous. Road and riverine transport had delayed the growth of trade forever in the past, but with the railroads, man was freed of this hindrance to commerce.

The expansion of the railroads directly led to the expansion of breweries and the establishment of many more pubs in England. This growth was most pronounced in the period 1840–1870, which corresponds neatly with the increase in track laid down. Before the railroads, 15–20mi was about the longest distance beer could be safely transported in one day by horse-drawn wagon. The rate is, obviously, slower than normal walking speed. Bumpy, rutted roads are not conducive to beer transport. With enough jarring, the barrels could explode, especially on warm days. Rail transport changed all that. In becomes apparent that breweries, especially those located at important rail junctions good now market and distribute their beers over an area never-before imagined.

To give you an idea about how quickly brewery expansion and output grew during this period, we'll look at the Bass Brewery at Burton-upon-Trent. From it's founding in 1776 until 1837 the annual output reached about

10,000 barrels. Two years later the Midland railroad was established in the area. By 1847, output increased to 60,000 barrels. During this decade the brewery was expanded. By 1853 a second brewery had to be built to handle the increase in demand, and annual output reached 130,000 barrels. Within ten years a third brewery had to be built because output now reached 400,000 barrels. By 1876 production reached 900,000 barrels and the brewery site had grown to such an extent that on it were 12m of track upon which 11 rail-engines operated. Beer grew to be, by 1880, the second largest industry in England (after cotton).

German immigrant brewers in the USA were also took advantage of the railroads. Instead of siting their breweries on the coastal periphery, they centrally placed them in the vast American mid-lands, at the heart of one of the world's greatest grain producing areas. Rail transport facilitated the shipment of grains to the breweries, and the distribution of beer from them. It is much easier to distribute anything from the centre of a country out to its boarders (blanket distribution) than the other way round. A brewer at New York, would have to ship his beer at least 1,000mi farther to California than would a brewer at St Louis. Too, centrally located brewers have markets in all directions by land. Coastal brewers have 180° of ocean to one side. It is easy, too, to understand why the Germans chose cities such as Cincinatti, St Louis and Milwaukee for their breweries, and why they had such a competitive advantage over breweries established at, say, New York, Dallas, or even Los Angeles, and why the former grew to be the HCBs they are today.

Looking at the problem from the opposite direction, brewers at the periphery were at a tremendous cost disadvantage to centrally located brewers because they had much-higher expenses shipping the grains and hops to their breweries from the interior. In effect, they were socked coming and going.

The final act that completed these events, and made it all possible, was the establishment of depots and warehouses along the rail routes where the beer could be kept cool until it was delivered on to its final destination.

German immigrants bring Lager to North America

PRIOR TO THE great influx of German immigrants beginning in the 1840s, in part due to social upheaval there, English brewers and their traditions held sway, as should be expected. Obviously these traditions and their techniques had to be somewhat modified to North American conditions of climate and agriculture.

The Germans, ever resourceful and energetic, brought with them to North America their great organizational and technical prowess, habits and skills. Much of this development stemmed from the fact that their homeland was surrounded by belligerent neighbours, with whom they were frequently warring. This pushed German creativity in many fields as a way of national defence.

Located, as she was, in Central Europe, Germany had many centuries behind her as a centre of trade and commerce. Her businessmen and farmers were skilled and looking for opportunities, which they found throughout Europe. For example, many German farmers were invited by Katherine the Great of Russia (herself a German), to settle and farm the Volga River area. They successfully did this. Especially, though, in North America, where business activities were relatively unfettered by anti-business attitudes, regulations and restrictions, were Germans spectacularly successful.

So, in the history of brewing in North America, we have many German-named brewers: Anheuser-Busch, Coors, Miller, Pabst, Schaffer, Schlitz, FX Matt, and Strohs, to name but a few. They became household names in the USA.

Chapter 3: Once around the Beer World

Country reviews

 WE WANT TO give readers an overview of the current state of beer in the different brewing countries of the world. At first thought, we figured this would be a relatively easy section to compile, but the further we got into it, the bigger it became. Part of the reason for this is, perhaps, contradictory. There is a scarcity of brewing information (especially in English) covering huge areas of the globe: Latin America, Africa, many parts of Asia and the Middle East, and parts of Eastern Europe and the Balkans. To even things up a bit, we decided to include population statistics of each country we reviewed, and to give brief, non-beer-related historical summaries of countries about which we had little brewing information. Whilst we realize this has caused us to drift (a bit) off track, we feel knowing some of each country's history is beneficial and fascinating. This still fits the overall thrust of this book—to educate the reader. Remember, too, that most all the tribes (peoples, nations) covered in this book have been making beer since before recorded history.

Too, some of our reference material is getting a bit dated (mid-80s), so we scoured, for fresher information, as many beer-related periodicals as we could lay hands on. Some were useless but, in others we found much information, covered, perhaps for the first time. To these intrepid writers, we owe thanks.

Along the way we have met some remarkable, dedicated people who, upon discovering the historical aspects of this book, volunteered either information they possessed, or offered to fact-check our data, or both. They are acknowledged elsewhere.

There were conflicting ways in which much of our information was organized geographically. Some writers did it by continent, and we followed that path at first. The problem was, not every place falls neatly in to place. There is North America and South America, but what about Central America? There is so little information on brewing there that we could hardly justify giving it its own subheading. We decided to stick with Canada and the United States in North America, and call everything south of the Rio Grande River Latin America, as it is most frequently called. Similarly, we decided to break Australia and New Zealand out of Asia and put them in their own area—commonly called Oceana. Similarly, the Arab countries of Africa and Asia are gathered in the Middle East, but even here there can be nit-picking. Sudan is mostly Arab (its power structure, majority of her territory and capital are firmly in Arab hands), but it does have black African southern provinces. We left it in Africa. There are a few other situations like this, but don't let them bother you.

Finally, as throughout much of this book, decisions had to be made on which units of measure to use: barrels, gallons (US or Imperial) or metric, &c. We chose the metric system because of its superiority to all others. For those who are a bit lacking on their knowledge of this stem, a litre is about equal to a quart, and a hectolitre is 100 litres. A hectolitre is an approximation of a US barrel. Besides, some statistics given are rounded to the nearest 1,000 hectolitres anyway.

Canada

Population (1991 est): 26,800,000; **density:** 2.7/sq km (7.0/sq mi); **distribution (1991):** 77% urban, 23% rural: **average annual growth (1990 est):** 1.1%.

Annual beer production is 22,135,000hl. Per person annual (1989) beer consumption is 80.6 litres.

HERE IS A strange bird, a hybrid. On one hand, Canada is more British in tradition and had a longer officially linked history than the USA. She is still tied to the British Commonwealth, and was granted her own Constitution only recently. Transfer of this power to Canada was achieved in 1982 with the British Parliament's passage of the Canada Act, authorizing the patriation of Canada's renamed and amended constitution. On the other hard, her economy is shaped in the European socialist mould with very high protectionist barriers. Worse yet, Canadian brewers adopted most of the bad habits of her American colleagues. Except her micro-brewed beers, Canadian beers generally fall into the same categories as American beers. They might be marginally stronger, but not nearly enough to give them categories of their own. That is why we call the styles "North American" whatever, as opposed to "American" whatever. Their marketing, too, emphasizes their beers' "smoothness", but in truth they are simply dull.

A welcomed change to the dullness mentioned above is a report that Molson has just launched a "Signature Selection" of all-malt beers. One is an Amber Lager with 5.3% ABV. The second is a bronze-coloured ale with 5.1 ABV. This follows on the heels of Millers introduction of all-malt beers. At least some of the HCBS are starting to take action after noticing the tremendous growth of micro-breweries and brew-pubs. We feel this is an excellent trend. The more the merrier, so long as the HCBS do not use their great competitive advantage to drive the micros out of business.

The 1914–18 war wreaked havoc on Canada, but she quickly regained her feet. In the 1920s she travelled a considerable distance forward from the decade before. Automobiles were by then commonplace; females won (1918) the vote; and the movement for prohibition of alcoholic beverages gained strength. The old saloons, with their sawdust and spittoons, had become casualties of the war and of prohibitionists' interests. The saloons never returned. Thankfully, however, Canada did not adopt peace-time prohibition, as did the United States, much to her beer-drinkers' ever-lasting embarrasment. Although banned by the end of the war in all provinces, the sale of beer, wine, and liquor gradually resumed after 1920 under provincial government control.

There are still some surviving ale brewers in Ontario and Quebec. One of the best is Wellington Country at Gulph, Ontario, which produces cask-conditioned Ale.

As just mentioned, Canada has high protective barriers not only to products produced in other countries, but also to products produced within Canada. Inter-provincial trade is stymied by restrictions. A beer produced in one province may not be sold in another unless a brewery is established there! Worse still, Canada imposes the highest duty on beer—53%. Because the income tax is one of the highest in the world, a worker must earn CAN$1.43 to pay each CAN$1.00 for beer. $0.96 of the $1.43 is tax. Outrageous, but most of the people there want and expect the government to take care of them, and this is but a result.

The Big Three breweries in Canada are Molson (the oldest), Labatt (the biggest), and Carling. A large regional with a presence in the USA is Moosehead, which has plants in New Brunswick and Nova Scotia. None of the products from these brewers, except perhaps the IPA from Labatt is remarkable or even notable.

Canada, like the USA, is also experiencing a boom of micro-brewery and brew-pub openings, which can only be considered a positive. Some of the newer ones are at Toronto, Halifax, in the Ottowa Valley, Montreal, and Quebec.

Canada has a total population (1990) of nearly 26.8m, or approximately one tenth that of the United States. About 80% of her people live within 160km (100mi) of the long border with the USA. Approximately 89% of the country is virtually unsettled. Due to her relatively small population (when compared to other industrial countries), Canada will never be able to support more than a few large breweries, unless she exports beer in huge volumes. This limits her impact on the international brewing scene.

An interesting segment of the Canadian brewing scene are "brew-on-premises" (BOP) facilities where people can brew their own beer. The BOPS provide all the equipment and brewing materials needed. The cost to the brewer is US$60–75 for a 48 litre (~ 12.5gal) batch, depending on quantities of ingredients used. Brewers can supply their own ingredients if the choose. Most BOPS are malt-extract oriented, but some are set up to brew using the all-grain method.

Customers do their own bottling. One-litre plastic pet bottles have become the standard because of glass's great weight disadvantage. bops do sell PET bottles for CAN$0.60 each, and Grolsch-type swing top glass bottles for CAN$1.10. Including a set of PET bottles, the cost for a first batch is about US$96 (CAN$120). This works out to about US$1.00 per pint.

BOPS have existed since 1988. There are about 250 in Ontario Province, quite a number considering it has only been six years since they were allowed to open. British Columbia has about 30. BOPS have evidently generate enough turnover that they have attracted the taxman's attention. Besides paying a 7.0% federal goods and services tax, and an 8.0% provincial sales tax on materials, Ontario has imposed a CAN$0.26 per litre tax (US$9.40 per 12.5gal batch). It's enough to make one scream and start searching for some place better to live.

☞ USA

Population (1990): 249,632,692 (including overseas US citizens); **density:** 27.1/sq km (70.3/sq mi); **distribution (1990):** 74% urban, 26% rural; (1980–90, resident

annual growth population): 0.98%.

ANNUAL BEER PRODUCTION is 237,286,000hl, placing her first in the world. Per person annual consumption is 87.8 litres. Consumption is just ahead of Finland (85.5) and just behind The Netherlands (90.5).

The micro-brewery trend started in the 1970s in response to the increasingly bland beers marketed by the HCBs. Entrepreneurial brewers sensed there was a demand for tasty European-style ales and lagers and began opening micro-breweries to meet this demand. Often they actually created the demand by producing excellent beers. In many ways this growth has been a word of mouth phenomenon—friends telling friends.

As of 1992 there were 285 independent brew-pubs and micro-brewers. Of this total, 184 were brew-pubs, the remaining 101 were micro-brewers. Excepting the six HCBS (Anheuser-Busch, Coors, Heileman, Millers, Pabst and Strohs), there are now more than 700 breweries. This reverses a trend that saw the number of breweries decline to about 80 from the 600 (or so) that were operating in 1940. This has been a benefit for distributors and retailers as well as beer drinkers. In fact, many thank yous should go to the beer importers who marketed foreign beers that helped educate Americans as to what good beer really is. Though many small breweries have targeted imported beer as their main competition, their real targets are the HCBS.

Beer consumption has remain flat recently. In 1992 the six HCBS experienced a 0.5% drop in sales, whilst beers made by contract breweries, micro-breweries and regional breweries had a combined increase of 17%. The total speciality beer industry shipped 1,229,000 barrels in 1992, an increase of 44.0%. The micro-brewed segment of the beer market has reached $300m per year. Some brewers are experiencing 45% annual growth rates.

To illuminate the changes occurring in the American beer market we'll look at Pittsburgh Brewing and their Iron City brand. They had been experiencing declining market share for a decade though they kept lowering the price of their beer to try to compete against Budweiser, Coors and Miller. New ownership noticed that the contract beer they were brewing for Samuel Adams was rapidly gaining market share. Pittsburgh Brewery realigned their Iron City brands: they localized them and raised the prices and launched a new advertising campaign starring locals who made their own commercials about drinking the beer. Then they launched a new darker-coloured brand named JJ Wainwright's Select Lager. It sold out in three weeks. These moves led to their first increase in market share after a decade of decline.

Their distributors loved the move too, because speciality beers have a greater profit margin than do mass-market brands. The price wars between the HCBS, squeeze the distributors' margins to the extreme.

One glaring error made by the previous owner (Bond Corp Holdings of Australia), was that they cheapened their image by lowering the price too much. As with any product, there is a minimum price at which consumer perceptions of the product change for the worse. Price any product too low, and no matter how well-made and great it is, consumers will think it cheap and somehow defective. What happens is the great middle class perceives the product as being for the poor or the riffraff of society, and they do not want that image (it rubs off). Image is so important.

An other example of the change for the better is the FX Matt Brewing Company of Utica,

NY. The brewery was founded in 1888, and their two flagship brands have been Matt's and Utica Club, both rather typical American fizzy water products. Coincidentally, they are a contract brewer of New Amsterdam Beer (Ale, Amber and Light), NYC; Prior Double Dark, NYC, Brooklyn Lager, Brooklyn; Dock Street, Philadelphia; Olde Heurich, Washington, DC; Harpoon Lager and Ale, Boston; and Columbus 1492, Ohio.

Noticing the growth in the beers they contract-brew for others, FX Matt joined the fray by introducing a new line of all-malt beers named Saranac. So far there are three brands in this line: Adirondack Lager, Black and Tan (a combination of Lager and Stout), and Golden, a Pilsenerbier, the last two being newly-introduced (May 1993 and April 1993 respectively).

Nicholas Matt, president of the firm said:

"As the national breweries continue to produce lighter and lighter beers in an attempt to satisfy the mass market, we find there is an increasing number of consumers who aren't satisfied with the products they are now finding on the market. They are looking for beers with more flavour and character, not something that tastes watered down. This trend is driving the growth of the speciality beer market, especially beers like our Saranac."

The HCBS are actually at a disadvantage brewing speciality beers compared to smaller breweries. The reason is their operations are so enormous that it is nearly impossible for them to brew small, less-frequent batches that speciality brands dictate. Too, the HCBS are geared to mass marketing, their area of expertise. Speciality beers do not lend themselves to be promoted in commercials depicting attractive young adults whooping it up at the beach, or similarly. The advertising budgets of the HCBS are enormous. Their economic strength is mighty. Their presence is almost everywhere, and they will continue, as before, for many generations to come. Then again, even the mighty may fall (or, at the least, stumble badly). Witness IBM, the computer giant. They've been taken down a rung or three recently.

LATIN AMERICA

EVERY COUNTRY IN this region produces its own beer. Most population centres large enough to support a brewery have one. Latins Americans are as enthusiastic about their local beers as the English or Germans are about theirs.

Like Africa, Latin America has been long ignored, except when they have conflicts or natural disasters. This applies equally to their beers. There isn't a large amount of material from which information can be drawn. What little information there is concerns itself mostly with Mexico, and to lesser extents with Brazil and Argentina. We'll cover these countries, and then wrap up this section with some beers and/or breweries from other countries in the region.

Too, it should be noted that most of this region's breweries were established in the 1880s and 1890s. Around the turn of this century, the brewing business was fairly thriving

☛ Mexico

Population (1990 est): 87,870,000; **density:** 45.2/sq km (117.2/sq mi); **distribution (1990):** 66% urban, 34% rural; **annual growth (1990):** 2.2%.

Annual consumption of beer is 47.0 litres per person.

MANY PEOPLE WOULD be surprised to know that the first commercial brewery established in the New World was in Mexico. It was founded in the mid-1500s. This was the time of the conquistadors and Cortez, who wrested control of the area from the Aztecs.

Mexico is the adoptive home of Vienna-style beer. More is produced here than in Austria, which may seem odd, but many of Mexico's brewers in the late 1800s were German or Swiss. They, naturally, brought with them the styles with which they were familiar. Much the same "take over" of the brewing industry by Germanic immigrants that occurred in the USA happened, too, in Mexico. The United States was not the only destination European emigrants sought. These people settled throughout the Americas, from the North of Canada to Tierra del Fuego at the tip of South America.

The three big breweries in Mexico are, by size, Modelo, Cuauhtétemoc, and Moctezuma. They own 17 breweries amongst themselves, and all the beer they make is Lager. As in other countries, the HCBs have been taking over the smaller regional and local breweries. Some of the better-known brands from these brewers are, Corona, Dos Equis (two xs), Hussongs, Negra Modelo, Nochebuena, Pacifica, Chihuahua, Superior, Tecate, and Victoria.

Beer is looked at, socially, more as a thirst-quencher than as an intoxicant. In fact, the alcohol content of beer is kept below ABV 5.0 so that it may be classified as a non-intoxicant (by law). Beer consumption is actually encouraged by the government, which is trying to steer people away from hard liquors such as Tequila.

Mexico is the largest beer exporter in Latin America.

☛ Argentina

Population (1989 est): 31,900,000; **distribution (1983):** 83% urban, 17% rural; **annual growth (1984-85):** 1.6%.

Argentina produces 8,300,000hl of beer per year. Consumption of annual domestic production is 26.0 litres per person.

HERE IS ANOTHER country with a huge European descended population. It, too, has a European brewing tradition, though its production doesn't match that of Brazil's or Mexico's. Expect to find Lagers—some with German brand names. Here are a few: Bieckert, Cordoba, Leon de Oro, Quilmes and Santa Fe.

Buenos Aires was originally founded in 1536 by Pedro de Mendoza, but because of Indian attacks, it was abandoned within a few years in favour of Ascuncion, Paraguay. From the mid-16th century to about 1700, Spanish colonists moved in from the Pacific coast over the Andes The pattern of settlement, from west to east, was opposite to that of the United States of America.

After Buenos Aires was permanently resettled (1580), it gradually began to reap the benefits of its advantageous location as both an east-coast port, and as a buffer to the southward expansion of the Portuguese colony of Brazil. The creation, in 1776, of the Vice-royalty of La Plata (including present-day Argentina, southern Bolivia, Paraguay, and Uruguay). Its capital was at Buenos Aires, which further enhanced the city's growth and status. Until then, Argentina had been administered under the Vice-royalty of Peru.

In 1806, during the Napoleonic wars, Buenos Aires was seized by the British. Although the colonial militia, led by Jacques de Liniers (1753–1810) restored Spanish rule, Spain's ties with its American colonies were weakened during this period of unrest, especially after Napoleon's deposition of Ferdinand VII. On 25 May 1810, a revolt occurred at Buenos Aires. A junta was installed in the name of the deposed king. A full-independence counter-movement led by Manuel Belgrano soon gathered force, however. The royalists were finally defeated. A proclamation of independence was signed at Tucuman on 9 July 1816.

☛ Brazil

Population (1990 est): 150,400,000; **density:** 17.7/sq km (45.8/sq mi); **distribution (1989):** 74% urban, 26% rural; **annual growth (1985-90):** 2.1%.

Per person annual consumption of domestic production is 43.2 litres. Total production is 65,000,000 hl.

BRAZIL IS THE largest brewing country in Latin America, and second largest after the USA in the Americas. World-wide it is fifth, after the USA, Deutschland, China and Japan (1991 figures). It's beer market is divided between two HCBS, Brahma and Antarctica Paulista. The first is based in Rio de Janeiro, the second in Sâo Paolo. Together they control around 90% of the market. The Brahma group has been controlled, since early in this century, by a family with roots in Germany.

Lagers predominate, as elsewhere. They aren't terribly strong, either, as Brazilians prefer a moderate alcohol content of about 5.0%. Two unique beers from Brazil are Brahma Porter, an ABV 8.6% top-fermented offering, and Xingu, a black beer.

Xingu is available in the USA. It is probably the darkest beers brewed anywhere in the world. It is made at the Cacador brewery, about 600 mi southwest of Rio do Janeiro. Alan Ames, has travelled the world to search out beer, tracked down the original black beers made by natives along the Xingu River of Brazil. After observing their production techniques, he found the small Cacador brewery to make it. It took four batches before the results were acceptable. In early 1988 the first 1,000 cases arrived in Boston. It sold out within two weeks

THE REST

☛ Belize

Population (1990 est): 193,000; **density (1986 est):** 7.3/sq km (18.9/sq mi); **distribution (1981):** 62% urban, 38% rural; **annual growth (1984):** 3.5%

Brand: Belikins

No production or consumption figures are available now.

BELIZE IS THE northern-most country of Central America. It is bordered by Mexico, Guatemala and the Caribbean Sea. Belmopan, a small inland town protected from the fury of tropical storms, became the capital in 1970, when it replaced the coastal Belize City, the nation's largest urban centre.

Known as British Honduras until 1973, the former British colony achieved self-government in 1964. On 21 September 1981, Belize was gained independence, which ended more than 300 years of British colonial rule on the American mainland.

☛ Bolivia

Population (1988 est): 6,448,297; **density:** 5.9/sq km (15.2/sq mi); **distribution (1988:** 49% urban, 51% rural; **annual growth (1987):** 2.6%.

Annual beer production is 1,450,000hl

Brand: Taquina

BETWEEN 600–900AD, INDIANS of Aymara origin lived at the southern end of Lake Titicaca, where they developed a highly advanced culture. Around 1400 the Quechua-speaking Incas invaded Bolivia from Peru, and incorporated the highlands into the Inca Empire.

The Spanish conquered the country in 1538, and were not driven out until independence from Spain was gained in 1825. Since independence, Bolivia has been plagued by many and frequent internal revolutions, and disastrous territorial losses have greatly reduced her original bounds. In the War of the Pacific, Bolivia lost her Pacific seacoast and the rich nitrate deposits in the Atacama Desert to Chile. In 1903 it lost the Acre Territory in her north to Brazil. The Chaco War (1928–30, 1933–35) cost her large areas of the Chaco region to Paraguay.

☛ Chile

Population (1990 est): 13,200,000; **density:** 17.4/sq km (45.2/sq mi); **distribution (1990):** 84% urban, 16% rural; **annual growth (1990):** 1.7%.

Annual beer production is 3,000,000hl. This ties Chile with Cuba in 9th place in American beer production.

Annual per person consumption of domestic production is 22.7 litres.

Brand: Escudo Chilean Pilsener

THE FIRST EUROPEAN exploration of this area was made by Diego de Almagro (1535). Unlike Peru, Chile yielded little gold, and the native Indians fiercely resisted. In 1541, Pedro de Valdivia established several settlements, including Santiago, which became the nation's capital. Sr Valdivia was killed (1553) by a native, who became the hero of the epic poem La Araucana.

Chilean-born Spaniards declared their autonomy, and established a governing junta on 18 September 1810. Although the Spanish crown regained control, its forces were eventually defeated by Chileans, and their Argentine allies, led by Bernardo O'Higgins and Jose de San Martin.

Independence was proclaimed on 12 February 1818. Sr O'Higgins was installed as supreme director. By 1830, Sr O'Higgins was in exile, and conservative landowners and merchants were in control of the central government.

A constitution adopted in 1833 remained in effect until 1925. After defeating Bolivia and Peru in the War of the Pacific (1879–84), victorious Chilean armies finally defeated Araucanian Indian forces to end the prolonged Indian wars.

A new constitution was introduced in 1925 by Arturo Alesandri. It provided for direct popular election of the president, separation of church and state, and compulsory primary education.

☞ Columbia

Population (1990 est): 31,800,000; **density;** 27.9/sq km (72.3/sq mi); **distribution (1989):** 67% urban, 33% rural; **annual growth (1989):** 2.0%.

Annual beer production in Colombia is 24,000,000hl, placing her fourth on the list of American brewing countries. She is behind Mexico and ahead of Canada.

Per person consumption of annual domestic production is 75.5 litres.

Brands: Clausen, Club and Colombia Gold.

THE FIRST SPANISH settlements were established here in 1509. After the interior had been conquered, Bogota was established in 1538. The area became the Spanish colony of Nueva Granada, which became a vice-royalty in 1717.

In 1810 the struggle for independence began. After 1812, it was led by Simon Bolivar, the "George Washington" of the region. The campaign was successful, and in 1819 the independent republic of Gran Colombia was declared. It was ruled by Sr Bolivar and Francisco Santander. It included the present-day states of Colombia, Ecuador, Panama, and Venezuela. By 1830, however, this republic had disintegrated, and Colombia (along with Panama), Ecuador, and Venezuela became independent nations. During this period, the Liberal and Conservative political parties were founded, composed of the followers of Srs Bolivar and Santander, respectively.

The rest of the 19th century was characterized by rivalry between the Conservative and Liberal factions. This rivalry escalated in to a series of armed struggles and then in to full-fledged civil war (1899–1903), during which Panama seized the opportunity to rebel and achieve her independence (with help from the USA).

☞ Costa Rica

Population (1989 est): 2,953,908; **density:** 59/sq km (151/sq mi); **distribution (1989):** 45% urban, 55% rural; **annual growth (1989):** 2.5%.

Annual beer production is 740,000hl. Per person consumption of domestic production is 25.1 litres.

Brand: Barvarian Gold

WHAT IS NOW Costa Rica had only a small Indian population when Christopher Columbus sighted it in 1502. For 300 years it was a Spanish colony, governed as part of the Mexican vice-royalty. When the colonies revolted in 1821, Costa Rica was included in the independent Central American Federation. This federation of states lasted until 1838, when each state decided to go its own way.

Her first free elections were held in 1889, and the country has, except for short-lived interruptions (1917 and 1948), remained a democratic republic. Two minor invasions by Nicaraguan rebels took place in 1948 and 1955, both of which provoked intervention by the Organization of American States.

☞ Ecuador

Population (1989 est): 10,262,271; **density:** 36.2/sq km (93.7/sq mi); **distribution (1989 est):** 54% urban, 46% rural; **annual growth (1989):** 2.4%.

Annual beer production is 1,750,000hl. Per person consumption of annual domestic production is 17.1 litres.

Brand: Club

ECUADOR WAS PART of the Inca lands at the time of the Spanish conquest (1530s). The last Inca king, Atahualpa, was partially Ecuadorian.

Under the Spaniards, Ecuador was part of the vice-royalty of Peru (except briefly) until 1739, when it became part of the new viceroyalty of Nueva Granada.

Immediately after liberation (1822), Ecuador became a province of the new republic of Gran Colombia, which comprised Colombia, Ecuador, Panama, and Venezuela, Simon Bolivar was president.

In 1830, the federation dissolved, and Ecuador became an independent republic. During most of the 19th and 20th centuries, she has been ruled by a series of dictators.

During the 20th century, commercial agriculture has expanded along the coast, and there has been a concomitant rise in the political power of that region. Nevertheless, the nature of national politics has not varied substantially. Military rule has tended to alternate with civilian governments chosen by an electorate, limited to the literate until 1984, when the voting age was lowered to 18 and illiterates were franchised. There were 14 presidents between 1931 and 1940. This instability diminished only briefly in the late 1940s and the 1950s.

☛ El Salvador

Population (1990 est): 5,300,000; **density:** 252/sq km (652/sq mi); **distribution (1989):** 43% urban, 57% rural; **average growth (1989):** 1.8%.

Annual beer production is 760,000 hl. Per person consumption of annual domestic production is 14.3 litres.

Brand: Pilsener

BEFORE THE SPANISH conquest in the 1500s, the area of El Salvador was divided among several Indian groups. The Pipil, whose culture resembled that of the Aztecs, were dominant. The region was under Spanish rule (1524–1821). In 1823, El Salvador joined the

Central American Federation. San Salvador was the capital from 1834 until dissolution of the federation. After the dissolution (1838-40), El Salvador was involved in a progression of other short-lived unions. She was subjected to almost constant interference from Guatemala and Nicaragua.

Military governments mainly have been in power since 1931, often responding to political unrest with violent repression. One serious problem is the demand for land. Tensions resulting from the large-scale emigration of Salvadorans into Honduras led to a brief border war (July 1969).

Under pressure from the USA to begin economic and human rights reforms, the junta named Jose Napoleon Duarte, leader of the moderate Christian Democratic party, as president in December 1980. A small land-reform program was begun as a concession. About 25% of the land, not including the coffee plantations, was redistributed to the land-lacking peasantry. A peace treaty, brokered by the un, designed to end the long civil war was finally concluded at the end of 1992.

☛ Guatemala

Population (1990 est): 9,200,000; **density:** 84.5/sq km (218.8/sq mi); **distribution (1990):** 40% urban, 60% rural; **annual growth (1989):** 2.4%.

Annual beer production is 1,300,000 hl. Per person consumption of annual domestic production is 14.1 litres.

Brands: Cabro Extra, Medalla do Oro, Monte Carlo and Moza Bock Beer

THERE ARE IMPRESSIVE Mayan ruins at Tikal, Uaxactun. More recent finds are at El Mirador and Nakbe. The latter may date back to as early as 600BC.

The territory was conquered (1523–24) by the Spanish under Pedro de Alvarado, who be-

51

came the first "Captain-general" of Guatemala. At one time it included most of Central America. Guatemala gained independence from Spain in 1821, and in 1824 became part of the Central Amarica Federation. In 1838 the union broke up, and in 1839, Guatemala became an independent country.

Until the 1939–45 war, she was ruled by military dictators. The most outstanding of these was Justo Rufino Barrios (president 1873–85), who enacted extensive anti-clerical legislation, and sponsored the beginning of the coffee industry.

The period of dictatorial rule ended in 1944. Following a provisional regime, Juan Jose Arevalo was elected president in 1945. A 10-year period of basic reforms began, including a new constitution, the country's first labour code, and a democratic political regime. In 1951, Sr Arevalo was succeeded as president by Coonel Jacobo Arbenz Guzman. His leftist regime began construction of a highway to the coast and carried out an extensive agrarian reform, which brought Presidente Arbenz into direct conflict with the powerful United Fruit Company.

In 1954, Carlos Castillo Armas led a us-supported revolt that overthrew Presidente Arbenz. For the next three decades, the government was dominated by the military. Many of the Arevalo-Arbenz reforms were undone, including the agrarian reform and much of the labour legislation. Tens of thousands of Guatemalans, most of them civilians, lost their lives in political violence. In the early 1980s, in an attempt to undermine support for leftist guerrillas, more than one million Indian peasants were moved into army-run villages, where some were enlisted in civil-defence patrols.

☛ Honduras

Population (1988 est): 4,972,287; **distribution (1986):** 40.7% urban, 59.3% rural; **average annual growth (1988):** 3.11%.

Annual beer production is 758,000hl. Per person consumption of annual domestic production is 15.2 litres.

Brand: Port Royal Export

HONDURAS WAS ONCE part of the Mayan empire, which flourished from about 250–950AD. The ruins of this highly advanced ancient civilization can still be seen at Copan.

Christopher Columbus reached the Honduran coast in 1502, and the area was later explored by Hernando Cortes. The Spanish settled southern Honduras in 1524, but the Indians of the north coast remained practically untouched by European influences, except during periods of British control, until the banana companies arrived. Throughout the colonial period Honduras was part of the Captaincy-general of Guatemala. Honduras declared independence from Spain (1821) and joined the other Central American colonies to form the Central American Federation. The federation dissolved in 1838. Honduras became an autonomous state. Francisco Morazon, the national hero, was unsuccessful in his attempts to maintain a united Central America.

☛ Peru

Population (1987 est): 20,700,000; **density (1987 est):** 16.1/sq km (41.7/sq mi); **distribution (1986):** 69% urban, 31% rural; **annual growth (1986):** 2.5%.

Annual beer production is 6,400,000hl. PER PERSON consumption of annual domestic production is 30.9 litres.

Brands: Callo Light, Callo Export Dark Beer, Cristal, Cuzon, Durango and Cervesa Maltina.

THE SPANISH ARRIVED in Peru in 1531. They discovered the flourishing Inca empire. By the time Francisco Pizarro arrived a year later, civil war had so weakened the empire that it was easily conquered by the Spanish. In 1535, Pizarro founded Lima. In 1544 it became the capital of the vice-royalty of Peru. This vice-royalty comprised all Spanish territory in South America until the establishment of the vice-royalties of Nueva Granada (1717) and La Plata (1776). Lima was the region's cultural and economic centre for many decades and continues as an important Latin capitol.

The conquest of Spain by Napoleon Bonaparte sparked independence movements in most of South America. Peru, however, remained strongly under Spanish authority. The independence movement, therefore, was led by foreigners. General Jose de San Martin, the revolutionary Argentine, entered Lima in July 1821, and proclaimed Peru's independence on the 28th of that month. General San Martin withdrew from Peru in 1822, and the task of driving out the remnants of the Spanish forces was left to the Colombian leader Simon Bolivar and his general, Antonio Jose de Sucre. He did so by winning two battles at Junin and Ayacucho (both 1824).

A succession of power-hungry generals kept Peru in turmoil until 1845. Border conflicts were frequent, and from 1836 to 1839, Peru was united with Bolivia under the presidency of Andres Santa Cruz. A period of civil war (1842–45) ended with the emergence of Ramon Castilla as Peru's president. Presidente Castilla, during two periods in office (1845–51 and 1855–62), brought about extensive economic and political reforms.

Presidente Castilla's retirement was followed by a period of renewed internal disorder, increased corruption, and rising foreign debt. In 1866, Peru, with the help of Bolivia, Chile and Ecuador, defeated a Spanish invasion, launched ostensibly because of Peru's debt. In the peace treaty (1879) that followed, Spain recognized Peru's independence for the first time. The first civilian government came to power in 1872. Manuel Pardo, its president, involved Peru in a secret defence alliance with Bolivia against Chile, which led to Peru's participation in the War of the Pacific (1879–83). This war was disastrous for Peru. It ended with the loss of valuable nitrate fields. The country was left bankrupt and politically unstable. The political instability has continued up to the present.

☛ Uruguay

Population (1989 est): 3,105,052; **density (1987 est):** 16/sq km (43.6/sq mi); **distribution (1984 est):** 84.5% urban, 15.5% rural; **annual growth (1987 est):** 0.39%.

Annual beer production is 710,000hl. Per person consumption of domestic production is 22.9 litres.

Brand: Doble Uruguaya

URUGUAY WAS THE last colony settled by Spain in the Americas. Spain sent missionaries among the natives in 1624. They founded Montevideo two years later, as a counter to Portuguese ambitions in the Rio de la Plata estuary. Revolutionaries from the Banda Orienta in 1811. It was led by Jose Gervasio Artigas. They joined forces with those of the Buenos Aires junta in expelling the Spanish. An attempted federal union with Argentina failed because the latter sought to impose a centralized government on the Banda Oriental. Sr Artigas, however, was unable to maintain Uruguayan independence against Brazil, which annexed the Banda Oriental in 1821.

In 1825 the group called the Thirty-three Immortals, led by Juan Antonio Lavalleja, declared URUGUAY's independence. Predictably, warfare followed. Finally, both Argentina and Brazil recognized Uruguay's independence in 1828, and approved her first constitution two years later.

☞ Venezuela

Population (1990 est): 19,750,000; **density:** 21.5/sq km (55.7/sq mi; **distribution (1990):** 83% urban, 17% rural; **annual growth (1990):** 2.3%.

Annual beer production is 12,900,000hl. This places Venezuela sixth in the Americas, following Canada, and just ahead of Argentina. Per person consumption of annual domestic production is 65.3 litres. A second source (Kirin Brewery) of figures has production at 15,179,000hl per year, which would make per person consumption of annual domestic production 76.9 litres. Per person consumption is 74.5 litres. This is not far behind that of the USA (87.4 litres).

Brands: Andes, Polar Light and Polar Dark.

INDIANS HAVE BEEN living in Venezuela for a very long time. It was discovered by Christopher Columbus in 1498. Settlements were established by the Spanish in 1523 on the coast of Cumana.

In 1535, Nikolaus Federmann, working for the Weiser brothers (German bankers who were granted rights to Venezuela by Holy Roman Emperor Charles v), led an expedition in Venezuela and Colombia. Settlements were eventually established in the northwest part of Venezuela. In 1556, the Weisers's contract was terminated. Spain resumed control.

Venezuelan Creoles were active in the movement for independence from Spain. In 1806, Francisco de Miranda landed in Venezuela with a revolutionary force recruited in the United States . He captured Coro, but was easily repulsed by loyalist troops. Venezuela's revolutionary congress declared its independence from Spain on 5 July 1811.

Ten years later, in 1821 the insurgent army of Simon Bolivar defeated the Spaniards decisively at Carabobo, ending their domination over Colombia and Venezuela. If one has the impression that Sr Bolivar was almost every-

where fighting for the independence of many countries form Spain, it is correct.

In 1830, Venezuela withdrew from Sr Bolivar's Federacion de Gran Colombia. She became a sovereign state. Political stability and economic growth proved difficult to sustain simultaneously, however, except under Jose Antonio Paez, Antonio Guzman Blanco, and Juan Vicente Gomez. Following the ouster of Sr Guzman (1888), the brief progressive period ended when Cipriano Castro seized control (1899). In 1908, when illness forced Sr Castro to seek medical treatment in Europe, he left the government in the hands of Sr Gomez. Sr Gomez's successors were faced with the demands of an increasingly urban society and the democratic aspirations of the people. A democratic period (1945–48) was sadly followed by more decades of military rule or interference with civilian governance.

A closing thought on Latin America: one must hope that the recent change to democracy in most countries of the region starting in the 1980s and 1990s continues. Most countries are now rid of military control of their governments (hopefully for good), though some are still plagued by centralized command economies of the same sort that plagued the Eastern Bloc in Europe, and elsewhere. Those countries in Latin America where democracy has won out, and where market economies have been established have been experiencing remarkable growth in many instances. This illustrates that people, in whatever country in which they may live, prosper and grow under this system. It is the only system that, by its nature, gives the opportunity of prosperity to all who seek it and are willing to work for it.

ASIA

☛ Japan's rise

Population (1991 est): 123,120,000; **density:** 326/sq km (844/sq mi); **distribution (1990):** 77% urban, 23% rural; **annual growth (1990):** 0.4%.

Annual beer production is 68,583,000hl. Per person annual consumption is 55.6 litres. Its consumption is not half that of Germany's, but she is solidly placed in the middle of the pack.

THE JAPANESE GOT a late jump on brewing, beginning only in 1853 when Commodore Perry arrived to "open" Japan to foreigners. As the storey goes, a Japanese visited one of the naval ships and was offered some beer. He was so overwhelmed by it that when he, later on, discovered a Dutch textbook of brewing, he translated it and began brewing—Japan's first brewer. Sapporo brewery credits this unidentified man with creating interest for this foreign beverage.

In 1869, the American firm of Wiegand & Copeland opened a brewery in Yokohama. The Japanese government got into the act in 1873 when it sent a man named Nakawara, as agent, to study brewing in Germany. When he returned in 1876, he was placed in charge of a brewery the government built in Sapporo, on the northern island of Hokkaido.

The government privatized the brewery a decade later. The new firm incorporated in 1888 as the Sapporo Brewing Company Ltd. In 1905 the company built a still-standing Victorian-style brewery. It now servers as a beer hall/garden. The replacement plant is beside it.

Kirin, another Japanese brewing company, traces its roots to back to the Wiegand & Copeland brewery. That brewery was later sold to English interests and became the Japan Brewing Company. It sold its first Kirin beer in 1888, too. The brewery was sold again, this

time to Japanese interests, who renamed it Kirin.

Until the turn of this century, most of the beer consumed in Japan was imported from Germany, but as the breweries grew, imports shrank. The breweries began exporting their beer to China, Hawaii, the Philippines and to Siberia. The Kirin firm now ranks as one of the largest international brewing firms, having recently moved ahead of another giant, Heineken.

Suntory is the third large Japanese brewer. They began as vintners around the turn of the century, and didn't begin brewing until 1963.

Asahi Breweries Ltd is Japan's fourth major brewery. This firm introduced "Dry" beer to the world, in 1987. It was such a success that other breweries round the word rushed to imitate it. Asahi's scientists developed (genetically engineered) a special yeast strain which can digest the normally indigestible sugars in the wort, thus fully attenuating it. The more fully attenuated a beer is, the dryer it is.

Though the early influence of the German brewers still exists (to some extent) in the taste of some Japanese beers, they have chosen to follow the lead of America's HCBs. Both use inexpensive rice as adjuncts. Most Japanese brands are unpasteurized, but they are heavily filtered. A recent trend, some call it a "craze", amongst Japan's brewers is to is to produce "extra-clean" taste profiles. It seems strange that these breweries would go through the bother and expense of brewing, with quality ingredients in technically awesome breweries, a fairly "legitamate" beer, and then filter it so heavily that it becomes extra-clean-tasting.

The Japanese people have taken to beer with great enthusiasm. It could be claimed that beer has displaced Sake as Japan's national drink. Roof-top beer gardens enjoy much popularity. Too, Japanese label art is some of the most beautiful in the world. Compare Japanese labels with Western graphic art.

From a late start brewing beer, Japan now has, demonstrably, the most advanced brewing technology anywhere. Miller developed their Miller Genuine Draft with technology from Sapporo. They were the developers of the technique of using ceramic filters as a method to avoid pasteurizing beer. Arguably, pasteurization can damage hop flavours and impart a slightly cooked flavour to beer.

☞ Chinese surprise

Population (1990): 1,133,682,501; **density:** 118.6/sq km (307/sq mi); **distribution (1988):** 46.6% urban, 53.4% rural; **annual growth (1990):** 1.47%.

Annual beer production is 80,000,000 hl. Per person consumption of annual domestic production is 7.0 litres. China is the number one brewing country in Asia.

CHINA HAS A LONG beer brewing history, one that modern nations can't come close to touching. Mongolians have been brewing beer for thousands of years, as have other ethnic groups within this huge and diverse country that could be called an empire (though, of course, communist regimes cannot, by their own warped definition, be imperialistic). For several millennia alcoholic beverages have been considered one of life's great pleasures, and a source of inspiration for artists and writers, especially poets.

Western Lager was introduced to China through 19th century traders. These were not early traders, if we recall that Marco Polo, the Venetian (1254–1324), is considered the earliest. The Germans established the first Lager brewery at Tsingtao in 1897. As the Western governments increased their "concessions" in China, the number of breweries also increased. Mostly, they supplied the colonists and colonial military forces stationed there to protect the colonies.

Of course, where there is alcohol, there are also prohibitionists doing their best to have it banned. Christian missionaries in China took up their anti-alcohol banners as they did in the West. The Western brewers struck back with advertising such as "American Alcohol Cures Opium" and "Sanitary Alcohol".

When China eventually regained possession of the Eur opean colonies, she nationalized the breweries (a typical reaction in most post-colonial countries. It lets them show the world they're made of tough stuff.). During this period China also increased the number of hop farms. All ingredients are internally produced.

As the communist government relaxes its grip on the economic sector, more entrepreneurs are seizing the chance by opening microbreweries to service small communities and towns. With a population of around one billion, there is plenty of opportunity if the government keeps its nose out of the economic picture. Already, many Western economic experts are fearing that within twenty or forty years (give or take) China will become the world's strongest economic power. The Japanese are worried, too, but they are taking advantage of the investment opportunities.

Virtually every eating establishment, from the simplest noodle stall on up, serves beer. Beer is cheaper than bottled water and soda, and easier to find.

One problem the Chinese face is that they have no understanding of "service". This was trampled by the communists, and the people need to be re-educated in even the simplest of things such as how to store and serve beer properly. Glass is almost unknown—paper or plastic cups are the substitutes. This should improve with time, but travellers to China should be aware of this.

The quality of the beer is inconsistent, but a good one is Peking Beer. Evidently, it is much sought-after, and therefore the stocks turnover is high.

Beer is inexpensive in China: 640ml bottles cost from $0.20–0.35.

Tsingtao beer is probably the most recognized Chinese brand in the USA. They have been exporting it since 1954, but it is hard to find inside the country. China, being hard-up for hard currency, exports most of this beer.

As the Chinese gain more Western expertise we expect to see them become more of a force in international brewing. When this will occur is anyone's guess.

☞ Hong Kong

Population: 5,812,000; **density:** 5,412/sq km (14,005/sq mi)

Annual beer production is 1,378,000hl.

BRITAIN SNATCHED HONG Kong to secure a base for the opium traders expelled from Canton. It was a barren rock occupied by a few communities of fishermen. Commercial development attracted thousands of migrants from the mainland. This immigration has continued ever since, especially whenever China has been convulsed by war or internal disorder.

In 1941 the Japanese invaded Hong Kong and occupied it until the end of the 1939–45 war, when colonial rule returned. Communist armies reached the frontier after their victory in the Chinese civil war (1949) but made no attempt to invade, although the new communist government repeatedly proclaimed that the treaties governing Hong Kong had been imposed by force and were, therefore, not binding. Still, the communists left the colony relatively undisturbed, probably because they didn't wish to provoke the West in to an armed conflict, and (as important) up to 40% of China's foreign exchange earnings are derived from trade and commercial transactions with it.

In 1982 negotiations began on Hong Kong's future. In 1984 China and Britain signed a joint declaration under which China would resume sovereignty over the whole colony in 1997, but promised to grant Hong Kong a high degree of autonomy, allowing capitalism and the inhabitants' life-style to continue undisturbed for 50 years (taken with a pound of salt).

The Chinese in Peking continue to play bully-boy with the British over the introduction of measures to strengthen democracy in the Territory. She has refused, because of the dispute, permission to the British to build a much-needed airport.

☞ Korea (South)

Population (1990 est): 43,045,098; **density:** 437/sq km (1,132/sq mi); **distribution (1989):** 64% urban, 36% rural; **annual growth (1990):** 0.8%.

Annual beer production is 16,400,000hl, placing it third in Asia. Per person annual beer consumption is 36.3 litres.

THERE ARE TWO brewing firms in Seoul, the capital of Korea, OB (Oriental Brewery co Ltd), and Crown. As expected, their main brands are lagers.

The Oriental Brewing Co Ltd was formed by Too Pyung Park in May, 1952. Distribution of ob commenced the next year. In 1966 they introduced canned beer to Korea, whilst expanding production to 75,000kl, three times original output. By 1976, OB opened a second brewery an Incheon with a production capacity of 50,000kl, increased to 150,000kl two years later, and doubled again the following year. In 1980, the brewery was expanded yet again, with production increasing to 430,000kl. As demand for OB Beer increased, so did the need for still another plant, so in 1985, construction started on a brewery at Kwangju. Completed in 1987, its capacity is 100,000kl annually. In 1987, Oriental Brewing entered into a marketing arrangement with Anheuser-Busch. 1988 saw a similar arrangement with Lowenbräu (Germany). The company now has over 60% market share in Korea.

OB operates its own research facility, founded in 1974. This has led to quality improvement in their beer list (OB Beer, OB Light, OB Draught Beer, NAB, Budweiser and Lowenbräu), and helped develop local raw materials (barley and hops) suppliers. In addition, they sent their brewers to study and gather knowledge in many established brewing countries.

In 1986, OB was designated the official beer of the Asian Games, and in 1988, the Oriental Brewery was the official sponsor of the 24th Olympi ad held at Seoul.

OB was first imported to the USA in 1982.

We have been unable, so far, to acquire any information about the Crown Brewery.

☞ India

Population (1991 preliminary census): 843,930,861; **density:** 267/sq km (692/sq mi); **distribution (1989 est):** 26% urban, 74% rural; **annual growth (1989):** 2.2%.

Annual beer production is 2,010,000hl.

THE NUMBER OF breweries in India has greatly fluctuated during the past two centuries. In colonial times there were 14. By Independence there were only four. Today there are about forty. Should Indian economic reforms continue, switching to a market economy from a socialist one (with outrageous restrictions on economic activities), there is no doubt more entrepreneurs will begin brewing. After all, the potential market is enormous. With a population of about 843m, it is the second largest following China. For entrepreneurs, that is a tempting amount of mouths to fill with beer.

Attitudes toward beer (and alcohol) vary from state to state.

A line of brewing cities stretching right up the middle: Bangalore, Hyderabad, Delhi and Solan (from south to north).

As far as styles are concerned, India has a mixed-bag of beers on offer, from lagers such as Lion (OG 1046) and Golden Eagle (OG 1050) to stouts such as Kingfisher (OG 1046).

☞ Indonesia

Population (1991 est): 181,400,000; **density:** 95.2/sq km (246.7/sq mi: **distribution (1990):** 30% urban, 70% rural; **annual growth (1990):** 1.8%.

Annual beer production is 1,195,000hl. Annual consumption of domestic production is an anaemic 0.66 litres. Obviously there is room for more brewers in Indonesia.

ONCE A COLONY of the Netherlands, Indonesia still has commercial brewing links between the two. Naturally, Heineken is a major player. They finally established an associated firm in Java at Surabaja. It produces a conventional-strength pilsener Heineken, and Bintang Lager.

Breda, part of Allied Breweries of Britain (now linked with Carlsberg), brews Anker Beer at Jakarta. It also brews the Skol brand, and a Stout.

The French even have a brewery there. Brasseries de l'Indochine, a Paris-based group has Brasseries de l'Indonésie at Medan, Sumatra, which brews "33" Export, Galion Pilsner and a lager.

☞ Malaysia & Singapore

Malaysia: Population (1991 est): 18,300,000; **density:** 55.5/sq km (144/sq mi); **distribution (1991):** 35% urban, 65% rural; **annual growth (1990):** 2.3%.

Singapore: Population (1991 est): 2,800,000; **density:** 4,531/sq km (11,735/sq mi); **distribution (1991):** 100% urban; **annual growth (1990):** 1.3%.

Annual beer production is 1,342,000hl. Consumption of annual domestic production is 6.4 litres.

CONSIDERING MALAYSIA AND Singapore used to be British colonies, it seems strange that the peninsula's largest brewery, Malayan Breweries Ltd (MBL), has had long-term links with the Dutch giant, Heineken dating to 1930. mbl grew out of Fraser & Neave, a soft drinks company, which distributed its products in Malaysia as well as Indonesia. Realizing that British colonists needed more than soft-drinks to douse their thirst, and with an eye towards profit, F&N hooked up with Heineken and started brewing. Their first product was the famous Tiger Stout.

MBL acquired a second brewery at Singapore in 1941, the year Imperial Japan invaded. In 1962, it built another brewery in Kuala Lumpur, Malaysia. That multi-million dollar brewery is where Anchor Beer, Anchor Draft and Tiger Stout are brewed. MBL also brews its abc Extra Stout. Anchor is the trade name of the brewery.

Malaysia is not an easy place to market beer. Half its 13m population is Muslim, and, therefore, do not drink. There are approximately 3.5m beer drinkers in Malaysia, but their per person consumption is only about 12 pints per year.

Anchor imports its hops from North America and its barley malts from Australia and Europe. It doesn't use adjuncts.

It takes about 16 years to become a Master Brewer at Anchor, but first apprentices must already possess a degree in engineering or science. Key employees are sent to advanced brewing courses at Heineken's facilities in the Netherlands.

Heineken twice a year sends brewery inspectors to Anchor examine every aspect of the brewery's operations. These inspections help maintain the brewery's high quality. Thirty-five quality control inspections are conducted on each batch brewed. In addition, each month MBL sends samples to Heineken for further testing.

Anchor's all-natural beers have won the much-coveted Monde International Trophy, awarded to beers that have been adjudged in three separate years as among the best in the world.

Carlsberg, the Danish brewer, has an associated company in Malaysia, too. They produce Carlsberg Green Label, a Pilsener-type. It also brews their extra-strong Carlsberg Special.

Guinness is also represented here. They brew, via an associated firm, Gold Harp, an all-malt beer, and Foreign Extra Stout with an ABV of 7.8%. Michael Jackson says of this beer:

"It is also one of the world's most unusual beer, combining a powerful body and dry roasted-malt palate, with a sharp acidity. Its full body ensures its local reputation as a beer that will build health and vitality, while its acidity is most quenching. All Guinness in South-East Asia is of the Foreign Extra Stout style."

☛ Sri Lanka (Ceylon)

Population (1989 est): 16,810,000; **density (1989 est):** 258/sq km (667/SQ MI); **distribution (1989 est):** 22% urban, 78% rural; **annual growth (1980-87):** 1.8%.

Annual production is 68,000hl. Per person consumption of annual domestic production is 0.40 litres, barely a blip on the scale.

THERE ARE TWO brewing firms on Sri Lanka. Ceylon Breweries brews Lion Lager, Pilsner Special and an excellent Stout, and two ales, Pale and Jubilee, both sweet.

The other firm is branded with the Three Coins name. The three styles it brews are a lager, a Pilsener-type and a bitter stout.

The ancient Greeks and Romans knew of Sri

Lanka. It has a recorded history dating to the fifth century bc. Buddhism was brought from India during the third century BC.

During its early history, the island was seldom united under a single ruler and, for a period during the 1400s, it was tributary to China.

The Portuguese arrived in 1505 and found seven indigenous kingdoms. The Dutch defeated and displaced the Portuguese in the mid-1600s and controlled most of the island until the British ousted them in 1796. This was the period of great competition between the rising European colonial powers. The country became an independent member of the Commonwealth in 1948.

☞ Taiwan

Population (1991 est): 20,401,174; **density:** 567/sq km (1,468/sq mi); **distribution (1990 est):** 71% urban, 29% rural; **annual growth (1990):** 1.1%.

Annual beer production is 4,544,000hl, placing Taiwan fifth in Asia. Per person annual beer consumption is 22.82 litres, or about the same as in Italy.

Exports are minimal: 17,000hl. Imports are quite a bit more: 178,500hl.

Information is scarce, to say the least.

TAIWAN FIRST BECAME known to the West in the 1500s by its Portuguese name, Formosa, which means "beautiful".

In the 1600s, Spaniards and Dutch briefly controlled parts of the island until the Dutch were driven out in 1661 by Koxinga, a pirate. He made Taiwan into a refuge (after 1644) for supporters of China's deposed Ming dynasty. In 1683, Taiwan surrendered to the Ch'ing dynasty and became part of China's Fukien (Fujian) Province.

Taiwan was ceded to Japan after the first Sino-

Japanese war (1895). She was developed as a colony by the Japanese. It reverted to Chinese sovereignty in 1945. Following the Communist takeover of the Chinese mainland, it became a refuge for the Republic of China's ousted Nationalist government (1949).

☞ Thailand (Siam)

Population (1991 est): 58,800,000; **density:** 115/sq km (297/sq mi); **distribution (1991):** 18% urban, 82% rural; **annual growth (1991):** 1.3%.

Annual beer production is 2,880,000hl. Thailand ranks seventh in Asia. Per person consumption of annual production is 4.9 litres.

THERE ARE TWO breweries at Bangkok, Thailand. They are named the Thai Amarit Brewery Limited and the Singha (Boon Rawd Brewery Co Ltd). Both produce lagers.

☞ The Philippines

Population (1991 est): 62,300,000; **density:** 208/sq km (538/sq mi); **distribution (1990):** 43% urban, 57% rural; **annual growth (1990):** 2.5%.

Annual beer production is 15,400,000hl. Per person consumption of annual domestic production is 24.7 litres. The Philippines ranks fourth in production in Asia.

HERE IS ANOTHER country with a centuries-old native brewing tradition, similar in some respects to those of the natives of Latin America. Looking at native brewing techniques is like taking a look back into brewing's ancient past: not much has changed.

European beer first started penetrating the Philippines during the mid-1800s. Those from America came a while later. Filipinos quickly took to the new styles. Thus, a new market was created, where the imported beer was meant for the colonialists.

Enrique Maria y de Yeaza opened his first brewery in the San Miguel district of Manila in 1890. This was the first commercial brewery in Southeast Asia. His first year's production was 500 barrels. He imported his hops and grains from Germany and North America. He must have been doing something right because by 1913 his beer had driven nearly all the imports out of business. Other brewers, too, tried to compete against his line of beers, but none lasted long.

The Japanese occupation was a very rough period for the Philippines. The occupiers seized the brewery, and started brewing an awful beer using 70% sugar and only 30% malt to give thirsty Japanese soldiers.

The liberation of the Philippines by American soldiers saw the return of the brewery to its rightful owners, and the beginning of an era of expansion. There are now three breweries in its homeland, one in Spain (which many people wrongly assume is headquarters), one in Djakarta, Indonesia, Honk Kong and Port Moresby, Papua New Guinea.

☛ **Note:** The San Miguel brewery at Hong Kong is branded as Sun Lik.

AFRICA

THE PEOPLES OF Africa are like those everywhere in our world when it comes to brewing beer. They have been at it a long time, using local ingredients and techniques developed over hundreds if not thousands of years. As everywhere, beer served as a dietary supplement. Some things have changed with the introduction of European brewing techniques and equipment. This is only natural.

Virtually every country in this region, even Arab lands where consumption of alcohol is discouraged, has local breweries catering to the desires of its peoples.

Too, like the countries of Latin America and Asia, the beers of Africa and the Middle East are widely unknown to Westerners, except perhaps to expatriates and businessmen who have settled or work in these areas. Historical information about brewing is scant in the West. We have fleshed out some of these country's histories with information about the countries themselves, not just their brewing histories.

A problem that adds to their scarcity is the light lagers produced by many African breweries simply do not travel well. An odd thing to say about Lager category beers. Once a beer has been finely filtered and pasteurized, it is a dead beer. Dead beer has a shelf life not much longer than six weeks. Consequently imported beers aren't as fresh as they should be. This hinders their efforts to attract and to keep loyal drinkers. Too, because much of the continent is beset by war and civil strife, supplies ranging from grain to bottle caps are often sporadic. All this effects consistency.

A last, and, perhaps greatest hinderence to the continent's development of a strong beer industry is lack of capital. In the north, the Arabs drink little beer, and though there is national wealth, but little of it into the brewing industry. South of the Sahara, there is little wealth, period. Annual production for the entire region roughly equals that of The Netherlands. What with famines, epidemics, fighting and wrecked economies (thanks to the great socialist economic experiments most of the countries conducted in the years immediately after gaining independence), and with little free capital available, little can be expected. Growth and increased prosperity are forecast for all the economic regions of the world—except Africa.

Pharonic Egypt kept excellent records of their daily life and much of this survives to this day. Then there is this enormous gap until the Colonial Era, when the Westerners recorded events. Despite the lack of written languages in "black" Africa, we can assume the natives of this area brewed for many hundreds or even thousands of years before they were discovered and colonized by the British (foremost), French, Portugese, Belgians, Dutch and the Germans who came late to the "Club".

The first foreign brewery was built in 1900 to satisfy German workers who demanded a quality daily beer rations. Since the weight of beer made it very costly to ship from Europe, it was natural that the colonists started their own breweries. By 1920, there were over 300. Today there are about 175.

Many large Western breweries such as Allied, Amstel, Becks, Carling, Carlsberg, Guinness, Heineken, Schultheiss, Union de Brasseries and Whitbread have links with local breweries throughout Africa.

All the breweries in Africa produce 58,500,000hl of beer per year (1991 figures). This places it fourth amongst the five great land areas.

☞ Algeria

Population (1991 est): 26,000,000; **density:** 11/sq km (28/sq mi); **distribution (1991 est):** 48% urban, 52% rural.

Annual beer production is 321,000hl. Annual per person consumption of domestic production is 1.2 litres.

No INFORMATION ON specific brands and breweries is available now

Until the 1500s, Algeria's history was linked to that of neighbouring Tunisia and Morocco. The region's earliest inhabitants were the Berbers. Phoenician traders arrived on the Algerian coast in the 12th century BC. The Phoenician city of Carthage, in present-day Tunisia, eventually dominated the entire western Mediterranean, including the coast of what is now Algeria. Northern Algeria was united under Masinissa, the tribal leader, after he supported Rome in the Second Punic War (218–201BC). Carthage's destruction in 146BC, and the defeat of King Jugurtha in 105BC left Rome in control of the Maghrib.

The prosperity of northern Algeria under Roman rule is evident from the ruins of thriving agricultural communities such as Timgad.

Later, Christianity flourished—Algerian-born Saint Augustine (354–430AD) was one of the most influential Christian thinkers. Invasions by Vandals ended Roman rule in the 5th century AD, although most of the area remained under Berber control. In the early 6th century the Byzantine Empire extended its influence as far west as present-day Algiers.

The Arabs forced the Byzantines from North Africa in the 7th and 8th centuries. The Berbers converted to Islam, but resisted Arab dominance. From the 10th to the 13th centuries, Algeria was ruled by a series of Muslim dynasties that originated in the Maghrib. The particularly prosperous Almohad period united North Africa and Spain under Muslim rule.

In the late 15th century Christian Spain, having expelled the Muslims from the Iberian Peninsula, captured several Algerian ports. They were forced off the coast with Turkish assistance, and Algeria became nominally part of the Ottoman Empire in 1518. The local rulers of the North African Barbary States had a high degree of autonomy. Piracy against European and American shipping led to British and American intervention in the early 19th century. This was followed by a French invasion (1830) and the deposition of the regent of Algiers.

The French campaign to conquer northern Algeria ended in 1847 with the defeat of Abd al-qadir, the Algerian leader. The French gradually extended their influence southward, despite local resistance, until Algeria's current boundaries were drawn in 1902.

France had encouraged European colonization of Algeria from about 1834; the area was declared an integral part of France in 1848. The European settlers confiscated Muslim land and created a flourishing colonial society removed from the Muslim majority. Muslims had almost no political rights and did not share in colonial prosperity. Organized Algerian nationalist movements arose after the first world war. European settlers, however, bitterly resisted any efforts to grant political and economic equality to the Muslims.

Algeria was under Vichy administration during the early years of the 1939–45 war After 1942, it served as a major base for the Allied North Africa campaign. Algiers was the capital of free France until the liberation of Paris.

The nationalist hopes aroused during the war were not met, and thousands of Muslims perished in bloody reprisals after 88 Frenchmen were massacred during a nationalist demonstration at Setif (1945). Although the French government granted Muslims the vote on a separate electoral roll in 1947, demands for full political equality and further reform were opposed by the European colonists. The nationalist movement gained support and became increasingly radicalized. In 1954 the nationalists proclaimed a war of liberation. They launched terrorist attacks against the French in both Algeria and France. The long Algerian War led to the fall of the Fourth Republic of France, and the return to power of Charles de Gaulle (1958). On 3 July, 1962, President de Gaulle proclaimed Algeria's independence.

☛ Burundi

Population (1990 est): 5,600,000; **density:** 201/sq km (521/sq mi); **distribution (1987):** 5% urban, 95% rural; **annual growth (1989):** 3.6%.

Together with Ruanda, Burundi produces 1,600,000hl of beer per year (1991 figures). Per person annual consumption of domestic production is 12.2 litres (combined with Rwanda).

IN CONJUNCTION WITH Heineken, Primus, the popular beer of Zaire, Burundi's neighbour, is brewed.

Burundi is a small country located at the northern end of Lake Tanganyika in East-Central Africa. It is bordered by Tanzania, Zaire, and Rwanda. It is located near the remotest headwaters of the Nile and Congo rivers.

Burundi history traditionally dates back to the 14th century, when the Tutsi invaded the region and made serfs of the local Hutu population. Tutsi domination continued, under successive mwamis, or kings, until recent times. In 1895 the region was designated a German sphere of interest by the Conference of Berlin.

European colonization was established in 1897 when Burundi was incorporated in German East Africa. In 1916, during the first world war, Burundi was occupied by Belgian troops, and was subsequently administered by Belgium as part of the Ruanda-Urundi mandate of the League of Nations (after the 1914–18 war), and as part of the United Nations Trust Territory of Ruanda-Urundi (after the 1939–45 war). It was formerly known as Urundi. Burundi gained independence as the Kingdom of Burundi on 1 July 1962. It became a republic on 29 November 1966.

Burundi is one of the smallest countries in Africa, but it has one of the continent's highest population densities. The capital and largest city is Bujumbura.

The economy of Burundi is based overwhelmingly on agricultural and pastoral activities.

☞ Cameroun

Population (1988 est.): 10,531,954; **density:** 22/sq km (57/sq mi); **distribution (1987):** 58% rural, 42% urban; **annual growth (1987):** 2.6%.

Beer production is 3,965,000hl per year (1991 figures). Per person annual consumption of domestic production is 37.6 litres.

UNION CAMEROUNAISE DE Brasseries brews both a Bock (ABV 5.0%) and a Super Bock. They also brew Pils 2000. Breda Bier is a Dutch connection, brewed under licence of the Three Horse Shoes Ltd of Breda, Holland.

Guinness also has an associated brewery here, where Foreign Extra Stout is brewed.

The Republic of Cameroun is an independent state in western Africa. It is bordered by Nigeria to the northwest; Chad to the northeast; the Central African Republic to the east; the Congo (Brazza), Equatorial Guinea, and Gabon to the south; and the Atlantic Ocean to the southwest. Most of Cameroun was once ruled by France. The rest was under British control. French influence remains strong, especially in Yaounde, the capital.

Little is known about the country's early history, but the population probably included migrants from the north who had abandoned the increasingly arid Sahara region. Too, it appears that the Bantu languages, now found throughout Africa to the southeast, spread from the Cameroun region. In recent centuries, the Fulani drifted into northern Cameroun, where they founded Muslim states with economies based on cattle keeping and slave-raiding among neighbouring non-Muslim peoples.

Germany proclaimed Cameroun a protectorate in 1884, and the country remained a German colony until the end of the 1914–18 war.

In 1919, treaties divided the territory into League of Nations mandates (1922) under the French and British. Following the 1939–45 war, the mandates became United Nations Trust Territories (1946) under the same powers. The French zone became a sovereign state in 1960, and a year later the southern half of the British territory federated with it. The federal system ended in 1972 when a new constitution was introduced.

☞ Central African Republic

Population (1986 est): 2,744,000; **density (1986 est):** 4.4/sq km (11.4/sq mi); **distribution (1983):** 44% urban, 56% rural; **annual growth (1983):** 2.3%.

The CAR is near the bottom of the list of African brewing nations. It produces 222,000hl of beer per year. The per person consumption of domestic production is 8.1 litres.

NO INFORMATION ON specific brands or breweries is available now.

Large stone formations near Bouar suggest the existence of an ancient civilization in the northwest, and stone tools found in the east indicate that people lived in this region several thousand years ago. However, most of the country's present-day inhabitants are refugees from Muslim slave-raiders in adjacent areas in the 19th century. The raiders' unrelenting hunt resulted in the depopulation of huge areas of the car between the 1880s and 1915.

About the same time, French military expeditions reached the area, and in the 1890s the region was annexed to the colony of the French Congo. Later it became a separate colony in French Equatorial Africa. Internal self-government was granted by the French in 1958. The Central African Republic became independent in 1960.

☛ Chad (Republic of)

Population (1990 est.): 5,000,000; **density:** 3.9/sq km (10.1/sq mi); **distribution (1987):** 27% urban, 73% rural.

Chad ranks next to last in beer production in Africa with 110,000hl per year. This translates to 2.2 litres per person annual consumption of domestic production only.

THE BRASSERIES DU Logone brew Gala "De Luxe" Export Beer.

The Republic of Chad is a landlocked state in north-central Africa. The largest country of the former French Equatorial Africa, it is bounded on the north by Libya, on the east by Sudan, on the south by the Central African Republic, on the southwest by Cameroun, and on the west by Nigeria and Niger. The capital is N' djamena (formerly Fort-Lamy).

In the pre-colonial period Muslim states controlled the northern and central parts of the country, but the French conquered them between 1897 and 1908. Chad was made part of French Equatorial Africa (FEA) in 1910 and a separate colony within the FEA in 1920. In the 1939–45 war, it was the first French territory to declare its loyalty to Gen. Charles de Gaulle and the Free French.

☛ Congo (Brazza)

Population (1991 est): 2,300,000; **density:** 6.7/sq km (17.4/sq mi); **distribution (1985):** 39.5% urban, 60.5% rural; **annual growth (1990):** 3.0%.

Congo (Brazza) ranks in the middle of the pack, producing 600,000hl of beer per year. Annual consumption of domestic production is 26.1 litres.

THE SOUTHERN REGION of the Congo formed part of the kingdom of Kongo, a state that flourished during the 16th century. Its king received the first Portuguese expeditions, and subsequently signed a cultural exchange treaty and welcomed missionaries.

Slave trading by the Portuguese destroyed the state. In the late 1800s, Pierre Savorgnan de Brazza (for whom the capital is named) led a French group that explored the area. In 1883 part of the Congo became a French protectorate, and in 1910 the Congo joined French Equatorial Africa (FEA), which had its capital at Brazzaville. It included what is now Chad, the Central African Republic, and Gabon.

In 1960 the Congo won independence. France dismantled its FEA. A labour uprising overturned the government (1963), and in 1968 a military coup was staged. Congo was declared a communist state in 1969, but by playing both ends against each other, it maintained close economic ties with France and other Western European nations. From 1970 to 1991 the country was renamed the People's Republic of the Congo, and the Congo Labour party (PCT) was the sole political party. The legislature, the National People's Congress, was re-established in 1979.

☛ Cote d'Ivoire

Population (1990 est.): 12,600,000; **density:** 39.1/sq km (101.2/sq mi); **distribution (1986):** 53% rural, 47% urban; **annual growth (1989):** 3.8%.

Annual beer production is 1,095,000hl. Per person annual consumption of domestic production is 8.7 litres.

FROM ABIDJAN COMES Mamba, a very strong beer, wrongly labelled a Malt Liquor in the USA. Michael Jackson describes Mamba as "smooth, sweetish" and is "full-bodied and robust—lusty, emergent beer[s]".

Cote d'Ivoire (Ivory Coast) is a West African nation, located on the Gulf of Guinea. It is bordered by Ghana on the east, Burkina Faso (formerly Upper Volta) and Mali on the north, and Guinea and Liberia on the west. Previously, it was a territory within French West Africa. It achieved independence on 7 August 1960. Its natural resource base and stable government give Cote d'Ivoire good potential for economic growth.

Little is known of the country's history before European involvement in the ivory and slave trades. French missionary contact in Cote d'Ivoire began as early as 1637, but an official French protectorate was not established until 1843–45, when treaties were concluded with local chiefs. Cote d'Ivoire became a French colony in 1893 and was a constituent of French West Africa from 1904 until 1958. It was made an overseas territory in 1946, and its inhabitants were given French citizenship. She was proclaimed a republic within the French Community in December 1958, and finally gained, in 1960, independence.

☛ Egypt

Population (1990 est): 54,700,000; **density:** 54.6/sq km (141.5/sq mi); **distribution (1989):** 45% urban, 55% rural; **annual growth (1989):** 2.6%.

Considering that Egyptians were some of the earliest brewers, their current production of 500,000hl could be considered surprising, if one forgets that the country's religion is Mohammedism, though it is a secular state.

Per person annual consumption of domestic production is 0.91 litre, surely one of the lowest figures.

No INFORMATION ON specific brands or breweries is available now.

☛ Ethiopia

Population (1991 est.): 53,200,000; **density:** 44/sq km (113/sq mi); **distribution (1990):** 11% urban, 89% rural; **annual growth (1990):** 3.5%.

Annual beer production is 460,000hl. Per person annual consumption of domestic production is a paltry 0.86 litres.

THERE ARE THREE breweries in this nation: the Melotti Brewery at Asmara, which brews Melotti Lager and a sweet Extra Stout; Meta Brewery at Addis Ababa, the capital, produces a lager; The St George Brewery, also at Addis Ababa brews a Pilsener.

Ethiopia, a country in eastern Africa bordered by Somalia and Djibouti to the east, Kenya to the south, and Sudan to the west, was one of the earliest world centres of agricultural innovation. Unlike most African nations, it was never a European colony. It has been important to the modern history of Africa as a symbol of independence. Addis Ababa is the headquarters of the Organization of African Unity (OAU), and the United Nations Economic Commission for Africa. The nation's recent history has been marked by the fall of one of the world's last emperors, Heile Selassi, a socialist revolution with its resultant civil horrors, a succession of devastating famines, and civil war between its central government and several of its regions. It has broken up now as a result of its long civil war, though a rump nation called Ethiopia remains.

☛ Gabon

Population (1990 est): 1,068,240; **density:** 4.0/sq km (10.3/sq mi); **distribution (1985):** 41% urban, 59% rural; **annual growth (1990):** 0.8%.

Annual beer production is 900,000hl, leaving Gabon tied for 9th place on the Continent. Per person annual consumption is a respectable 84.3 litres.

THE SOCIÉTÉ DES Brasseries de Haut Ogooué at Franceville brews an ABV 6.0% Pils called Bière Régab.

Gabon is on the west coast of Africa. It straddles the Equator. It is bounded the Congo (Brazza), Cameroun, and Equatorial Guinea. Located on its 885km (550mi) Atlantic coastline is Libreville, the capital and principal port.

In 1839, France signed a treaty with local chiefs that gave it powers over the southern coastal regions of Gabon. The Berlin Conference of 1885 awarded all of the territory discovered by Pierre de Brazza to France. This area was organized (in 1910) into French Equatorial Africa, and the separate colonies of Gabon, Congo, Chad, and Ubangi-Shari were formed.

Gabon achieved its independence from France in 1960.

☞ Ghana

Population (1990 est): 15,165,243; **density:** 63.6/sq km (164.7/sq mi); **distribution (1990):** 32% urban, 68% rural; **annual growth (1990):** 3.2%.

Annual beer production is 602,000hl. Annual per person consumption of domestic production is 39.7 litres.

GHANA IS HOME to three breweries: Accra Brewery, Kumasi Brewery and Gulder International. All three produce lager beers. Club Mini is the brand of the Accra Brewery, established in 1931. Gulder's lager is under its own name, and the brand from Kumasi Brewery Ltd is named simply Star.

Ghana is located on the Gulf of Guinea of the Atlantic Ocean. It is bounded on the west by the Cote d'Ivoire, on the north by Burkina Faso (formerly Upper Volta), and on the east by Togo. Ghana is an independent nation of West Africa located on the Gulf of Guinea of the Atlantic Ocean. It is bounded on the west by the Ivory Coast, on the north by Burkina Faso (formerly Upper Volta), and on the east by Togo. Its capital city, Accra, is on the southern coast. A developing country, it is rich in natural resources. It is among the world's leading producers of cacao. Ghana was formerly the British colony of the Gold Coast. The emergence of a small, educated African elite, combined with a changed world opinion, ultimately led to independence, the first black African colony to gain it. This was in 1957.

The country takes its name from the medieval empire that was located to the northwest of the present state. Migrants from there may have settled present-day Ghana, although the two should not be confused. Initial contact with Europeans occurred when the Portuguese reached West Africa in the early 1400s. They soon established trade relations with the people of the Gold Coast. The West African slave trade began in the mid-1400s, when the Portuguese transported some Africans to meet their own labour shortage. In 1482 the Portuguese built Elmina Castle on the coast. Then the Dutch got into the act. Seeing the profits to be made from the slave trade, they conquered the Portuguese bases in West Africa and, by 1642 they controlled the Gold Coast's forts. Between 1500 and 1870, an estimated 10m slaves, bought from Arab slave traders and black African tribes, were taken from Africa. About 19% of them departed from the Gold Coast.

British interests were, from about 1660 on, the chief competitors of the Dutch. They greatly increased their involvement in the Gold Coast between 1850 and 1874, by which time they had practically broken the authority of traditional African rulers. By 1898 the boundaries of the British Gold Coast were established. Throughout the colonial period, the British developed the infrastructure of the colony to lure British private investments to the area.

☞ Kenya

Population (1990 est): 24,639,261; **density:** 42.3/sq km (109.5/sq mi); **distribution (1986):** 16% urban, 84% rural; **annual growth (1990):** 3.8%.

Annual beer production is 3,300,000hl, which places Kenya fourth on the Continent. Per person annual consumption of domestic production is 13.4 litres.

EAST AFRICAN BREWERIES Ltd (established in 1922) is one of Kenya's biggest companies with three breweries in Nairobi and one in Mombasa. In addition it acts as advisors to the Tanzania Breweries in which it has a 45% stake. In turn, Allied Breweries has a stake in East African Breweries.

Some of the brands from this brewery are City Lager (OG 1042), Tusker Lager (OG 1038) and White Cap Lager (OG 1038). It also brews Guinness Foreign Extra Stout under licence.

Lager brewing began in 1930. Denmark supplies their yeast, and the brewery's brands have been successful, winning two gold- and one silver medal at the 1968 World Beer Competition at Nürnberg, Germany.

Kenya is named for Mount Kenya, the second highest mountain in Africa, located in the south central part of the country at the equator. It is located in East Africa, and is bordered by Tanzania on the south, the Indian Ocean on the southeast, Somalia on the east, Ethiopia on the north, Sudan on the northeast and Uganda on the west. Kenya was a colony of Great Britain before becoming independent on 12 December 1963.

Swahili became the official language of Kenya in 1974. It is grammatically a Bantu language, although it is heavily influenced by Arabic, but is written with the Roman alphabet. English is also an official language and is still widely used.

Modern European interest in Kenya began in the 1850s, when Europeans explored the interior in search of the source of the Nile. Christian missionaries began their efforts to convert the inhabitants and to end the Arabs' lucrative slave-trade. By 1855 there were about 300 missionaries in East Africa and, in 1873 the slave-trade was ended by the sultan.

In 1885, Karl Peters received a charter for his German East Africa Company. He initiated a mad scramble among the European nations to establish colonies in East Africa. The Anglo-German agreements of 1886 recognized the sultan's authority over the coastal areas, but divvied up the rest: the southern coastal strip (now Tanzania) in the German sphere of influence, and the northern coastal strip (now Kenya) in the British sphere of influence.

In 1887 the sultan leased the valuable northern coastal strip to the Imperial British East Africa Company. When that company was dissolved in 1895 the British government established the East Africa Protectorate. They were too smart to let go.

The railroad from Mombasa to Nairobi and Lake Victoria was built in the last decade of the 19th century, and as white settlers began to enter Kenya, large areas of the Kenya Highlands--later known as the White Highlands--were subsequently alienated from the Africans and reserved for white-only settlement. In 1920 the interior regions were organized as the British crown colony of Kenya while the coastal strip remained a British protectorate over lands nominally ruled by the sultan of Zanzibar.

☞ Liberia

Population (1990 est): 2,600,000; **density:** 23.3/sq km (60.5/sq mi); **distribution (1987):** 42% urban, 58% rural; **annual growth (1985–90):** 3.2%.

Liberia ranks dead last in beer production with 50,000hl made annually. Per person annual consumption of national output is 1.9 litres.

Monrovia Breweries Inc brew Monrovia African Lager, Monrovia Club Beer and Monrovia Dark beer. They are all lagers. The brewery has suffered damage in their recent civil war.

The Republic of Liberia is located on the Atlantic coast of West Africa and is bordered by Sierra Leone, Guinea, and Cote d'Ivoire. An independent nation since 1847, Liberia is the oldest republic in Africa and the only nation in black Africa never to have been under colonial rule. It was partially settled by freed American slaves during between 1820 and 1865. Liberia maintained close ties with the USA until the late 1980s.

The population embodies 16 ethnic groups, each with its own language, as well as the English-speaking Americo-Liberians.

Liberia's tribes migrated to the area between the 12th and 16th centuries. The Portuguese arrived in 1461 and began a trade in ivory and pepper, and later in slaves. In 1816 the American Colonization Society was founded in the United States to resettle former slaves in Africa. Four years later the first colonists arrived, and their successful settlement was named Monrovia (for James Monroe, the US president) in 1824. Gradually, more colonists arrived and established separate colonies. In 1847 the colonies merged, and Liberia became the first independent republic in black Africa.

The new nation faced many problems: resistance to the government by the indigenous tribes, declining demand for her exports, and territorial encroachment by the British, French, and Germans. She was able to maintain her independence only with help from the USA. In 1926, to restore the failing Liberian economy, a 99–year rubber-plantation concession was granted to the Firestone Company. This was in exchange for a large long-term loan from the US government. After the 1939–45 war, a modern airport, cargo port, hospitals, a hydroelectric station, &c, all financed by the USA, were opened.

☞ Malawi

Population (1989 est): 8,700,000; **density**: 73/sq km (190/sq mi); **distribution (1988)**: 13% urban, 87% rural; **annual growth (1989 est)**: 3.3%.

No production figures available.

With the government of Malawi, Carlsberg operates a brewery. They produce Carlsberg Beer and Carlsberg Lager.

Malawi is a landlocked nation in southeastern Africa. Approximately equal in size to Pennsylvania, it is bordered by Mozambique, Zambia, and Tanzania. Malawi was a British protectorate until 1964, when it became independent. Since then, while remaining primarily an agrarian nation, it has achieved steady economic growth. Unlike most African nations, Malawi has chosen a path of neutrality in international affairs, maintaining ties with both black African nations and South Africa.

The Maravi kingdom, centred in the Shire River Valley, arose during the 15th century. At its peak, it reached as far south as Rhodesia, present-day Zimbabwe. During the late 18th century, the kingdom faded as a result of warfare and internal conflicts.

In 1859, David Livingstone, the great British explorer and medical man, came to the region. This led to the arrival of British settlers. In 1891 the British protectorate of Nyasaland was created. In 1953, Nyasaland became part of the Federation of Rhodesia and Nyasaland. Internal hostility to the federation led to the birth of a nationalist movement, and in 1963 the federation was dissolved. In 1964 the independent nation of Malawi was declared.

☞ Mauritius (in the Indian Ocean) and Reunion Island

Mauritius: population (1991 est): 1,100,000; **density:** 539/sq km (1,396/sq mi); **distribution (1990):** 41% urban, 59% rural; **annual growth (1990):** 1.8%.

Reunion Island: population (1987): 560,004.

Beer production on both islands is 505,000hl, placing just ahead of Egypt. Annual per person consumption of domestic production is 30.4 litres.

MAURITIUS BREWERIES LTD produces The Phoenix Beer (OG 1049) and Stella Pils (OG 1044). In addition, they brew Guinness Foreign Export Stout.

Mauritius is an independent island state in the Indian Ocean. It is 805 km (500mi) east of Madagascar. Its outlying territories include the island of Rodrigues, situated 554km (344mi) eastward. It is about 104 sq km (40 sq mi), and two clusters of islets. She has had a history of successive colonization and immigration by French, East Africans, British, Indians, and Chinese because of her location on important ocean trade routes,.

Although it was explored by the Portuguese (1510) and Dutch (1598), previously uninhabited Mauritius was not permanently settled until 1721, when the French occupied the island. They established sugar plantations, and brought East African slaves to work them. In 1810, during the Napoleonic wars, the British captured the island and brought Indian servants to work on the plantations.

She gained her independence in 1968.

The island of Mauritius itself is volcanic and is surrounded by dangerous coral reefs.

Reunion is an island in the western Indian Ocean located about 645km (400mi) east of Madagascar. The island covers an area of 2,512 sq km (970 sq mi). Saint-Denis is the capital.

☞ Morocco

Population (1989 est): 25,605,579; **density:** 57.3/sq km (148.5/sq mi); **distribution (1989):** 43% urban, 57% rural; **annual growth (1989):** 2.5%.

Morocco produces 625,000hl of beer annually. Per person consumption of annual domestic production is 2.4 litres.

☞ Namibia (ex-Southwest Africa)

Population (1989 est): 1,372,425; **density:** 1.7/sq km (4.3/sq mi); **distribution (1988):** 30% urban, 70% rural; **annual growth (1985–90):** 3.2%.

Annual beer production is 556,000hl. Annual per person consumption of domestic production is 40.5 litres.

THIS COUNTRY, BEING a German colony for a while, still has much German influence in its beers styles. Hansa Brewery, one of two majors in the country, produces Hansa Pilsener, Export and Tafel brands. All have an OG of 1040. Hansa also brews a strong (OG 1080) Urbock of the dark style.

Hansa's rival is the South-West Breweries Ltd (SWB), also at Windhoek, the capital. Windhoek Export and Windhoek Lager are both brewed at OG 1044. To match Hansa's Urbock, swb has their Windhoek Mai-Bock in addition to Windhoek Extra-Stout (OG 1050).

Namibia is one of the most sparsely populated countries in Africa.

The earliest known inhabitants of Namibia are the San. They were hunters and gatherers whose presence goes back some 11,000 years. In the mid–1400s, Bantu-speaking peoples from East Africa began migrating southwestward to Angola and northern Namibia. They had pushed southward into the central Namibian plateau by the early 1700s.

The first European to visit the area, Diego Cao, the Portuguese explorer, arrived at Cape Cross in 1485. Shortly thereafter, the Dutch East India Company began exploring the Namibian coast from their station at Table Bay (now Cape Town). In 1773 the Cape government proclaimed Dutch sovereignty over Angra Pequina (Ludderitz), Halifax Island, and Walvis Bay. The Cape Colony and all its possessions were formally ceded to Britain in 1814.

By the early 1800s, British and German missionaries spread across the interior. Namibia became a German colony (German South West Africa) in 1884, although the British had annexed Walvis Bay in 1878. The German settlers expropriated African lands and assigned Africans to reservations. Between 1904 and 1907, Herero and Nama rebellions against German land policies were brutally suppressed. The Herero were reduced from 80,000 to 15,000, and the Nama from 20,000 to 9,000.

During the 1914–18 war, South African troops invaded Namibia and forced the Germans to surrender. Namibia (now South West Africa) was administered by South Africa under a League of Nations mandate. After the 1939–45 war, as the clamour to end apartheid in South Africa grew to a crescendo, and in defiance of the international community, the South African government refused to hand over administration of Namibia to the United Nations. It ruled the territory directly for much of the period before independence. In the meantime they established a society based on separation of the races. This has finally ended under a Russian- and American-brokered peace and free elections.

☛ Nigeria

Population (1992 census): 88,500,000; **distribution (1986 est):** 28% urban, 72% rural; **annual growth (1987):** 2.9%.

Annual beer production is 8,386,000 hl, placing Nigeria second in Africa after the Republic of South Africa. Annual per person consumption of domestic production is 9.5 litres.

FOR MANY YEARS, central Africa led the continent in brewing output, but in 1974, Nigeria took the lead and west Africa now holds the distinction. It has more breweries, about 50, than any other nation on the continent.

Nigerian Breweries Ltd produces Guilder Lager and Star Lager. The firm has financial ties with Heineken.

West African and Golden Guinea are two other breweries. West African Breweries Ltd produces TOP Lager Beer. Golden Guinea Breweries Ltd brews New Eagle Stout.

Nigeria is located on the Atlantic coast in West Africa. It is bordered by Benin on the west, Niger and Chad on the north, and Cameroun on the east. Nigeria has a population of 88,500,000 (1992 census), making it the most populous nation in Africa. Lagos, the capital, is the second largest city in sub-Saharan Africa (after Kinshasa, Zaire). Nigeria derives its name from the Niger River. The country attained its independence on 1 October 1960, but has been plagued by numerous changes of government.

Northern and southern Nigeria (savanna and forest, respectively) each have their own history. Arab traders, as early as the 8th century, found African peoples who were highly organized, with cities and towns, a trading network, and a monarchical government. The earliest first-hand account is that of the Arab traveller Ibn Battutta, who visited the western savanna zone from 1352 to 1353. A series of kingdoms flourished in the savanna zone, beginning with the kingdom of Ghana (700–1350) in the west and moving eastward to the Hausa emirates (emerged C.1000AD), located in present-day northern Nigeria.

In Yorubaland, in the southeast, archaeological evidence suggests a high degree of urbanization by the 11th century. Sophisticated bronze and brass sculptures by the Yoruba and the Benin tribes indicate a high level of metallurgical skill. In southeastern Nigeria, the Ibo had, by the 9th century, developed a sophisticated society that was involved in trade and supported artistic endeavours, including bronze sculpture.

The first Europeans to visit the Nigerian coast were the Portuguese seeking routes to India. As early as the 1440s the Portuguese began taking slaves to Portugal. The slave-trade was well established by the early 1500s.

British acquisition of Nigeria was accomplished by the Royal Niger Company, under Sir George Goldie. British claims to the Niger Basin were recognized by the other European powers at the Conference of Berlin in 1885. In 1914 the Colony and Protectorate of Nigeria was established, and Sir (later, First Baron) Frederick Lugard was installed as governor-general. He established the policy of indirect rule: rule through the pre-existing chieftain structure. A precursor of the proxy wars strategies managed by the ex-Soviet Union and the USA decades later?

In 1960, Nigeria gained its independence and became a federation.

☞ Rwanda

Population (1991 est): 7,500,000; **density:** 285/sq km (738/sq mi); **distribution (1985):** 6% urban, 94% rural; **annual growth (1990):** 3.8%.

Together with Burundi, Rwanda produces 1,600,000hl of beer per year (1991 figures). Per person annual consumption of domestic production is 12.2 litres (combined with Burundi).

IN CONJUNCTION WITH Heineken, Primus, the popular beer of Zaire, Rwanda's neighbour, is brewed.

☞ Senegal

Population (1990 est): 7,400,000; **density:** 37.7 persons/sq km (97.7/sq mi); **distribution (1989):** 36% urban, 64% rural; **annual growth (1989):** 2.7%.

Senagal is second from bottom of the African list, ahead of only Chad and Liberia. It produces 150,000hl of beer per year. Per person consumption of annual production is 2.0 litres.

THE BRASSEE A Dakar par Sibras produces Sibras brand beer.

During the 14th century the Mali empire expanded westward into present-day Senegal. In the 15th century the Wolof united several small states into the Jolof empire, which lasted into the 18th century.

French colonists founded Saint-Louis, on the Senegal River, in 1658, though French traders had been in the area since 1637. The colony passed back and forth between the French and the British during the 18th century, and was finally restored to France in 1815. The French gradually extended their control inland.

In 1895 the Federation of French West Africa was formed with Dakar as its capital. Although local self-governing institutions existed at Saint Louis and at Dakar in the 19th century, Senegal was not granted internal self-government until 1956. In 1959, Senegal and the French Soudan (Mali) merged as the Mali Federation, but Senegal broke up the federation soon after independence (1960).

In the 1980s, Senegal faced economic problems and political turmoil. A border incident with Mauritania in 1989 resulted in violent riots, and displacement of thousands of people from both countries. Senegal also has been engaged in a 12-year territorial dispute with Guinea-

Bissau. In 1989 an international panel ruled in Senegal's favour, but Guinea-Bissau rejected the decision. Senegal joined the us-led anti-Iraq coalition during the Gulf war of 1991.

☞ Seychelle Islands

Population (1990 est): 67,378; **density (1988):** 151.5/sq km (392/sq mi); **distribution (1989):** 52% urban, 48% rural; **annual growth (1988):** 1.6%.

No production figures are available.

IT MIGHT BE hard to imagine, but 1,450km (900mi) out in the Indian Ocean off the East African coast, Guinness produces their Foreign Export Stout. Brauhaase, of the Schultheiss group, set up a micro-brewery that produces a fine Pilsener (unpasteurized). Schultheiss, through Brauhaase, markets breweries around the world.

As early as 1505 the Seychelles islands were first charted by the Portuguese, although Arab traders may have visited them before that. In 1742, the French took possession, and French settlement began during the 1770s. After the defeat of Napoleon Bonaparte, the islands officially passed into British hands by the Treaty of Paris (1814).

Under both the French and the British, the islands were regarded as a dependency of Mauritius, an island located about 1,800km (1,100mi) to the southwest. In 1903, Seychelles became a separate British crown colony. Pressure for independence began in the 1970s and led to the Seychelles becoming an independent republic on 29 June 1976

☞ South Africa

Population (1991 est): 40,600,000; **density:** 33.3/sq km (86.1/sq mi); **distribution (1989):** 56% urban, 44% rural; **annual growth (1990):** 2.7%.

Annual beer production is 22,500,000hl. Per person annual consumption of domestic production is 55.4 litres.

INTERCONTINENTAL AND SOUTH African Breweries Ltd (SAB) are the two big breweries in South Africa.

SAB (founded in 1895) brews Amstel Lager and Carling Black Label under licence. Their local brands consist of Schaft (ABV 6.0%), Castle Lager, Castle Milk Stout, Lion Lager, Hansa Lager, and Lion Ale. sab is the largest brewing firm in Africa. Far from being just a brewery, it has diversified into foods, hotels, property, retail businesses and manufacturing.

Intercontinental was established in 1973 by Rupert International. Rupert has ties with Carlsberg, and controls the original Carling in Canada though it is brewed by its rival, SAB, in South Africa.

Intercontinental brews a selection of beers, both its own brands and some under licence. They are all lagers: Sportsman, Heidelberg, Becks and Kronenbrau 1308.

The first known inhabitants of present-day South Africa were the San and the Khoikhoi, who were hunters and gatherers. They were followed southward by Bantu-speaking peoples between 1000–1500AD. In 1488, Bartolomeu Dias, a Portuguese mariner rounded the Cape of Good Hope. In 1652 Jan van Riebeeck, a Dutchman, established the first European settlement at Table Bay (now Cape Town) as a station for the Dutch East India Company. Dutch pioneers spread eastward, and in 1779 war broke out between Xhosas migrating south and the Dutch near the Great Fish River.

Britain controlled the Cape sporadically during the Napoleonic wars, and formally received the territory (1814) under provisions made by the Congress of Vienna. Large-scale British settlement began in 1820.

To preserve their Calvinist way of life and to keep distance between themselves and "government", the Dutch (Boer) farmers began (1836) to move into the interior on the "Great Trek". In 1838 approximately 70 of the Voortrekkers were massacred by Zulus. Seeking vengeance, Andries Pretorious led the Boers against the Zulus, defeating them in the Battle of Blood River. The Voortrekkers eventually established independent republics, including the Orange Free State (1854) and the South African Republic (1852; later the Transvaal).

Discovery of diamonds and gold in the late 1800s drew British immigrant entrepreneurs (Uitlanders, or "foreigners") into the interior, and conflict over ownership ensued. Paul Kruger (Oom Paul), leader of the Transvaal, resisted British attempts to claim the area, including those by Cecil Rhodes, prime minister of the British-controlled Cape Colony, who encouraged the Uitlanders to take over the Transvaal. The unsuccessful Jameson Raid, engineered by the British, and intended to aid the Uitlanders in an uprising, added to the mounting tension. Eventually, the Boer War (1899-1902) erupted between the British and the Boers. After an arduous and vicious campaign, the British won. In 1910, Jan Smuts helped create the Union of South Africa, with dominion status, out of the former British colonies and the two defeated Boer republics. Louis Botha, a moderate Afrikaner advocating close co-operation with the British, became the first prime minister.

☛ Sudan

Population (1991 est): 25,900,000; **density:** 10/sq km (27/ sq mi); **distribution (1985):** 29% urban, 71% rural; **annual growth (1990):** 2.9%.

Annual beer production is unavailable.

THERE IS THE Blue Nile Brewery at Kharthoum. It brews Camel, a lager (OG 1044). The brewery is state-owned, but it use to be linked with Courage.

Egypt first unified the small, independent Sudanese states, some of which had existed since the early Christian Era, in 1820–21. Later in that century, the Muslim Mahdi ("messiah"), Muhammad Ahmed, led a religious revolt. He captured El Obeid (1883) and Khartoum (1885) after a long siege in which Charles George Gordon, the British general, was killed. The Mahdi died the same year, but his successor formed an autocratic state that lasted for the next 13 years. The Mahdist state was overthrown, however, by British and Egyptian forces led by Lord Kitchener (1898). Sudan then came under the joint rule of Britain and Egypt, and remained so for more than 50 years.

Independence was achieved on 1 January 1956, but the governments during the first 13 years of independence, both civilian and military, were unstable. The country has been undergoing a prolonged civil war between the Arab Muslim north and the Black Christian (and native-religions) South.

☛ Tanzania

Population (1987 est): 23,500,000; **density:** (1987 est): 24.9/sq km (64.4/sq mi); **distribution (1986 est):** 18% urban, 82% rural; **annual growth (1987 est):** 3.5%.

Annual beer production is 667,000hl. Annual per person consumption of domestic production is 2.8 litres.

TANZANIA NDOVU LAGER and Snow Cap Lager are brands of Tanzania Breweries Ltd. The brewery has links with East African Breweries Ltd of Kenya.

By around 500BC, people lived at various places along the Tanzanian coast. Accounts of the coastal area in the 1st century AD describe several settlements where commerce took place. For the next millennium Arab traders plied the coast, trading with Zanzibar and with settlements on the Tanzanian mainland.

Tanzania principally settled by migrating waves of Bantus. These tribes probably moved along the Congo River network into the southern portion of present-day Zaire. By the 10th century the areas around Lake Victoria and Lake Tanganyika had been settled.

Vasco da Gama was the first recorded European to visit the coast of Tanzania (1498). Portuguese conducted trade along the coast until 1698, when they were expelled by Arabs from Oman. European missionaries and explorers such as David Livingstone arrived in the 1850s. The Anglo-German Agreements (1886 and 1900) divided spheres of influence along the present Kenya-Tanzania border, giving Germany control of the southern portion (today's Tanzania).

German East Africa was, at first, administered by the German East Africa Company, but in 1891 the German government assumed control. The region became a protectorate. Opposition to foreign rule mounted, leading to a quasi-religious Maji Maji rebellion, which lasted from 1905 to 1907. As a result of Germany's defeat in the 1914–18 war, Britain took over German East Africa in 1920.

In 1954, Julius Nyerere was one of the founders of the Tanganyika African National Union (tanu), which led the nationalist movement. The movement won independence for Tanganyika in 1961, and Nyerere became head of state. Zanzibar, which gained independence in 1963, joined Tanganyika (1964). Finally, the nation was renamed Tanzania in 1965.

☛ Uganda

Population (1989 est): 17,000,000; **density:** 72/sq km (187/ sq mi); **distribution (1987):** 43% urban, 57% rural; **annual growth (1980–85):** 3.35%.

Annual beer production is 247,000hl, placing Uganda sixth from the bottom of the list. The almost constant civil strife and war in the country can only have been harmful to the nation's economy and people.

Per person annual consumption of domestic production is 1.45 litres.

NILE BREWERIES , AT Jinja, produces Source of the Nile Lager (OG 1040), and Source of the Nile Pilsener (OG 1042).

The native people of what is now Uganda ranged from the ancient centralized and rival kingdoms of Buganda and Bunyoro to the decentralized Acholi and Amba. Extensive migration and trade relations previously existing among peoples throughout Uganda, but British rule tended to freeze these groups into their present places.

British explorer John Hanning Speke reached Buganda in 1862 during his successful search for the source of the Nile. Missionaries followed, and shortly after there were rivalries at the court of the *Ganda kabaka* (king), which led first to religious persecution and then to religious wars. By siding with one faction, Capt. Frederick D Lugard (later, 1st Baron Lugard) established a military presence that committed a reluctant British government to make Uganda a protectorate (1894). In 1900, Buganda's leading chiefs signed an agreement accepting British protection in return for freehold rights in land for themselves. This provided Britain with a base from which to consolidate colonial rule over the rest of Uganda, and helped create the opportunity for Buganda to reinforce its cultural separation from (and more rapid economic growth than) its neighbours.

The too-complicated federal constitution under which Uganda received formal independence on 9 October 1962, recognized four kingdoms, ten customary districts, and one "special" district.

Milton Obote, a Langi, became prime minister in an uneasy coalition with Kabaka Yekka, a Ganda, following two sharply contested national elections. The coalition predictably broke down, and a battle between the national and Buganda governments led to the exile of the kabaka, the elimination of federalism, and a direct role for the army in national life, which has characterized the country up to the present (recall the wicked and disgraceful rule of Idi Amin).

☛ Zaire

Population (1990 est): 36,600,000; **density:** 15.6/sq km (40.4/sq mi); **distribution (1985):** 56% rural, 44% urban; **annual growth (1989):** 2.9%.

Zaire is fifth on the list, producing 3,000,000 hl of beer each year. Per person annual consumption of domestic production is 8.2 litres.

PRIMUS IS THE biggest national brand. Heineken lends a technical helping hand. Zaire is a huge country, and there are a few local brands within different provinces.

Long before Europeans arrived during the 15th century, Zaire had developed an iron technology, an agrarian culture, trade, and a measure of political centralization in the states of Kongo, Kuba, Luba, and Lunda.

The Portuguese navigator Diogo Cao reached the estuary of the Congo River in 1482. Commercial and diplomatic relations were established between Portugal and the Kongo kingdom, and some trade was conducted with neighbouring Portuguese colonies in Angola.

In 1877, Henry Stanley was the first European to travel down the river. After this arduous and dangerous journey, King Leopold II of Belgium commissioned Mr Stanley to undertake additional explorations, and to establish stations along the Congo. In 1884–85, King Leopold's claims to the Congo River basin were recognized at the Conference of Berlin. He then established the Independent State of Congo under his personal rule. In 1908, following international criticism of brutalities tolerated by King Leopold, the territory became a colony under the direct control of the Belgian government. Although development took place, the Belgians made little effort to involve black Africans in administration or the economy, using them principally as cheap labour.

During the 1950s, opposition to Belgian control grew. It erupted (January 1959) into nationalist rioting in Kinshasa. Independence was granted by Belgium on 30 June 1960, after only a minimum of preparation, as was often the case with other colonies.

☛ Zambia

Population (1991 est): 8,400,000; **density:** 11/sq km (29/sq mi); **distribution (1986):** 43% urban, 57% rural; **annual growth (1990):** 3.2%.

Zambia is tied with Gabon at ninth on the list of African beer-producing countries. Annual beer production amounts to 900,000 hl. Per person annual consumption of domestic production is 10.7 litres.

IN 1851, DAVID Livingstone crossed the Zambezi River from the south, and spent the next 20 years exploring what is now Zambia. In the late 19th century the British South Africa Company began making treaties with the local chiefs in what was then called Northern Rhodesia. Following the British administrative takeover of the region (1924), and the discovery of copper in the late 1920s, many Europeans immigrated to the area.

In 1953, Northern Rhodesia, Southern Rhodesia (now Zimbabwe), and Nyasaland (now Malawi) were brought together by the British into the Federation of Rhodesia and Nyasaland. This federation lasted until 1962, when Nyasaland pulled out, followed by Northern Rhodesia in 1963. Independence for Zambia followed on 24 October 1964.

☛ Zimbabwe (ex-Rhodesia)

Population (1988 est): 9,700,000; **density:** 24.7/sq km (62.2/sq mi); **distribution (1987):** 24% urban, 76% rural; **annual growth (1987):** 3.5%.

Annual beer production is 2,800,000 hl, placing the country 6th in Africa. Annual per person consumption of domestic production is 28.9 litres.

RHODESIAN BREWERIES LTD produces the same Castle and Lion brands as in South Africa.

White settlement dates back to 1890, when the Pioneer Column led by Leander Starr Jameson, of Cecil Rhodes's British South Africa Company, trekked north from South Africa in search of gold and land and open spaces. The Company acquired land by treaty and by battle against the Mashona and the Matabele tribes.

Rhodesia was administered by the company until 1923, when it became the (self-governing) British colony of Southern Rhodesia. The United Kingdom retained the right to intervene on constitutional issues and matters affecting the African population. In 1953, Southern Rhodesia was joined with Northern Rhodesia and Nyasaland to form the Federation of Rhodesia and Nyasaland. Salisbury was the capital of the federation.

Under a 1961 constitution, limited voting rights were extended to blacks, but the whites remained in actual control. In 1963, after black governments were established in Northern Rhodesia (now Zambia) and Nyasaland (now Malawi), the federation was dissolved. No agreement could be reached with the British on the issue of black participation in the government of an independent Rhodesia, and on 11 November 1965, Prime Minister Ian Smith made an unilateral declaration of Rhodesia's independence. A constitution preserving white control of the government was adopted.

This move drove the country into isolation as no country other than South Africa recognized the breakaway colony. The British government, which termed the secession an illegal act, and the United Nations imposed trade sanctions, including an embargo on petroleum shipments. Rhodesia held out because Portuguese-ruled Mozambique and South Africa opposed the economic sanctions, and petroleum continued to enter Rhodesia until Mozambique gained independence (1975).

In 1969, after further fruitless negotiations with London, a new constitution ruled out future black majority rule, and Rhodesia was proclaimed a republic in March 1970.

Black nationalists continued to seek greater representation in government throughout the 1960s and '70s despite detention and exile of prominent leaders and other forms of repression. Guerrilla attacks on European farms and road and rail links intensified in the mid-1970s, especially after Mozambique became independent and closed its borders with Rhodesia. In 1978, seeking to end the war, Prime Minister Smith negotiated an "internal settlement" with black leaders, which led to an interim coalition government led by the four leaders. In elections held in April 1979, the principle of universal suffrage was accepted for the first time. Mr Muzorewa became the nation's first black prime minister, and the country was renamed Zimbabwe Rhodesia.

EUROPE

THE BREWING INDUSTRY in Europe is undergoing change. All industries are changing because of the European Union, to which most Western European countries are members, and many of the rest are rushing to join. Much of this is due to directives issued from Brussels that are intended to increase competition by removing inter-European barriers to trade and competition. Germany was forced to admit beers that did not conform to the *Reinheitsgebot*. It did not mean Germans had to drink these beers. It did mean that the German government could not keep them from being offered within Germany. The tied-house system, in which breweries are allowed to own pubs and restaurants is being looked at with an eye towards abolishing the practise. Some argue that large breweries with more cash to spend can control the outlets to the detriment of small brewers. After all, a brewer needs to sell his product to pubs, but if the pubs are owned by the other brewers, how can he sell his beer? On the other hand, some small brewers and consumer organizations, such as CAMRA, feel the abolition of the tied-estate will bring the ruination of small brewers because the large brewers will simply cut their prices to the point where small brewers will no longer be able to compete, because they have higher costs per unit.

Too, the recent social revolution in Europe, which few expected ever to see in our lifetime, freed the countries of the ex-Warsaw Bloc from communist domination. This has opened many doors to renewed commercial efforts. The brewing industry has not been slow to respond. One of the first items western Germany sent to her rejoined *länder* to the east was beer. To the Western breweries quickly formed links with ones in the east or laid plans to establish new breweries in those depressed lands. The countries of Eastern Europe are fertile grounds for renewed investments by brewing companies, both established and newly formed ones.

As modern Western equipment is installed in these breweries, the standards of the beers they produce can do nothing but improve.

There have been some serious discussions of establishing a two-level tax structure to help brew-pubs and micro-breweries remain competitive with the HCBs. Though much of what comes down from Brussels is socialist in nature, the bureaucrats there do realize that the most dynamic sector of any economy is the small to medium-sized business one.

Even pubs are slowly coming under the regulating influence of the European Community based at Brussels. Regulations concerning method of dispense, the measure, sanitation and other ways of pub life are coming under scrutiny. There even was a move to replace the venerable Pint with metric standards of measure.

There is an anomaly about beer consumption in Europe. This occurred to us as we researched the different countries in this section. There is a fat band across the centre of Europe, Its western edge is France's Atlantic and Channel coasts; its eastern edge is out in Ukraine and Russia; its southern boundary lies north of Italy; and its northern one takes in Denmark. To the south of this band, the peoples of southern France, Greece and Spain have a wine drinking tradition. We discussed the Beer Line elsewhere. To the far north, the peoples of Finland, Iceland and Scandinavia had long ale- and mead-drinking traditions, yet these formerly fierce tribes have been cowered by their governments and churches into near abstinence from alcohol. The more power the people give up to their government and religious leaders, the more Church and State treat their citizens as babies, unable to think clearly or choose for themselves. There's a lesson here.

A hunch is that membership in the EU will force change upon these northern countries, change that, as things now stand, would be politically slow in coming. Cowardly legislatures and bureaucrats could then say (oily) to prohibitionists, "Of course we are on your side, but Community directives (laws) mandate that we must loosen our grip on the throats of alcohol producers and drinkers. We have no option but compliance." (There is now a European Court with powers of enforcement). What a joyous day that would be for brewers and beer-drinkers alike.

Finally, Europe, taken in totality, is the biggest beer producing continent. It is just ahead of the Americas, producing 445,687,000hl per year versus New World production of 437,453,000hl. (See charts in Appendix for national production figures.)

☛ Albania (Republic of)

Population (1990 est.): 3,262,000; **density:** 132/sq km (341.4/sq mi); **distribution (1989):** 35% urban, 65% rural; **annual growth (1989):** 2.0%.

Annual beer production is 100,000hl. Per person consumption of annual domestic production is 3.06 litres. This figure surely isn't a threat to even the Fourth Division.

LITTLE IS KNOWN in the West about brewing (or much else for that matter) in Albania. For decades it was one of the most isolated, secretive and totalitarian. For much of that period, her only "friends" were communist China and North Korea. She shunned the Soviets, much to their chagrin, but being so small, she wasn't worth any effort to influence her.

Albania, one of Europe's smallest countries, and it's poorest, is situated in the western part of the Balkan Peninsula. She has a 360km (225mi) coastline on both the Adriatic and Ionian seas. She's bounded on the north and east by the ex-Yugoslavia and by Greece on the southeast. The Albanians' name for their country, *Shqiperi* means "eagles' land", aptly suggests Albania's isolated, rugged terrain and its strongly independent-minded people. Albania began the painful process of changing from a one-party dictatorship to a multiparty democracy, and from a centrally controlled economy to a free-market system in 1990, after

four decades of rigid Communist rule,

For a Balkan state, Albania, fortuanately, has an highly homogeneous ethnic composition. Albanians comprise 96% of the population. They are believed to be descendants of the ancient Illyrians, who were among the earliest inhabitants of the Balkan Peninsula. Despite centuries of foreign domination, the Albanians have managed to preserve their national identity and language. Albanians comprise two major subgroups: the Ghegs (or Gegs) to the north of the Shkumbi River and the Tosks to the south.

☛ Austria

Population (1990 est): 7,600,000; **density:** 90.6/sq km (234.7/sq mi); **distribution (1990):** 55% urban, 45% rural; **average annual growth:** 0.1%.

Annual beer production is 10,184,000hl. Per person annual beer consumption is 123.7 litres.

Austria exports 807,000hl and imports 290,000hl each year.

EVEN THOUGH AUSTRIA isn't the brewing nation it once was, we have much for which to be thankful to her.

Austria and her Empire occupied a unique position in Europe though she is landlocked. First, she WAS part OF the Roman Empire, and influenced by the Romans' love of wine. She was the Holy Roman Empire of the German Nation. She is located south of the Beer Line. Austria is Southern European. Second, the Austrian Empire included Hungary, bits of Poland and other Slavonic peoples, and Bohemia. She was an earlier (and less successful) version of the American melting pot. In addition she incorporated other German lands to her north until knocked back by the Prussians. Austria is Central European. Third, she had been under great influence and pressure from the more aggressive Germans to her north. Austria is Teutonic—German, so her people also were influenced by their own beer-drinking customs.

Any mention of Austrian brewing would be incomplete without first mentioning the great Dreher brewing family. Some accounts say the family began brewing in the early 1600s. Others, that the tradition did not begin until the end of the 1700s, when they bought a brewery from a nobleman at Klein Schwechat.

Anton Dreher built a huge brewing empire. He bought or opened breweries at Michelob in Bohemia, Budapest, Hungary and Trieste, Italy. Only the brewery at Pilsen was larger than his plant at Vienna.

He worked closely with Gabriel Sedlmyer, the great brewer of München, and separately, but in collaboration, developed the equipment that turned the tide in Lager's favour—refrigeration. Anton Dreher is credited with brewing the first modern lager in 1841 at his brewery at Vienna. A German commission ruled on this in 1941. Gabriel Sedlmyer was right behind, and the Bohemians changed over to lager-brewing the very next year.

The Austro-Hungarian Empire was going through upheaval. She was dead on her feet, but did not realize it, nor did the other countries of Europe. She was running out of strength and falling apart at the seams. Simultaneously, the Dreher brewing empire had begun to merge with that of another Austrian family, that of Mautner-Markhof. The Austro-Hungarian Empire collapsed at the end of the first world war and, Austria, again, at the end of the second. Her population now stands about 7.5m. The brewery at Trieste was acquired by Heineken and Whitbread. The Mautner-Markhof's lost control of the brewery during the 1939–45 war, only to regain it in 1976. It operates under the name Schwechat. Since then, they have acquired many smaller breweries.

They brew Steffl Export, Austria's number-one draught beer, and have several other brands such as Skol Pils, Lager, Hopfenperle,

Schwarzquelle Spezial and Easter and Christmas Bocks.

The largest brewery group in Austria today is Österreichische Bräu, based at Linz, and with seven other breweries round the country. Their best-selling brand is Kaiser Bier.

Gösser Bräu is another fairly large brewery. It is based at Loeben in Styria, the region with Austria's highest per-person beer drinking rate: 145 litres per year. The national average is about 100 litres. Next to the firms headquarters is a Benedictine monastery, which has a brewing museum. The firm supports the museum, and one of their popular brands is Stiftsbräu, an Abbey Beer.

There are about 60 active breweries left in Austria today. Though they produce a wide range of styles, hardly any are in the classic Wiener style. Sadly, one must go elsewhere to drink it.

Finally, though it doesn't have a *Reinheitsgebot* of their own, there is a law derived from the old Hapsburg *Codex Alimentarius*, which forbids the use of artificial colouring being added to beer. It declares that beer must be made from cereals, hops and water, but it does not specify which cereals are acceptable. Whilst adjuncts may be used, Austrian beers are of high quality.

☛ Belgium (Kingdom of)

Population (1990 est): 9,958,000; **density (1990 est):** 326.3/sq km (845.1/sq mi); **distribution (1991):** 95% urban, 5% rural; **annual growth (1990):** 0.1%.

Annual beer production is 13,799,000. Per person annual beer consumption is 112.0 litres.

Belgium exports annually 3,145,000hl, and imports 459,000hl. Obviously there is a much higher demand for Belgian beer in the world than the demand Belgians have for foreign beer. Why should they, when the styles they brew are so distinctive and delicious? Nowhere else are so many different styles brewed.

THE NUMBER OF Belgian breweries as declined from 3,223 in 1900 to just 126 in 1992. Actual production has decreased from 14,617,000hl to 14,259,000hl, a reduction of 358,000hl. The amount of imports and exports have flip-flopped, though. In 1900, Belgium imported 5,149,000hl of beer. The 1910s were most cruel (the 1939–1950 period was likewise), and Belgium almost ceased importing beer. Since then, the peak year for imports was around 1980 when 969,000hl was brought into the country. It has since declined to its present level. Exports, on the other hand, rose from a paltry 5,000hl in 1900 to the present (1992) 3,458hl. Export or wither.

Belgium is a beer-lover's paradise—provided, that is, that you enjoy unusual-tasting (to a non-Belgian's palate!) beers. According to the Belgian Brewers Association, Belgium offers "400 different kinds of beer, often still artisanal, characterized by more than 200 original tastes". This is not a land of light-coloured Pilseners or Cream Ales (although Pilsener-style beer is brewed there). Rather, if you enjoy or are willing to try fruited beers, unique ales (some very sour and some extremely strong), Scotch Ales not brewed in Scotland, beers made by monks, beers fermented by air-borne yeast and beers made in other unusual ways, then Belgian beers are for you. They are an acquired taste, but once acquired, they will hold you for a lifetime.

Except for Belgium's HCBs, with their modern plants, looking at most of the other breweries is like peering back through brewing's history. Many of the practices, techniques and equipment are centuries old. Yet world-class beers are produced with them. There is something warm and comforting in these old-style beers. They are unlike the cold, almost antiseptic image that Helles and Pilsener have become.

One centuries old practice is to ferment different beers from the first and second runnings from the mash tun. The first runnings are made into strong beers, and the second into weaker ones. This practice dates to the Middle Ages.

Perhaps the Great Spirit is being kind to the Belgians, repaying them for all the horrible battles that have raged across her landscape since recorded history. The Romans fought here, as did the Spanish, French, British, Prussians, Russians, Germans, Americans, Canadians and others. It was here, at Oudenarde, that John Churchill led the British to victory over the French in 1708. Waterloo (1815) was fought in southern Belgium, about 20km South of Brussels. The British, with last minute help from the Prussians finally ended Napoleon's tyranny. The Germans invaded twice, with horrible destruction. Dunkirk, the site of the evacuation of the bef in 1940, is also in Belgium. The North Americans chased the Germans out in the 1939–45 war. Thankfully, peace has reigned since 1945, and the Belgians are back brewing and consuming their favourite beverage to the tune of 145 litres per year, which places them consistently in the top three with Germany and the ex-Czechoslovakia. She has, at times, headed the list.

By legend, the King of Beers is Jan Primus, the first duke of Brabant, Louvain and Antwerp. He also goes by the name Jean Primus, in French and Gambrinus, a corruption, throughout most of the rest of Europe. By this latter name he is honoured at some breweries, either with a brand using his name, or as the name of the brewery itself. He is credited with introducing the Toast as social custom.

Belgium (and the rest of the world) isn't restricted, as is Germany, with a *Reinheitsgebot*. This frees the Belgians to brew many more styles of beer than elsewhere. Why don't other countries commercially brew like the Belgians? It isn't that other countries are restricted from brewing the same type beers as the Belgians. It simply that these styles have no traditions or commercially exploitable followings in other countries. We do note, however, that quite a few brew-pubs are adding some Belgian styles, especially Fruit Beers. These don't, yet, have the character and depth of Belgian examples, probably because they are brewed with fruit syrup instead of going through the long process of producing the "real thing", but we must applaud the start. We recently had a Chocolate Mint Stout at a brew-pub in San Diego, California. The mint was a little over accented, but the beer was very tasty, and we noticed other patrons drinking it as well. This is a good sign.

Cafés are a way of life in Belgium, though half their beer drinking takes place at home. In a country smaller than Ohio or about the same size as Wales, there are 60.000 cafés serving beer, an incredible number.

☛ Czech Republic & Slovakia

Population (1990 est): 15,700,000; **density:** 123.3/sq km (318.9/sq mi); **distribution (1990 est):** 75% urban, 25% rural; **annual growth (1990):** 0.2%.

Combined annual beer production is 23,855,000hl. This ranks fifth in Europe between Spain and France. Per person annual consumption is 120.8 litres. This is third in Europe behind Germany and Denmark. She has one of the most disparate ratios between imports and exports: exports are 1,752,900hl and imports are a minuscule 8,400hl. When a country's brewers are making great beer, there's scant incentive to drink foreign beer.

THESE TWO COUNTRIES, recently separated and going their own ways, are at the heart of Europe. They are bordered by Poland on the north, Germany on the north and west, Ukraine on the east, and Hungary and Austria on the south. They have long been called the crossroads of the East and the West.

The Czechs, being closer to the free-wheeling Germans have chosen a market economy path, whilst Slavic Slovakia has kept to a socialist one.

With the opening of the Czech economy by

selling off state-owned firms, Westerners have come looking for opportunities. Many have been looking to acquire the Czech breweries, especially the Budwar Brewery (by you know who) and Pilsner Urquell, by far the two best-know Czech brands. These takeover attempts are being resisted because the Czechs are certain the HCBs (particularly American ones) will force bean-counter mandated changes upon them, thus ruining their classic beers (a not unreasonable fear). The Czech government seems convinced of this and have opposed such take-overs. The management are determined that Pilsner Urquell will forever be brewed only in Pilsen. Surely this must be one of the most enlightened governments in the history of beer. Imagine how much better the brewing culture in the USA would be today if the brewing industry hadn't been destroyed by Prohibition.

A problem Pilsner Urquell will face is expansion. They plan to double production in six years from 1991, but their present plant is too small to allow this. The bottle neck is in the underground lagering cellars (not nearly large enough), and in coopering (finding enough of the proper type wood to simply maintain the barrels is hard enough, let alone to plan to make new ones). So, it is inevitable that stainless steel lagering vessels will be installed as the brewery modernizes.

As we were going to press, we learnt that Bass, the British giant, has, for £9m, bought 10% of the market in the Czech Republic via Prague Breweries, that country's second-largest brewery. Bass gets exclusive marketing rights in the EU to *Staropramen*, PB's leading brand. Bass, for its part (and, of course the £s), is sending in a management team, directors, marketing men and technicians. (We wonder if they are going to Prague to learn how to brew a proper lager? They could have asked the Germans a century ago.) Look for *Staropramen* to be brewed in England by Bass, under licence.

The Czechs a cash hungry, but they do not necessarily want to give up their breweries to foreign interets, but $s & £s & D-marks will usually win out in the end.

☞ Denmark (Kingdom of)

Population (1989 est): 5,100,000; **density:** 118.4/sq km (306.7/sq mi); **distribution (1989):** 84% urban, 16% rural; **annual growth (1989):** 0.0%.

Annual beer production is 9,672,000hl. Per person annual consumption is 126.2 litres. The number of active breweries is 19. Denmark exports 2,560,000hl of beer and imports 16,000hl, the lowest figure in the EU. Barley, is grown on about 50% of all farmland.

HERE IS SMALL Germanic country (with virtually no population growth) with the huge Carlsberg A/S (formerly United Breweries Ltd) group comprising the Carlsberg, Frederika, Neptune, Wiibroes and Tuborg breweries. It controls about 80% of the Danish national market. Tuborg, the other large brewery in Denmark, and Carlsberg had been co-operating since the beginning of this century. It is a natural that they combine. The overarching thought was that they wanted to be strong enough to compete in the ever more competitive EU. The concern has interests all over the world. Recently, it merged with Allied-Tetley of Britain to form one of the largest HCBS in that country. It is based in Copenhagen, the capital.

Any history of brewing must praise the Carlsberg brewery, for it was there, in 1883 that lager yeast cells were first isolated after years of tenacious and dedicated research. Since its founding, Carlsberg has always been at the forefront of the industry in the adaptation of technology to brewing. Incidentally, the name Carlsberg came about in this way. Jacob Christian Jacobson founded a new brewery, with money inherited from his mother, upon a hill, berg in Danish. He had a five-year old son he had named Carl. He put the two together. The first Carlsberg beer was brewed in the November of 1847.

Years later, there was a split between father and son. This brewery came to be called the Old Carlsberg, and the one Carl founded as New Carlsberg. Years later, the two breweries re-combined.

Let us back up and describe some of the significant history of this brewery in a more orderly manner.

Sometime in the late 1700s, Christian Jacobsen, a farmer's son, set out from Jutland to Copenhagen. He soon started brewing. Setting what was to become a family characteristic, he sought out technology to help him brew better beers. He was one of the first brewers to use a thermometer. This was an enormous step.

Christian Jacobsen's son, Jacob Christian Jacobsen (Norse naming patterns are a bit convoluted), further examined the ways science could help brewing.

In 1854 Jacob Christian set off on a remarkable journey from Copenhagen to München by stagecoach. His mission was to return with lager yeast. He convinced Gabriel Sedlmyer, whom he previously had studied under, to give him a couple of small containers of yeast. To keep the yeast from drying out, he kept his stovepipe hat over the containers, and at every stage stop he poured water over the yeast. In this manner he successfully completed his return journey.

He used the yeast to brew the first good-quality lager beer in Denmark. He lagered the beer in storage areas in the city's ramparts, which served a secondary purpose.

Jacob Christian was relentless in his pursuit of scientific excellence. Amongst his friends and colleagues were Anton Dreher, Louis Pasteur, Gabriel Sedlmyer and Eugene Velten of Marseilles, a brewer. In 1875 he set up the Carlsberg Laboratories. Besides its obvious interest in brewing sciences, it is an endowment that pursues research of benefit. The next year, the Carlsberg Foundation began operations to "benefit science and honour the country".

One of the single-most important discoveries at the laboratory was made by Emil Christian Hansen, a scientist who had worked at the New Carlsberg. His contribution is not small. He isolated the first single-cell yeast culture. Once the trick of isolating different yeast species was known, it became a matter of experimenting to find which ones make acceptable beers and which don't. His experimenting was successful in 1883. To understand their better: not all yeast strains produce tasty beer. Before the isolation of single yeast cultures, the yeast brewers used was not pure but, rather, made up of two or more yeast strains. It was more or less haphazard how they were combined. Brewers kept trying different combinations until they hit a "good" one. This accomplishment of Emil Hansen's allowed brewers to eliminate bad yeast strains. This went a long way to ensuring brand consistency.

Denmark is a small country of 5m souls. The Carlsberg concern controls about 80% of the domestic market. Consequently, the 19 remaining breweries are very small and divvy up the remaining market between themselves.

Denmark's brewers produce many different styles of beer in both the lager and the ale categories. Though Carlsberg/Tuborg are known for their high-quality lagers, there are quite a few ales produced, including an Imperial Stout. Two particular styles of note are tax-free because they are under ABV 2.5%. The two are White Ale and Ships Ale. What makes these a bit peculiar is that they are brewed as normal-strength beers, but have low alcohol content. As an example, Carlsberg brews an OG 1048 White Ale, that would normally have an ABV of 4.6–4.9%. This brand's ABV is only 1.65%.

From a small land came a gigantic effort by the Jacobsen family at the Carlsberg breweries. Their hunger for scientific knowledge led to some of the most important advances in brewing. Beer lovers the world over have gained much for which to be thankful of them.

☞ Finland (Suomi)

Population (1988 est): 4,954,359; **density (1988 est.):** 15/sq km (39/sq mi); **distribution (1989 est):** 62% urban, 38% rural; **annual growth (1980-87):** 0.5%.

Annual beer production is 4,408,000hl, placing it immediately behind Ireland. Per person annual consumption is 85.5 litres, on par with the USA.

Finland exports 142,600hl of beer per year, and imports 63,400hl.

FINLAND IS SOMETIMES grouped with Denmark, Norway and Sweden in Scandinavia, but it is not. The latter three are Nordic/Germanic linguistically and genetically. The Finns were originally central Asiatics, forced northward by larger tribes, especially the Russians, with whom they have had a rocky relationship for many centuries. They are related in some ways linguistically with Estonians across the sea, and the Hungarians are some distant far-removed cousins but, in reality, the Finns stand alone. Over the years they have mixed with Eastern Balts and the Nordics.

Finland is the fifth largest country in Europe, excluding Russia, and Helsinki, its capital, is the world's second most northern capital after Reykjavik, Iceland.

The Finns were one of the tribes that brought brewing to Central Europe from Central Asia when they migrated westward and northward in 100–200AD. Elsewhere in this book, we previously noted that the *Kalevala* devotes more versus to beer brewing than it does to Creation.

Hops were introduced to Finland very early on. Fifty years before Columbus discovered the Americas (1492), King Christopher decreed that every Finnish farmer should maintain a hop-garden of at least 40 plants. This was to reduce a drain on the national hard currency that was used to buy imported hops.

After years of Swedish domination, Finland passed to Russia and became a Grand Duchy under the Czars. By the end of the 1800s, the Finns were the most-advanced brewers in the Russian Empire. One of her best breweries was at Viborg, Karelia Province. This was the land the ex-Soviet Union stole by force of arms from Finland in the winter wars of 1939–41. After 50 years of communist devastation, there is talk of the lands reverting to Finland, but the Finns don't want them any longer. The cost of bringing them up to Finnish standards would bankrupt the 5m citizens in Finland proper. They have taken heed of what reunification is costing the Germans, and smartly want no part of it.

The Finns are mostly Lutheran, hard-working and pious. They are also fun-loving and hard-drinking. A story goes that three Finns got together for a serious drinking bout. Bottle after bottle of spirits were consumed. Not a word passed among them. On the third dawn, one said, "Oh, look! Here comes the sun again." One of the other two shouted, "Shut up! We came here to drink, not to hear a sermon!"

Perhaps this is why they were the only European country to legally enact Prohibition (hiss!), as did the USA. This period lasted from 1919 to 1933. Today, even by strict Scandinavian standards, Finnish laws about drinking (and their high tax rate) are severe by almost anyone's standards. Local government has veto rights on any changes to national law: of Finland's 500 communities, 40 ban class III and IV beer. Class I beer (ABV < 2.8%) is the most accessible. Brewers don't even bother with class II. They refuse to brew class II beer (ABV < 3.75%). Class III beers have ABV < 4.64% and, finally, Class IV beers have ABV < 5.65%. There is a new class, VI-b, Export, as of 1993, that allows ABV 7.0%.

When Finland joins the EU soon, her laws will have to come into compliance with Euroregulations. Perhaps there will be a lightening of restrictions. Counterbalancing all this (somewhat) is a law, similar to Germany's *Reinheitsgebot*, that states that grains other than barley are banned. It does permit he use of brewer's sugar.

Traditionally, Finns often used rye in their beers, but this is a grain which imparts a harsh taste. It is a hearty local grain and that was one reason it was used. Home-brewing is very popular. Here rye malt is used with barley malt. Both home-brewers and commercial firms make *sahti*. In addition to hops, traditional berries and branches of the Juniper are used along with straw. The branches and straw act as a filter on the wort. *Sahti* is often brewed strong, up to about ABV 12.25%. There are many sahti breweries, and their product is sold through the state-owned monopoly shops. Another tradition that hasn't, thankfully, died is the female brewer. Women still are the main brewers in Finland. This is almost foreign in the USA where brewing is now looked on as an almost exclusive male activity. We are founding members of a home-brew club. There are about 150 members. To our best reckoning, just two are females who actively brew. Yes, there are some women involved in the brewing industry, some owning breweries, like Marcia King at the New England Brewing Company, but their numbers are small beer.

Finland's biggest brewing firms are Mallasjuoma, Sinebrychoff and Hartwall.

Mallasjuoma has breweries at Heinola, Lahti and Oulu.

Sinebrychoff is based at Helsinki, the capital, with another brewery at Pori.

Hartwall has breweries at Turku, Vasa and at Lappeenranta in Finnish Karelia.

In addition, Pyynikki has a brewery at Tampere, Oivi has one at Lisalmi and Lapin has one at Tornio.

Too, as of 1993, Finland has legalized brewpubs. As of this writing, there are two. One, *Kappeli,* is in Helsinki and brews unfiltered and unpasteurized lagers. The other, *Vanha Apteekki* (Old Drug Store), is in a "protected" building in Turku. It brews ales. As in many countries, the Finns are active to protect historic buildings. So much so, that the new brewpub owners can't change the name of the building! So, even though it is now a brewery, the signage still says *Vanha Apteekki*. A bit of bureaucratic nonsense, to say the least.

☛ France (Republic of)

Population (1990 est): 56,556,000; **density:** 104/sq km (269.3/sq mi); **distribution (1990):** 74% urban, 26% rural; **average annual growth (1990):** 0.5%.

Annual beer production is 20,991,000hl. Per person annual consumption is 40.5 litres, down from 44.31 litres in 1980.

France exports 1,016,790hl of beer annually. This is up from the 615,829hl she exported in 1980. She exports most of her beer to Switzerland, Spain, Italy and the UK. Imports are 2,906,000hl, up from 2,676,222 in 1980.

FRANCE HAS 33 active breweries (1991).

France? France et bière? Non, non, Monsieur! C'est impossible!

Wait! If this isn't so, then how come the patron saint of beer is St Arnou de Lorrain? There are several versions of this Saint Arnoul and his lineage, but this is what our research has revealed. Actually, his name was Arnulf, Bishop of Metz, and that is how you will find him listed in the *Encyclopædia Brittanica*, not under Arnoul.

He was an Austrasian noble who gained the Bishopric of Metz in 613 as reward for going into the service of King Clotaire II of Neustria against Brunhilda. In 623, Clotaire decided to pass his kingdom to Dagobert, his son. Clotair appointed Arnulf and Pippin I (The Old) as mentors to his son. Arnulf had a son, Adalgiselus, afterward called Anchis, before he received the Bishopric. Pippin had a daughter called Begga. Anchis married Begga, and they

had a son named Pippin II.

When Pippin II grew up he waged war against the Ebroïn, the mayor of the palace, and Neustria. He won a great victory at Tertry, near St Quentin in 687. From that date he was sole master of the Frankish kingdom. Pippin II had several sons and grandsons whom he appointed to several positions of power. However, his illegitimate son by a concubine, Charles Martel, seized power, and continued the lineage. It was Charles Martel's son, Pippin III, who fathered Charlemagne or Karl I der Grosse, as he is known to the Germans. Charlemage was one of the greatest rulers the Franks ever had.

Now, let us return to St Arnulf in 613. He remained Bishop of Metz for fifteen years. He then retired to a monastery at Remiront. He died there on 16 August 640. The next year, the citizens of Metz asked for the return of his body so they could inter it at the Church of the Holy Apostles. It is said that during the journey the tired porters and hangers-on stopped to rest and to have a drink at the village of Champigneulles. However, there was only one mug of beer for the whole throng. It was passed round, but the mug was never drunk empty, and everyone had their fill of beer.

A miracle! A new Saint.

Since the Franks are a German tribe, it is only befitting that they, too, are beer drinkers. Actually, Julius Ceasar found the Gauls to be brewing beer when he arrived as Conqueror. Over many centuries, the Romans managed to pacify and latinize the Gauls and most of the Franks. Part of this taming of the wild tribes included wine as the drink of choice, rather than beer. Today the main beer-drinking and brewing areas of France are in her borderlands with Germany, and in the north by the Germanic Flemish and Dutch.

The French now drink only about 45 litres of beer per person per year. This is one of the lowest figures in the EU, besting only the Italians at 16 litres. Germany consumes about 147 litres per person annually and the Belgians are next at 143 litres.

Another of France's sons made great contributions to brewing science. His name was Louis Pasteur. He was directly involved with the difficulties of brewery production, and he loved to work "hands on". His greatest contribution was making brewers comprehend the fermentation process.

Lille is the "capital" of the beer-drinking Région du Nord, which runs up to the Belgian borderlands. It is in this area that the most distinctive beers in France are brewed—namely, Bière de Garde. This style was brewed by farmers for their workers. They are ales with a distinctly "earthy" taste, and they are real treats.

France's second brewing region is Alsace, a territory that has passed back and forth between France and Germany for centuries. It is French now, and given the modern situation, it is likely to remain so. It is a little strange to meet people named Pierre Fräbel or Karl-Heinz Potvin, but that is how it is. Many of the breweries and their brands in this region bear German names, such as Kronenbourg, Fischer and Kanterbräu.

Lager is the primary style brewed in Alsace. The words *de luxe* are often on the labels. The style accounts for about three-quarters of output. One big difference between French lager and that across the border in Germany is that the French aren't tied to the *Reinheitsgebot*. This allows them to make cheaper beer than their neighbours. The alcohol content of these de luxe beers is about ABV 5.0%.

There has been a resurgence in beer drinking in France, led by the you people. Production has been increasing in the last thirty years, after many when it simply foundered. Of interest: women consume more than half the output. Middle-aged and the elderly continue to prefer wine, but as they pass they will be replaced by beer-drinkers. The future bodes

well for France's brewers, even if they are consolidated in the hands of a few HCBs. To, France has is share of entrepreneurs opening micro-breweries, such as the Two Rivers at Morlaix in Brittany, which brews three cask-conditioned ales, or Le Micro Brasserie at Paris.

In the ten years from 1965 to 1975 more than 50 breweries consolidated into just six groups. They are Albra (Heineken), Artrois (Motte-Cordonnier), Brasseries du Pêcheur, BSN Bières, Pelforth and Union de Brasseries.

☞ Germany (Deutschland)

Population (1991 est): 79,500,000; **density:** 223/sq km (577/sq mi); **distribution (1991):** 83% urban, 17% rural; **annual growth (1990):** 0.0%.

Annual beer production is 117,993,000 hl, up from 92,342,000 hl in 1980, and 18,176,000 hl in 1950. Deutschland ranks second in the world after the USA. Per person annual consumption is 142.7 litres, which makes it first in the world.

Deutschland exported (1991) 6,755,000 hl, up from 2,244,029 hl in 1980, and 104,425 hl in 1950. Imports have grown from 2,464 hl in 1950 to 826,384 hl in 1980 to 2,809,000 hl in 1991. There are 1,315 active breweries. She buys more beer from Denmark than any other country, and Great Britain is the biggest export market for her beer.

Frankreich? Vergessen sie Frankreich. Wir haben bier hier!

THE SHEER NUMBER of breweries in Germany almost overwhelms the mind. There are over 1,300 of them, with more on the way as the eastern *länder* are brought up to speed. At times, it seems every village and town has a brewery, though this can be misleading because the density of breweries varies from land to land. The heaviest concentration is in Bayer (Bavaria) with somewhere in the neighbourhood of 800. To Bavaria's west, Baden–Württemberg is next with about 250 breweries. By the time one reaches Schleshwig-Holstein, in the north, there are only a light handful scattered about. Although almost all Germans drink beer, (it would seem a prerequisite to be considered a German), the fun-loving Porsche-, Mercedes- and BMW-building Bavarians and Baden–Württembergers absolutely relish their beer (they are also quite keen on their excellent wines).

Germans remain loyal to their local brands. There still isn't a true "national" brewer in the sense of Anheuser-Busch, Carlsberg or Allied-Tetley (with the latter two recently merged). Becks, in North America, gives the image that it is Germany's national brewer, but this is mere propaganda for ignorant Americans. The Germans have even less stomach for imported beer. The purists amongst them consider any beer not made to the *Reinheitsgebot* to be ersatz. Less than 4% of the beer Germans drink is foreign.

The evaporation rate of beer is highest in Germany: the annual per person beer consumption rate is about 150 litres.

It is staggering, the number of words written about German beer and brewing: Germany and Beer are almost synonymous. Her brewers have gone to all parts of the world to teach others how to brew in the German style; her breweries have links with many breweries in other countries; her beer styles have been copied (in some countries, none to well) the world over. Since the end of the 1939–45 war, millions of foreign soldiers stationed there have brought home tales of the marvellous beer the Germans drink. Too often these tales have been a lament, an indictment of the quality of beer brewed at home. This is beginning to change in other countries, thanks to the efforts of micro- and pub-brewers.

An interesting habit taken up in the USA is the adoption of the German Oktoberfest (most are correctly celebrated in late September). These appear to be proliferating and growing in scope, though we doubt anyone keeps count on how many "Oktoberfest" are held in the States. The best of these even offer Imported German beer or, with growing frequency, Real North American Lagers supplied by a local micro-brewery. This is appropriate.

The two big German Oktoberfests are at München (the one everybody knows) and at Canstatt, a district of Stuttgart. Actually, the event at Canstatt is not called Oktoberfest but, rather, Canstatter Wasen. The one and only true "Oktoberfest" is at München. Other brewers, German ones included, are trying to capitalize on the Oktoberfest name by branding their beers as such. True Oktoberfest beers must come from München brewers.

The celebration at München began in 1810 to honour Queen Theresia, wife of King Ludwig. The site is called *Theresienwiese* (Theresia's Meadow). Only brewers located in München proper can participate. They are Augustiner-Bräu Wagner, Forschungsbrauerei München, Gabriel Sedlmyer Spaten-Franziskaner-Bräu, Hacker-Pschoor-Bräu, Lowenbräu, Paulaner-Salvator, Thomas-Bräu and Staatlisches Hofbräuhaus in München. Recently, a big brew-ha-ha developed when the brewing prince, Luitpold of Bavaria, was barred from participating. The good prince complied by opening a brewery in the city. The organisers, turned the tables. They declared that only breweries established before a certain date were eligible. Wouldn't you know it. The cut-off was before the date the prince opened his brewery. The brotherhood of Münchener brewers is evidently a closed shop.

The king of Württemberg began the *Canstatter Wasen* in 1818. This annual event has the distinction of being held at Germany's largest fairgrounds.

All the different German styles are discussed in the chapter on beer profiles. It is fair to note that most brewers the world over (the notable exceptions being Great Britain and Belgium) tend to pay homage to the great German styles by imitating them, some remarkable well, and others the similarity ends at the name on the bottle. One segment, brew-pubs, contrarily concentrate on brewing ales. There are several reasons for this. First, Ales can be turned over much quicker. This increases profit. Lagering a bottom-fermented beer, by its very nature, takes longer than to condition an ale. Long lagering creates problems of storage space, another big expense most businessmen consider well worth avoiding. Second, lagers are harder to brew, and are more prone to have something go wrong during the brewing process that will seriously taint a batch, making it unsaleable. This is costly. Third, pub-brewers wisely stay away from brewing light lagers because of the similarity to the beers produced so cheaply by the HCBS.

A custom that is falling by the wayside is the stoneware steins. Many of us have at least one in our collections, or at the least we've seen pictures of happy Germans toasting with their steins or, perhaps more frequently, the serving girl carrying more of these steins than seems humanly possible. These steins are going the way of steam locomotives. They are being replaced by (often) distinctive glassware. We would be remiss if we did not mention Böckling of Neudenau, Rastal and Sahm, both of Höhr-Grenzhausen. They are some of the foremost designers and manufacturers of stoneware, glass and porcelain drinking vessels. Just looking through the Rastal catalog makes ones mouth thirst for a beer.

Beer has been serious business (and a source of great pleasure) in Germany for many centuries, if not millennia. The practise of brewing fell under the watchful eyes of kings, princes and other nobles. There are still several breweries in Germany owned by counts. Of interest, Friedrich the Great, Prussia's finest leader and king, was trained, at his father's direction, to be a master brewer.

☛ Greece (Ellas)

Population (1991 est): 10,100,000; **density:** 76.5/sq km (198.2/sq mi); **distribution (1990):** 58% urban, 42% rural; **annual growth (1990):** 0.1%.

The name Greece is derived from the Latin name Graeci, applied to a people who lived in ancient times in the northwest part of the country.

GREECE'S SEVEN BREWERIES produce 3,500,000hl of beer per year, ranking it between Switzerland and Norway. Provisional 1992 figures show this increasing to about 4m/hl. Per person annual consumption is about 40 litres, or about the same as in France. She exports 130,000hl and imports 182,000hl (provisional 1992 figures),

There is very little brewing information available on Greece, drawing not a single mention in Michael Jackson's *The World Guide to Beer.*

☛ Hungary

Population (1989 est): 10,600,000; **density:** 114/sq km (295/sq mi); **distribution (1989 est):** 59% urban, 41% rural; **annual growth (1989):** −0.2%

Annual beer production is 9,302,000hl. Per person annual consumption is about 99 litres, placing her citizens as some of the more thirsty ones in the world. We have no figures on exports, but she imports 1,120,000hl (1991). It could be that all domestic production goes to feed domestic demand.

HUNGARY GAINED MUCH of her modern-day brewing heritage when she was part of the Austro-Hungarian Empire. When Pest, the second half of the city Budapest was built, enormous quantities of stone had to be quarried. What an ideal situation. Quarry caverns often make excellent lagering cellars, and that was the case here. In 1854 the Köbánya brewery was established in the city. This attracted German and Austrian brewers who brought with them knowledge of the lagering process (remember, lagering was a new technique at that time). The Köbánya brewery still exists with several others: Pécs, Sopron, Nagykanizsa and Borsod. Most of our information dates from the late communist period, and there is a good likelihood that even more breweries and brew-pubs are now established, or working in co-operation with German and other foreign-breweries. In 1991 Heineken bought 50% of Komaromi Sorgyor, another brewery. As the second largest brewery firm in the world, Heineken contiues its international expantion.

The most popular "session" beer is Pale Lager of fairly low gravities called Világos (3.0% ABV) and Kiniszi (3.5% ABV).

There are also some dark beers called Barna (5.0% ABV) and a stronger Bak, which might be their equivalent of a German Bockbier.

Hungary has been pushing ahead with market reforms, such as privatization, in the post-communist era. She is also keen to get into the eu to gain complete access to its markets for exports. Don't be surprised if at least one Hungarian brewery makes a good mark for itself in the export market sometime in future.

At the last possible moment for inclusion, as we were finishing this book, we read that South African Brweries (SAB) has bought 80% of the Köbánya brewery. SAB paid us$50m for the stake. Over the next five years, it intends to invest a further $40m.

☛ Iceland (Republic of)

Population (1990): 256,000; **density:** 2.5 /sq km (6.4 per sq mi); **distribution (1990):** 90% urban, 10% rural; **annual growth (l990):** 0.9%.

Annual beer production is only 61,000hl, placeing Iseland dead last in the European League list, behind Albania. Per person consumption of annual domestic production is 23.83 litres.

ICELAND IS THE second largest island in Europe, after Great Britain, with just asmall fraction of the latter's population. Located in the North Atlantic Ocean immediately south of the Arctic Circle, Iceland lies about 965km (600 mi) west of Norway, 800km (500mi) northwest of Scotland, and 260km (160mi) southeast of Greenland. Reykjavik, its capital, is on the southwest coast. She had been under Denmark's control since the late 14th century, and became a separate, independent kingdom under the Danish crown in 1918. In 1944. she bacame a republic.

Iceland's population is predominantly Scandinavian. The rest is of Celtic origin. A high degree of homogeneity characterizes the inhabitants of an island. Not many people think of Iceland as a place to move to. Their Icelandic language is distinct, having evolved from Old Norse, but belongs to the same North Germanic group as the other Scandinavian languages. More than 95% of the population is Evangelical Lutheran.

The Lutherans have almost eradicated all traces of the once-great beer drinking traditions of their ancestors. Let's face it, ~24 litres annual consumption per person doesn't even begin to take the chill from their bodies. A good German drinks that in under one month.

☛ Ireland (Republic of) (Eire)

Population (1991 est): 3,500,000; **density:** 49.8/sq km (129/sq mi); **distribution (1991 est):** 56% urban, 44% rural; **annual growth (1991):** 0.6%.

Annual beer production is 4.870,000hl. This figure places her between Sweden and Finland. Per person annual beer consumptionis 117.0 litres, up from 105.0 litres in 1985. This places her people between Belgians and New Zealanders. There are seven breweries. on the island. In 1991 she exported 2,615,000hl, placing her fourth in Europe between Belgium and Denmark. She imported only 65,000hl.

IRELAND IS KNOWN for her world-famous, and now classic, Guinness Stout. It is brewed under licence in many countries besides Ireland, and to different gravities. About 40% of the Guinness's Stout is exported, much of it going to Britain, even though a substantial Guinness brewery is at London. One sad passing this year was the discontinuance of bottle-conditioned Guinness Stout, which, argueably, was the best of the Guinness brands. A great source of commercial-quality yeast for home-brewers has vanished, except as sediment in the bottoms of unconsumed bottles.

Contrary to popular notion, Stout is not a native beer to Ireland. She adopted it as one of her own. Stout developed across the Irish Sea by the large commercial Porter-brewers of London. Until her independence, Ireland was part of Britain for many centuries, so it wasn't an outright theft. Stout's popularity was, no doubt, spread round the world in no small way by Irish emmirants. It got its start in Ireland when Arthur Guinness bought a clapped out brewery in Dublin in 1759. His goal was to brew Porter and Stout. He succeeded. Today the Guinness "dynasty" is the fruits of his efforts.

Porter, on the other hand, has died out in Ireland, as it had elsewhere until its current revival.

Stout has about 60% of the Irish market, but other styles of ale are making a comeback. It remains to be seen if the Real Ale revolution in Britain will carry over to Ireland.

Lager brewing takes a back seat to Stout. The most-known lager is Harp Lager, which Guinness started. It is a second division beer that is mostly used as the "tan" in Black and Tans in America.

Other breweries in the Republic are at Dundalk (Macardles) in the Northeast, Kilkenny (Smithwicks and Perry) and Waterford (Cherry and Phoenix) in the Southeast, and Cork (Beamish and Crawford, and Murphys) in the South. Both Beamish and Crawfords and Murphys are owned by agressive international breweries, so the prospects of their Stouts getting incleased foreign exposure are excellent.

☛ Italy

Population (1991 est): 57,742,241; **density:** 191.6/sq km (496/sq mi); **distribution (1991):** 72% urban, 28% rural; **annual growth (1990):** 0.5%

Italy produces 10,699,000hl of beer per year. It ranks between Poland and Österreich (Austria).

ITALIANS DRINK LESS beer per person than any other European nation. Their national drink is wine. Since Italians make exceptional wines, this is only natural. This doesn't mean Italy is a soulless desert for one looking for beer. All beers brewed in this land of wine, popes, very old buildings and famous artists are lagers.

Italians have Anton Dreher, the great Austrian brewer who opened a brewery at Trieste in 1868. He continued to expand, opening beer shops throughout the Adriatic and the Italian peninsula. The company, Dreher of Italy, and headquartered in Milano, have been owned (since 1974) by Heineken and Whitbread. It has four other breweries in Italy in addition to the one still operating at Trieste.

The biggest Italian brewing firm is the Peroni Group, which has eight breweries. Both Prinz Bräu (owned by Oetker Group, a German firm) and the Wuhrer Group have four breweries. Weighing in with two breweries each are Moretti and Poretti. There are handful of other smaller-still breweries.

Two firms, Moretti and Peroni brew possibly the only two beers with which people outside Italy might be somewhat familiar. Better-class Italian restaurants in the USA and pubs that specialise in offering beer from "around the world" often have them.

☞ Malta

Population (1986 est): 354,000; **density (1986 est):** 1,120/sq km (2,902/sq mi). **distribution (1985):** 85% urban, 15% rural.

Annual beer production is 170,000hl. Per person annual consumption of domestic production is 48.0 litres.

MALTA IS A country composed of a group of islands lying 93km (58mi) south of Sicily in the Mediterranean Sea between Italy and North Africa. The islands are Malta (the largest), Gozo, Comino, and the uninhabited rocks of Comminotto and Filfla. Historically, Malta's location has been of great strategic importance in the Mediterranean. Valletta, the capital, possesses one of the finest harbours in southern Europe. Malta has been subject to numerous invasions and foreign domination because of these factors, which has left a legacy of foreign influences. Most recently, Malta was a British colony. It became self-governing in 1947. This self-government was revoked in 1959, but was restored in 1962. Full independence was achieved in 1964, and Malta became a member of the Commonwealth of Nations. In 1979, Britain's naval base on the island was closed.

Malta's population has been increasing rapidly. It has one of the highest population densities in the world. Her people are mixed ethnically, absorbing Arabs, Italians and British. The main spoken language is Maltese. It is the only Semitic language in the world using the Latin alphabet. Most of the inhabitants are Roman Catholic, the official religion.

This island nation is one of the few ale strongholds in the world, and has Farsons (Ferrugia), probably the only ale brewery in the Mediterranean. This is a legacy of the island's period of colonization by the British. The brewery imports all the ingredients from Britain. Some of their styles include a dark Mild (at OG 1040, it is almost too strong to be called a modern Mild), a Bitter at OG 1052, a Pale Ale at OG 1040, and an English-style Sweet Stout. They do produce a pale Lager. The yeast for this last mentioned beer comes from Denmark, and the hops come from Belgium, Germany and Slovenia, once part of the ex-Yugoslavia.

☞ Norway (Kingdom of)

Population (1990 est.: 4,246,000; **density:** 13.1/sq km (34/sq mi); **distribution (1990):** 71% urban, 29% rural; **average annual growth (1988):** 0.28%.

Annual beer production is 2,236,000 litres. This places her behind Greece and ahead of Lithuania. Per person annual consumption is 52.8 litres. She exports 17,800hl and imports just 2,300hl.

THE REINHEITSGEBOT IS also in effect in Norway. The brewing industry and alcohol are under strict government regulation, and severe restrictions exist on the sale of alcohol, similar to conditions in Iceland, Finland and Sweden. A tenth of the population life in areas where alcohol sales are banned, mostly in the South and the West Coasts. The main cities, interior areas and the East Coast are the most liberal. It is the Christian Democrats, a rightist party, that takes the strong temperance stand is this country.

Only NABLAB beers may be advertised. This includes class I, < 2.2% ABV. Tax Class II encompasses 2.5–4.75% ABV. Tax Class III beer has up to 6.3% ABV, and are designated as Export beer or Bokk or Jule (Christmas beers).

New small micro-breweries are, indeed, opening and they often mirror trends in other countries in that they are re-introducing ales that were swept away by Lagerbier many generations ago.

All of Norway's 300-plus breweries in 1842 brewed ales (practically every brewery in the world did then). The major customers were the merchant marines, Norway being a great seafaring nation (remember the Vikings) The public tended towards strong spirits.

Lager yeast made its way to Norway via Denmark and, quickly, all Norwegian breweries made the switch. Lager brewing and consumption was encouraged by the government to change the population's drinking habits from hard spirits to beer—the lesser of two evils approach promoted by more than one government. England, for instance, urged ale drinking to the populous rather than bathtub gin, when the latter was ruining the health of the lower classes, especially the women and children.

There is a new brewery, Akershus Bryggeri, at Enebakk, a suburb of Oslo. What makes this brewery special is that it as an all-ale plant, producing 5,000hl. This is a small but needed reversal in the fortunes of ale brewing, which has been dormant for 150 years. Akershus brews a Pale Ale and an Irish Stout. All the brewery's beers are all-malt, in keeping with Norway's *Reinheitsgebot*. Bard Thanem is the head-brewer and used to work at the Mikkro Bryggeri, Oslo's first brew-pub.

Norway has a long tradition (since the 12th century) of home-brewing, an especially strong rural tradition. By the 1800s, most farms had their own brewing equipment. Most of Norway's home-brewers prepare their own malt rather than buy it, and brew to mark all cultural and religious holidays, especially Christmas, weddings, christenings and funerals. Old people, expecting to die, often prepared their own funeral beer. If they didn't die when expected, they would consume it and make another batch when, again, they felt their time approaching. Often, finely-chopped young twigs of the adler or juniper are used. Norway was the prime source of Juniper berries used by the Dutch gin distillers. The Norwegians swapped their berries for some finished product.

Home-brewing is no small thing in Norway. Government statistics indicate 12m litres (and frequently much more) of home-brew are brewed on average each year. There is also a lively, and quite illegal, home-distilling activity in the country.

There are about twenty breweries and brew-pubs of different sizes ranging from the rather large Ringnes to a very tiny brewery at Sandefjord. Besides Ringnes, Oslo is also home to the Frydenlund and the Schou breweries. None of these has made much of a mark in the export market except, perhaps, Ringnes, which is sold in the USA.

☛ Poland (Republic of)

Population (1990 est): 37,800,000; **density:** 120.8/sq km (313.1/sq mi); **distribution (1990):** 61% urban, 39% rural; **annual growth (1990):** 0.6%.

Annual beer production is 12,000,000hl. There are about 95 breweries in Poland, though, perhaps, this number will increase as the country moves to a market economy. German brewers, and other foreigners will undoubtedly make investments in the country.

POLAND'S BREWING HISTORY is long. Hops were introduced by way of Bayern in the 1200s, and much Germanic influence is evident in Polish beer. Her primary brewing regions are Silesia with its centre at Breslau (Wroclaw). The city has three breweries, typical of a large German city, though the Germans were driven out after the 1939–1945 war ("ethnic cleansing", before it was ever called that). The Soviets stole a huge slice of Eastern Poland after the war, then the Poles took a similar slice off of Eastern Germany, in effect shifting her round 120 miles to the west. Similarly, much of Prussia is now in Poland and Russia. These were also prime barley-, rye- and oat-growing lands.

Galicia, too, is a noteworthy brewing region. The beers in this region were more influenced by Austria-Hungary to her south than by Germany to the west. Krakow is the regional brewing centre. Two of the more familiar brands (in the West) are Krakus and Zywiek, both from this region.

Her breweries produce several different styles. Two are low-alcohol: Slodowe is dark and sweet; Jasne is an amber-coloured lager that is bitter. Their equivalent to Pilsner is Pelne. Unusual for the area is Porter, which is heavy and has 7.5% ABV (compare with modern Western Porters at round 5.0% ABV).

☞ Portugal (Portugese Republic)

Population (1991 est): 10,400,000; **density:** 112.6/sq km (291.5/sq mi); **distribution (1991):** 30% urban, 70% rural; **annual growth (1990):** 0.2%.

Annual beer production is 6,882,000hl. Per person annual consumption is 65.9 litres

Portugal has eight breweries that produce 6,892,823hl. She exports 131,716hl (probably to her ex-colonies in Africa), and she imports 160,000hl.

LARGE-SCALE COMMERCIAL brewing began in the early 1800s. Lisbon at one time had six competing breweries. Seven were at Oporto. That city had a lively trade swapping its port wine for British beer. Both side made out well.

Frenchmen formed the first two commercial breweries in Lisbon. Another foreigner, the Dane John Henri Jansen, also operated a brewery there in the late 1800s. Two of his employees set out on their own, and this effort eventually led, through several name changes, to what is now Sociedade Central de Cervejas, Portugals largest brewing group. It has about 70% of the domestic market. It's breweries are at Vialonga and Coimbra. German style lagers are produced: a Dortmunder-style named *Sagres*, and a dark Münchener-style named *Preta*.

Companhia União Fabril Portuense grew out of the mergers of the several breweries at Oporto. This is the second big brewing group in the country. They produce a *Cristal*, a Pilsener-style.

Most of the brands are Lagers, but a brewer on Madeira produces a Sweet Stout. Another

Portugese posession, the Azores, also is home to a brewery.

☞ Romania (Republic of)

Population (1989 est): 23,168,000; **density:** 97.5/sq km (252.7/sq mi); **distribution (1987 est):** 49% urban, 51% rural; **annual growth (1989):** 0.5%.

Annual beer production was 9,727,000hl in 1991. Per person consumption of annual domestic production is 41.98 litres.

We have no additional information now.

☞ Russia (Russian Federation)

Population (1989): 147,386,000; **ethnic composition:** Russians (82.6%); Tatars (3.6%); Ukrainians (2.7%); Chuvash (1.2%); and more than 100 other ethnic groups.

HERE IS THE prime example of how communism and socialism prostrates, to the point of tears, a great nation. There are somewhere between 300 and 400 breweries in Russia and the other lands that made up the ex-Soviet Union. Travel restrictions were so severe, and transport so shoddy that little is know of these breweries except that they were state-owned. As Russia privitizes their industries, these breweries will surly pass into commercial hands or be shut. *The Economist* reported, in passing, that the three largsest breweries in St Petersburg were recently bought by foreign concerns.

Large scale brewing developed in Russia in the 1800s. Great Britain was a huge exporter of beer to Russia by the 1780s. Porter and Stout were the favourites. One style, Russian Imperial Stout, was brewed for the Russian imperial court. Courage's Imperial Stout is still available. It has an OG of about 1105 and 10.5% ABV. It wasn first brewed at the Anchor Brewery at London. This brewery was sold to Perkins, which was later gobbled up by Courage.

As an aside, this beer, though labelled a Stout, would more appropriately be called a Barley Wine. Much of this trade came about because Empress Catherine (The Great), herself anorth German took a fancy to strong English beers. As is often the case, products rulers use become desired by the great masses, and so it was with Porter and Stout. The trade continued until the 1914–18 war. There wasn't much call for it after the Bolsheviks eliminated the Royal family and the nobility.

Russia ranks somewhere around third in the world list of brewing countries, but accurate figures are probably non-existant due to the state of confusion in the country. This should change as Russia pulls herself out of the economic and politcal mess she is in as she makes the transformation to a market economy.

Much help is coming from the West. This will lead to a remarked improvement in the quality of Russian beer which, in the main, can only be described as abysmal.

To ween people from vodka and other spirits, beer drinking is encouraged, much as it was in England and Norway. Cheap gin was the culprit there. Brewing is local in nature in Russia because of the chronically weak transport network. Simply handling the grain and vegetable harvests is still a near-hopeless task, and until this is all sorted out, the possibility of Russian HCBS developing are practically nil.

Though, and perhaps because, Russia is an enormous country with over one hundred ethnically different tribes living within her borders a national market for beer might never develope. Large sections prefer wine, others tea or different beverages. If one limits one's view of Russia to the portion west of the Ural Mountains, meaning European Russia, then the situation looks better. Some of the northern and western regions could reach German levels of per person annual beer consumption, for it is there that beer drinking traditions are strongest.

☞ Spain (Kingdom of)

Population (1990 est): 39,618,000; **density:** 78.5/sq km (203.3/sq mi); **distribution (1990):** 91% urban, 9% rural; **annual growth (1990):** 0.2%

Annual beer production is 26,081,795 hl. Per person annual consumption is 70.54 litres, a respectable figure.

SPAIN, SURPRISINGLY, HAS 30 breweries. She exports 316,216 hl and imports 1,806,277 hl. These are respectable figures for a Mediterranean country known more for it s wine than its beer.

Spain is not the "home" of San Miguel beer, the Philippines is, though it has been brewed in Spain since 1957. It has breweries at Burgas, Lérida and Málaga.

The largest Spanish brewing group is called Damm. It was organized with help from Oetker, the German firm. Damm is based in Barcelona, site of the 1992 summer Olympics, which Spain heavily promoted.

Spain also has breweries, CCC and Tropical, in the Canary Islands and the Baleares.

☞ Sweden (Kingdom of)

Population (1990 est): 8,529,000; **density:** 19/sq km (49/sq mi); **distribution (1990):** 83% urban, 17% rural; **annual growth (1990):** 0.3%.

Annual beer production is 4,738,000 hl. Annual consumption is 61.0 litres. She exports but 30,800 hl and imports 506,400 hl, which would seem to indicate there is plenty of room for her domestic breweries to expand.

"Even if you can afford the exorbitant prices, Swedish brewers do their damndest to ensure you stay sober. Most beer is low in alcohol, and so fizzy that drinking sufficient to make you drunk would defeat all but those with the most hardy of digestive systems."

So wrote Andrew Sangster in *What's Brewing*.

SCANDINAVIA HAS LONG been a lager bastion, but one corrupted by socialist government interference. In 1977, for instance, the Swedish government banned the most popular beer tax category simply because it was annoyed at beer advertising. Regulation and tax are starting to be rolled back slowly, under a more understanding centrist government, but the price of a pint of beer still hovers around £5.00 (@ $8.50). The Swedish import monopoly charges SKr8.5–12.5 ($1.45–2.13) per litre. The government distribution monopoly adds on 18%, and there is a 25% sales tax. Then the pub owners must mark-up the beer by 80–125% to make a profit (which is heavily taxed). All this adds up to a very expensive pint. Mr Sangster reports a downward trend in prices. In September 1992 a half-litre glass of beer cost £4.00 ($6.80). In July 1993 the same half-litre glass sold for £3.00 ($5.10), still outrageous by standards elsewhere. He attributes this decline to growing retail competition as state regulation unravels, thus liberating entrepreneurial endeavours.

There are four classes of beer in Sweden, similar to those in Finland. We will tell you straight away that no beer may be stronger than 5.5% ABV. Also, beers stronger than 3.5% ABV are excluded from being sold in supermarkets. This has led importers, such as Budweiser Budvar of the Czech Republic to water down their classic Pilsener. Class I beer is < 2.25% ABV. Class II can have up to 3.5% ABV. Class III can have up to 4.5% ABV, and Class IV up to 5.5% ABV. Classes III and IV can only be bought at licensed establishments for on-site consumption or at Systembolagets, the state-owned off-licences.

Sweden is undergoing an ale revival of sorts. Several British breweries such as Arkells, Batemans and Shepherd Neame are exporting to Sweden. Some is cask ale, but often it is bottled or kegged versions. Since there is, so far, no domestic alternatives to lagers in the Swedish market, British exporters of low gravity (< 3.5% ABV) ale are seeking to take advantage of the situation and gain entry before inevitable competitive forces rise against them.

What of Sweden's brewers? Pripps is the biggest. Their BLÅ is the best-selling brand in that country. It is brewed to Class I, II and III specifications. The original Pripps was founded in 1828 at Gothenburg. In 1963 it merged with the Stockholm Brewing Company. It has breweries at Malmö, Stockholm and Gothenburg, plus around 50 distribution depots, many of which were former breweries that were bought and closed. The Swedish government, in 1965, took a 60% stake in the firm. Guess who calls the shots.

Nordik Wolf, is, perhaps, its most internationally well-known brand. It is a rather bland lager with 4.75% ABV.

The Falken brewery at Falkenberg is the second largest beer producer. It is a private corporation.

There are several breweries run by consumer co-operatives. The largest is named Wårby and is located in a Stockholm suburb. It has a network of outlets through which it sells its beer. There are other co-ops at Skruv and at Sollefteå.

There are about 15 brewing companies, with breweries at Malmö, located at Sweden's lower tip, all the way up to Gällivare, well above the Arctic Circle. Being a northern country, it is not surprising that about two-thirds of the breweries are situated on or below the line Gälve–Torsby, in the lower third of the country.

As in Finland, and other places with severe restrictions on access to alcohol, (often in conjunction with excessively high taxes and a strong neo-prohibitionist movement) home-brewing and illegal home-distillation is common. Sweden is no exception.

☛ Swiss Confederation

Population (1989 est): 6,700,000; **density (1986 est):** 157/sq km (406/sq mi); **distribution (1980):** 60% urban, 40% rural; **annual growth (1983 est):** 0.35%

Annual beer production is 4,183,000hl. This places her between Finland and Greece on the European league list. Per person annual consumption is 69.8 litres, ahead of Bulgaria, but behind Spain. This lastfigure has decreased by about two litres per person since the 1970s.

SWITZERLAND'S CONSUMPTION FIGURE is skewed because the country is a combination of French-, Italian- and German-speaking regions. The French region is in the west and the Italian region in the south. These two, when campared to the Germanic north, where most of the breweries are located, prefer wine, bring the average down. This is a legacy of Roman domination. There was no national brewing heritage before the Middle Ages when Irish missionary monks brought their knowledge to the area. The monks brewedseveral types of beer: a weak beer for the riffraff, regular beer for themselves and a special style reserved for the upper classes of Church and State. The tradition has developed since then. The main brewing cantons are Appenzall, Glarus, St Gallen and Thurgau. Consumption is very heavy at ski resorts, no matter where located.

Swiss brewers, like some in other countries, adhere to the *Reinheitsgebot*, but in this country, compliance is voluntary.

One of the big Swiss brewing group is Sibra, which brews using the Cardinal brand name. The brewery was founded in 1788 at Fribourg on the border between French- and German-speaking Switzerland. Sibra took over three other breweries in 1973. They were located at Fribourg (eliminating much local competition), Rheinfelden and at Wädenswil. Sibra choose the Cardinal name in 1890 when the local archbishop was elevated to a cardinal, a significant event then.

A second large brewing group is Feldschlössen at Rheinfelden. (These first two groups could be considered national brands.) Feldschlössen ceonsists of Gertens at Bern, Müllers at Neuchatel and Valaisanne at Sion. In addition, the group co-operates with Calanda at Chur, andHaldenguts at Winterthur, bothof which are big regional breweries.

The Swiss are fond of co-operatives. It is no different in the brewing industry where Falkens at Schaffhausen, Hürlimann and Löwenbräu both at Zürich and Schützengarten at St Galen formed a co-operative named Interbeva. Together they buy ingredients, market and promote themselves.

All but a few very independent brewers are members of the Swiss Brewers Society, a cartel which works to control the price of beer. Evidently the government feels the brewing indusry is small and, therefore, vulnerable, so it continues to allow price-fixing to the detriment of consumers. This is a clear example of hidden subsidy—every country is guilty of this somewhere or another in their markets. Worldwide, these subsidies cost consumers billons of dollers each year.

Regional tastes in beer vary. The French-speaking people prefer their beers light, dry and chilled. The Italian-speaking people prefer a somewhat heavier and hoppy lager, whilst the German-speakers like a lightly-hoped sweet beer served chilled just ever so slightly.

Most of the beer styles found in Germany, Bock, Lager, Starkbier, Weisse, are also brewed in Switzerland, but the stronger ones are seldom up to German strengths. One Swiss brewer, Hürlimanns is ahead of Erste Kulmbacher Union (EKU), their German opposite. Hurlimann's *Samiclaus* (Santa Claus, a Christmas beer), 13.71% ABV is the current Guinness Book Of Records record holder for World's Strongest Beer, beating out EKU–28, 13.5% ABV. ECU claims theirs is the stronger beer, based on an original wort gravity of 28° Plato versus 27.6° for Hurlimann's brand. EKU–28's wort has been measured as high as 30.54°. Both beers are extremely difficult, expensive and time-consuming to produce. It appears that Hurliman's yeast does a better job of reducing the og than does eku's, thus the slight advantage to Hurlimann's *Samiclaus*.

The only styles native to Switzerland are diet-beer and NABLAB s, where the process was developed.

☞ The Grand Duchy of Luxembourg

Population (1990 est): 379,000; **density**: 146.6/sq km (380/sq mi); **distribution**: 78% urban, 22% rural; **annual growth (1985-89)**: 0.1%.

Annual beer production is 572,000hl. Per person annual consumption is 121.4 litres. There are five active breweries in Luxembourg. She exports 181,000hl, and imports just 42,000hl.

THERE ARE FIVE breweries in this small sovereign nation. It is one of the three countries, along with Belgium and the Netherlands, that comprise the Benelux group. Laying strategically between Germany and Belgium it was fought over for centuries. Finally, it was declared eternally neutral. It's beer styles are definitely German: Pils, a stronger lager resembling Dortmunder and the odd Strong Lagers.

The Luxembourgers are fifth on the per person annual beer consumption list of European countries, at 121.4 litres. They also consume much wine and spirits, so they're most definitely not a nation of teatotals.

The five breweries are Brasserie Diekirch at Diekirch, Mousel et Clausen, Brasserie Nationale at Bascharage, the family-owned Brasserie Simon at Wiltz, and Battin at Esch. A sixth, Brauerei Funck, appears to have ceased brewing.

☞ The Netherlands (Holland)

Population (1990 est): 14,936,032; **density**: 356.7/sq km (924/sq mi); **distribution (1989 est)**: 89% urban, 11% rural; **annual growth (1990 est)**: 0.4%.

Annual beer production is 20,658,810hl, and perperson annual consumption is 90.5 litres. She has a big trade surplus in beer: exports ran 7,495,445hl and imports were 528.534hl, less than a tenth of exports (1992 figures).

THERE ARE 16 breweries, mostly along the frontier with Belgiun and Germany. The borderlands (to the south) with Belgium were, until the countries split in 1830, the same region, the Brabant. The Netherland's only Trappist brewery at Tilburg, is but a short distance from the border. With EU harmonization, the Brabant will, no doubt, revert to its historical position.

Northern regions of The Netherlands are the opposite of the South. Per person annual beer consumption is only in the 70–80 liter range, whilst Southerners consume well over 100 litres per year. Several northern provinces, Groningen, Friesland, Drenthe and Utrecht, don't even have a brewery. Gelderland and Overijssel's three breweries are near the German border.

The Dutch like their beers served cool and with a "two finger" depth to the head. They are serious people who take their drinking seriously. Passing a six-month training course for bar owners is madatory. After successful completion, they are then certified to practise their trade. To Americans this sounds like bureaucratic overkill, but the process does promote pride in profession.

Some more internationally known brands are Amstel, part of Heineken, Brand, a brewery that dates before 1340 and is one of the oldest, if not the oldest in the world. It received the "Royal" title from the queen in 1971. Other well-known brands are Breda (an Anglo-Dutch concern), Oranjeboom, Skol (another

Anglo-Dutch firm), Grolsche and Alfa, located close to Germany, in lower Limburg Province.

Heinz may have 57 varieties of condiments, but Heineken has affiliations with 57 different breweries around the world. Any discussion of brewing in The Netherlands must center round Heineken as the firm is so dominant. Too, internationally it is a major league brewer. In many parts of the world, it is the most popular import.

Heineken is headquartered in Amsterdam, where it was founded in the 16th century. It has always been in the Heineken family. In 1868 the brewery was moved to its present site. In Holland, the firm now has its second and third breweries at Zoeterwoude in South Holland Province, and at Hertogenbosch in North Brabant respectively. Heineken bought rival Amstel (1968), whose Amstel Pils is the second best-selling beer in the country. A controlling stake was taken (1972) in the French Albra Group, and in coup, they, with Whitbread, acquired the Dreher brewing concern in Italy (1974). The great Dreher firm is the offspring of the Austrian company that was one of the pioneers of lager brewing.

The most recent (November 1993) industry scuttlebutt is that Heineken will join with Whitbread, similar to the recent joining of Carlsberg and Tetley. This merger might be necessitated by other joint efforts by Heineken's rivals, Carling, Coors and Fosters, all very busy competing in the world market. Heineken wouldn't want to lose its position in the "Brewers League" standings to others.

One of the biggest, and most pleasant, surprises from Heineken is that they have abandoned the use of adjuncts and switched to all-malt brewing. Perhaps they sense which way the wind is blowing. It has, in fact, changed directions during the last decade, what with the explosion of micro-breweries and brew-pubs catering to the tastes of those who demand better. We do not know if this change is universal. Perhaps the beer they ship to North America will be the same adjunct-

laden beer as before, though it would be nice to think them fair.

One pitfall of the switch will be how they will (or won't) promote the change. If they claim the new beer is better and all-natural, it puts them in the position to be accused of selling inferior beer previously. Afterall, they surely could have brewed real beer, as the Germans and others, have done. According to Mr Jackson, the changes in character are not obvious.

Heineken has been introducing beers, too. One of note, Heineken Tarwebok (*tarwe* means wheat in Dutch), is a seasonal dark wheat Bok (Bock), with OG 1064, 7.0% ABV. Another seasonal beer, this one to celebrate the new year, is their 1994. It will be sold only during December. It is an OG 1064, 6.5% ABV dark amber-brown coloured Bok with a Guiness-like head. If the brand is successful, they will repeat it with a 1995, and so on.

The Netherland's second HCB is Skol. Its big domestic markets are Rotterdam and the North Brabant. The firm is 90% owned by Allied Breweries, the British group. Skol was begun in 1964. The idea was to produce an international brand with breweries, franchisees and licensees in a dozen or so scattered countries, such as Sweden and Canada, and in Africa and Asia.

Grolsche Brewery whose home is at Groenlo in Eastern Gelderland close to the German border. The town's name used to be Grolle. It is from this that the brewery took its name. The brand, Grolsch (without the final "e") Pilsner, is appreciated all over the world for its fine taste, even if it is more remembered for its ceramic swing-top. In the United States, the ceramic stopper is being repalecd with plastic. The ceramic was damaging the bottle recycling equipment. The extra fermenting and lagering time the brewery uses to produce their Pilsener definitely enhances its taste.

The beer industry appears to be very healthy. Production has increased from 3,551,653hl in

1960 to 20,658,810 in 1992. Imports rose during the same period from 103,712 hl to 528,534 hl, whilst exports increased from 916,314 hl to 7,495,445 hl. One figure that caught our eyes was per person beer consumption. In 1960 consumption was a paltry 23.8 litres. It increased nearly four times to 90.2 litres in 1992—truly remarkable.

☞ United Kingdom

Population (1991 est): 57,500,000; **density:** 235.5/sq km (610/sq mi); **distribution (1989):** 90% urban, 10% rural; **annual growth (1990):** 0.3%.

Annual production (1992) was 55,888,000 hl. Annual consumption per person was 105.7 litres, placing her sixth in Europe after Germany, Denmark, Ireland, Luxembourg and Belgium. Exports were 2,084,000 hl, and Imports were 5,534,000 hl. Most imported beer came from Ireland, Germany and The Netherlands. Her exported beer went mainly to North America, Ireland and The Netherlands. In 1991 Great Britain had 99 breweries.

BRITAIN, IN REGARDS beer, seems to be going in two opposite directions, one good, one bad, simultaneously. We'll look at the bad, the so-so, and then the good.

On the sombre side of the ledger, people who drink beer in Britain pay, by far, the highest taxes on it than anywhere else in the EU. In fact, they pay more than the rest of the EU combined, and Germany, second behind Britain, pays just one quarter as much. Fifty-five percent of all beer duty collected in the EU is levied in Great Britain. This is great for the Exchequer (or so the think) and horrendous for the drinker, the brewer and the publican because, as duty has increased, the amount of beer consumed per person has decreased. To the anti-drinks crowd, this is delightful news, though high alcohol taxes do nothing to stop alcohol abuse, acording to a report, *A Disorderly House*, produced by the Adam Smith Institute.. It is a sad fact that many govern-

ments, not just Britain's, of allegedly market-economies ignore the economic fact that high tax rates can halt business growth (indeed, it can put it into decline), and cause unemployment. Too, since all taxes imposed on business is passed through to consumers, it is they who are left holding the bag, much to their dismay and frustration. This does not keep a populace happy, which is supposed to be a primary goal of government. Pity so few of them try to achieve this. Unless duty rates are cut, CAMRA feels the brewing industry faces "a bleak future". They are hoping Kenneth Clarke, the chancellor, will cut rates to revitalize the industry.

Government isn't the only party to blame for high beer prices. Many of the breweries are as well. During the 1980s, the major breweries pushed up the wholesale price of beer at double the rate of inflation. After eliminating Britain's outrageously high duty on beer from calculation, wholesale beer prices are twice those in France and The Netherlands. They also increased pub rents by several hundred percent, leaving up to publicans to decide whether or not to raise their mark-up (prices). Some choice, eh!

Many Britons find it cheaper to cross the Channel to buy their beer (in quantity) than to buy it at home. In France, drinkers pay just 3 pence per pint, the British pay 33 pence. Some 12% of the beer consumed in-home is now bought in in the Continent. Similarly, there is the absurd situation of smugglers and merchants bringing British beer back in to Great Britain, spurred by the price differential and potential for profit. These activities cost the Exchequer some £12.5bn, and they cost British mercants some £500m per year in sales lost to the Continent. The loss of such sums costs jobs as well, which especially hurts a country suffering from high unemployment.

Britian's creaking and endangered tied-house system of pub ownership is also under great attock. This attack comes not from within, but from the eu. The system of tied-house is being examined throughout the Union, and indications are that tied-houses will be ruled illegal, or rather, that the breweries will have to sell off the pubs they own. Speaking in general economic terms, tied-houses are a hinderance to competition, since small brewers are often shut out of pubs owned by other breweries. For a brewery to survive, it must have retail outlets (pubs) through which it can sell its beer to the public. If this route is closed, what to do? The obvious answers are to buy a pub or ten or fifty (a very expensive proposition beyond the reach of most start-up breweries) or to sell through the limited free-house sector (if one can get one's foot in the door). Most small breweries have a small tied-estate. The problem the British see with abolishing the tied-estate is that small brewers will not be able to compete with the HCBs on price (they can't now), and consequntly they will lose their outlets, thus forcing them out of business and depriving beer drinkers with quality alternatives to the HCB's product. Compromise talk, called a "block exemption", is that small indepyndant breweries will be able to keep their estates, but the HCBs will be forced to dispose of theirs. If a compromise is not reached, even regional brewers are predicted to go out of business "over night".

Further consolidation of the British HCBs seems inevitable, either through mergers with other brewers or via joining with foreign HCBs such as Forters, which already controls Courage, Coors, Millers, Heineken, Anheuser-Busch, Interbrew and others. It is definitely a Big Boys league. Scottish & Newcastle has rejoined the Big Boys with their acquisition of Chef & Brewer chain of pubs from Grand Met. This gives the northern-based company a big presence in the South, which it lacked. Scottish & Newcastle was formed in late 1960 withthe merger of Scottish Brewers based in Edinburgh, and Newcastle Breweries. Both had long histeries. Scottish Breweries can trace their ancestry back via William Younger of the Abbey and Holyrood breweries founded in 1749, and via William McEwan of the Fountain Brewery, founded 1856. Other merger talk is of Whitbread merging with Heineken, the Dutch giant.

On the positive side, there are more microbreweries and brew-pubs have been opening. Some of these brew beer to tastes traditionally associated with the areas in which they are located, but abandoned by the HCBs. Fizzy lager consumption is in decline, and Britain's traditional beer, cask conditioned ale, is increasing. Some large brewers who had abandoned cask-ale when lager sales were soaring have rejoined the Real-Ale fold.

Finally, all-malt brewing is again gaining favour with British brewers. One manner of fighting competition is to make one's product better than one's competitiors, and publicise the hell out of that fact. Samuel Smiths recently went back to all-malt brewing, which went into decline after 1847, when the use of sugar in beer was leagalized (under pressure from the sugar lobby). Perhaps it is too much to expect every brewer to produce beer to the *Reinheitsgebot*,

Scotland

SCOTTISH BEER DEVELOPED differenly than did its English cousin. The main difference is that they are much maltier than Bitter because Scotland is far from hop-growing areas causing Scottish brewers to use it sparingly. They are much more inclined than are English brewers to use roasted barley, dark and chocolate malts. These create a darker, nutty-tasting and sweeter beer that is an alternative to Dark Lagers. It is often said that Scottish Ales are the corresponding ale to Bavaian Dunkles lagers. The Scots use different terms for their beers as well. Light Ale refers to low-gravity beer, regardless of colour; Heavy Ale refers to medium-strength ale; and Export Ale refers to the strongest ales.

Most Scottish breweries are in the Lowlands. They are concentrated around Alloa, Edinburgh and Glasgow. This happened becouse malting barley grew in the Borders and Northeast England. The malt that survives the harsh North is best-suited for distilling, another Scottish speciality.

Wales

THE FIRST (1882) lager brewery in Britain was located at Wrexham in Wales to cater to thirsty steelworkers and miners. The pits are all, but one, closed, as are the steelworks. The brewery at Wrexham is part of Carlsberg-Tetley, and produces 300,000 barrels a year.

THE OLDEST ALE brewery still surviving is at Palssey, North Wales.

It would be fair to say that Wales has been devasted by brewery take overs and closures. There but but a handful left, the main supply coming from English brewers. Brains seems to be the one well-known Welsh brewery.

Wales's newest brewery is Dyffryn Clywd Brewery at Clywd.

Isle of Mann

THERE ARE TWO breweries on the Isle of Mann, which islocated between england and Ireland. The breweries are Bushy's Brewery at Braddan, and Isle of Mann Breweries Ltd.at Douglas. The latter is a result of a merger in 1986 between Castletown Brewery and Okells Brewery. The Island has a *Reinheitsgebot* of their own. The one difference with the German version is that only minute amounts of brewing sugar is permitted.

Channel Islands

THERE SEEMS TO be some excellent brewing happening on the Channel Islands. The Ann Street Brewery on Jersey, long a keg-only brewery has begun brewing cask-ale. Their Old Jersey Ale has OG 1035, 3.6% ABV, and their Winter Ale is OG 1068, 7.5% ABV.

One difference from Britain is that duty is paid on volume not gravity (read original gravity of the wort) of the beer.

Besides the Ann Street Brewery, there are the Guernsey Brewing Company (1920) Ltd, and the RW Randall Ltd's Vauxlaurens Brewery, both on Geunrsey. Guernsey Brewing produces a 3.7% ABV LBA Mild, and a 4.1% ABV Real Draught Bitter. Two brands from Vauxlaurens are their OG 1033 Best Mild and OG 1046 Best Bitter.

Northern Ireland

BASS SELLS KEG versions of their ale and lager, and Stout and other bland keg beers from the Irish Republic are imported.

Cask ale is being test marketed by Scottish & Newcastle, but the land is not a cask-ale bastion. There is only one Real Ale brewery in Northern Ireland and that is the Hilden Brewery at Lisburn. Its brands are an OG 1039 Hilden Ale, and an OG 1040 Porter.

THE MIDDLE EAST

LYING BETWEEN AFRICA, Europe and Asia is the Middle EAST. Starting at the Red Sea and the Levant, and stretching towards India and China, the countries, except Israel, are Muslim. Some, like Turkey, are secular and tolerate alcohol consumption. Others, such as Saudi ARABIA, are theist and ban it. The other countries lie between the extremes.

Some of our reference material is getting a bit dated, and we've found little with which to replace it (a trip to Brussels in August 1993 netted us "Statistics 1993" from the Confédération des Brasseries de Belgique. To the cbb, we are indebted.). For instance, Beirut, Lebanon is listed as the site of the Almaza brewery, which produces a Pilsener. However, much of Beirut was destroyed in their long civil war, and odds are the brewery was, likewise, destroyed. In Iran, Muslim militants overthrew the Shah, and a theist regimen was imposed on the people. Was alcohol banned? Surely, it was, and the breweries were closed.

All we can give is a very brief review.

☛ Cyprus

Population (1990 est): 700,000; **density:** 75.7/sq km (196/sq mi); **distribution (1990):** 62% urban, 38% rural; **annual growth (1990):** 1.0%.

Annual beer production is 340,000 hl. Per person consumption of annual domestic production is 48.6 litres.

ALL WE HAVE IS that a beer called Keo Lager is brewed on the island.

Cyprus has played an important role in the history of civilization, because of its key location in the eastern Mediterranean. During the second millennium BC, Cyprus was an important source of copper for Egypt and the Middle East. Greek cultural influences spread to the island, but from about 800 BC, Phoenician influence became more prominent. In 709 BC, Cyprus submitted to the Assyrian king Sargon II. The falling off of Assyrian power was followed by a period of Persian domination. When Alexander the Great conquered the area in the 4th century BC, Cyprus was united politically with the rest of the Greek world. Cyprus, then, consisted mainly of city-states held together under the sovereignty of Alexander's successors. In 58 BC, the island was annexed by the Romans and held for many centuries before being passed about like a single pint being shared amongst several very thirsty men.

St Paul travelled to Cyprus. The people were converted to Christianity at an early date. Ruins of several early churches exist. With the split of the Roman Empire, Cyprus came under the control of Byzantine emperors at Constantinople, who continued to rule it until it was occupied (1191) during the Third Crusade by Richard I (the Lion Hearted) of England. Cyprus was given (1192) to Guy de Lusignan, who founded a French-speaking monarchy. From this time, Italian merchants assumed an increasingly important role on the island. She came under Venetian control in 1489. The ruined castles and Gothic churches of Cyprus date from this period.

The Turks, led by Suleiman the Magnificent, overran the island in 1570–71. It remained under Turkish rule until 1878. During this time many Turks settled on the island. The British occupied Cyprus, by agreement with the Turkish sultan (1878), to support Turkey against Russia.

In 1914 it was formally annexed by Great Britain. Soon afterward a movement developed among the Greek Cypriots for union with Greece, a movement that became more powerful after the 1939–45 war.

Cyprus gained independence (1959) after a period of guerrilla war, though Great Britain retained her military bases.

☛ Iran

Population (1991 est): 58,600,000; **density:** 35.6/sq KM (92.1/sq mi); **distribution (1990 est):** 54% urban, 46% rural; **annual growth (1990):** 3.1%.

Annual beer production is 200,000hl. Per person consumption of annual domestic production is a meagre 0.34 litres.

WE HAVE NO information on any active breweries now, though there must be at least one in the ugbf figures from 1991 are correct.

Many dynasties and empires have ruled Persia. At times she has been at the centre of vast empires extending through much of the Middle East. The modern Persian state traces its beginnings to Cyrus, who became the first of the Achaemenid emperors in 549BC. In 330bc, Persia became part of Alexander the Great's empire. It was subsequently part of the Seluecid kingdom, and then, beginning in 250bc, of the Parthian empire. Around 224AD, the Parthian Arsacid dynasty was overthrown by the Sassanians, a Persian dynasty that ruled until the Arab conquest (641). The Arabs introduced Islam. During the 1100-1200s, the country came under the rule of the Turks, who laid down the administrative and economic structure that persisted until the 1900s.

Persia was overrun by the Mongols under Genghis Khan in the 1200s. In fact, the French refer to the country as Iran-Mongolie.

From the 1500s to the overthrow of the most recent Shah, Persia/Iran has been ruled by a series of "dynasties" such as the Safavid, Afshar, Zand and the Qajars. Some were more despotic than others

During the past century, Iran came under increasing pressure from Russia (in the north) and from Britain (from the westward from India and northward from the Gulf). The Anglo-Russian Entente (1907) divided the country into a Russian zone of influence, a British zone, and a neutral zone.

In 1908 petroleum was discovered, which led to even more internal (and external) intrigue, which has lasted up to the present.

☛ Iraq

Population (1991 est): 17,100,000; **density:** 39/sq km (102/sq mi); **distribution (1991):** 73% urban, 27% rural; **annual growth (1990):** 3.9%.

Annual beer production is 100,000hl. Per person consumption of annual domestic production is a paltry 0.58 litres.

THE LAND OF the original brewers has fallen on hard times. Baghdad is home to the Eastern Brewery Company, if our rather dated information is correct.

Iraq was one of the most ancient centres of civilization and settled cultivation. Sumer, Akkad, Assyria, and Babylonia all developed major civilizations in ancient Mesopotamia. During the early centuries AD, the area was part of various Persian empires. After the Arab conquest in the seventh century, Baghdad (founded in 762AD) became the seat of the Caliphate of the Abbasids. The Arabs, and their religion, ruined the brewing industry in the area. The Mongol conquest (1258), virtually ruined the rest of the country.

During the 1500–1600s, control over Iraq was contested by the Ottoman and the Persian empires. From 1638 Iraq was part of the Ottoman Empire, though frequently with some degree of autonomy. During the 1914–18 war, a British force occupied Iraq, and in 1920 it became a British mandate of the League of Nations. The mandate was ended in 1932, following civil disturbances during the 1920s, but the British maintained strong influence over Iraq until 1958.

☛ Israel

Population (1991 est): 4,900,000; **density:** 236/sq km (612.5/sq mi); **distribution (1990):** 90% urban, 10% rural; **annual growth (1989):** 1.5%.

Annual beer production is 533,000hl. Per person consumption of domestic production is 10.9 litres.

TWO BREWERIES ARE active in Israel. Goldstar, Maccabee and Maltstar brands are made by Tempo Brewing Industries. They are all lagers.

☛ Jordan

Population (1991 est): 3,400,000; **density:** 37 sq km (96 per sq mi); **distribution (1988):** 59% urban, 41% rural; **annual growth (1990):** 3.6%.

Annual beer production is 60,000hl, which places Jordan next to last in the region. Per person consumption of annual domestic production is 1.76 litres.

THERE ARE TWO brewing companies in the kingdom. The Arab Breweries Company and the General Investment Company (!). Both are in Amman, the capital. GIC brews Amstel under licence.

☛ Lebanon

Population (1991 est): 3,400,000; **density:** 325/sq km (842/sq mi); **distribution (1987):** 80% urban, 20% rural; **annual growth (1990):** 1.3%.

Lebanon produces the least amount of beer of any country in the region. Annual production is only 40,000hl. Per person consumption of annual domestic production is about 1.2 litres.

LEBANON HAS BEEN in the mainstream of history since history began. Its strategic location has made it a transporter and transmitter of civilization, culture, and religion.

The earliest inhabitants of coastal Lebanon were a Semitic people related to the Canaanites who came to coastal Lebanon from the Arabian Peninsula about 3500BC. The Greeks named these seafaring people Phoenicians. They established city-states (including Baalbek, Beirut, Byblos, Tyre and Sidon). Their 22-letter alphabet was used throughout the region.

It is to these people that we beer drinkers owe thanks because it was their seafaring and trading ways that spread beer and brewing throughout the area: from Mesopotamia westward.

After being successively ruled by the Egyptians, Assyrians, Neo-Babylonians, Persians, and Greeks, Lebanon came under Roman rule in 64BC. Christianity was firmly established there by 395AD, when Lebanon became part of the Byzantine Empire.

During the early Christian Era, when theological controversies bred numerous sects and antagonisms, Lebanon became a safe harbour for persecuted minorities fleeing the authority of the "great" empires. In the 660s, one of these sects, which later became the Maronite Church, settled in the rugged mountains of Lebanon to avoid forcible conversion to Islam by the Arabs, who had completed their conquest of the region by 640AD. The attractiveness of Lebanon as a refuge persisted into Islamic times.

The coastal plain and the Lebanon Mountains fell temporarily to the Christian Crusaders early in the 1100s. Many Lebanese Christians fought alongside the Crusaders, and thousands of them were slaughtered by Muslims once the Crusaders had been driven out in the late 1200s by the Mamelukes of Egypt. Generally, however, the mosaic of religions that Lebanon had become offered some freedom from persecution for its various groups, each of which concentrated in specific areas that are still their "homelands" today.

From 1516 to 1918, when Lebanon was formally part of the Ottoman Empire, local leaders were granted relative autonomy as long as they paid taxes to their Ottoman rulers.

As an Ottoman fiefdom, Lebanon developed commercial, educational, and religious links with Europe. Opened to the West, it became a centre for political rivalries between various foreign colonial powers, including France, Britain, and Russia. France and Britain pressured the Turks to establish, in the Mount Lebanon area (1864), a semi-autonomous Christian-dominated province.

After the 1914–18 war, Lebanon became a French mandate, as promised by the secret Sykes-Picot Agreement of 1916. In 1920 the French created Lebanon's current boundaries by adding the al-Biqa Valley, the coastal cities, and areas to the north and south. The Republic of Lebanon, established by the Constitution of 1926, remained under French mandate until 1943, when it gained independence.

Various factional and civil wars have almost completely ruined Lebanon, and her economy. So, too, have Israeli incursions, and gross interference from Iran and Syria. It is hard to do business when fighting rages all about. Beirut, once a main financial centre of the region, and a beautiful city, was reduced to rubble. It is slowly recovering.

☞ Syria

Population (1986 est): 10,931,000; **density (1986 est):** 59/sq km (152.9/sq mi); **distribution (1986):** 49% urban, 51% rural; **annual growth (1986):** 3.9%.

Syria doesn't brew much beer. Annual production is 90,000 hl. Per person consumption of annual domestic production is 0.82 litres.

ALL WE KNOW is there is a state-owned brewery called Al-Chark, which was established in 1954. It was taken over by the government in 1965.

Once a client state of the ex-Soviet Union, and propped up by her, Syria has had to steer a more moderate course since the disintegration of her patron. Strict domestic repression has been in force since the socialist Baath Party assumed power (1963). They quickly moved to redistribute the land and nationalize the economy. The sad state it is in is a reflection of these sorry policies.

☞ Turkey

Population (1991 est): 58,500,000; **density:** 75/sq km (194.4/sq mi); **distribution (1990):** 53% urban, 47% rural; **annual growth (1990):** 2.1%

Annual beer production is 3,000,000 hl, placing it first in the region. Per person consumption of domestic production is 5.1 litres.

WE HAVE BETTER luck with Turkey. Of all the countries in the region, Turkey is the most open to the West. It has been a loyal member of nato, the western defence alliance, for many years, though it has often been given second-class treatment by its Western "partners".

The brewing industry in Turkey is healthy and robust. At Adana, the Guney Biracilik Malt Sanayii produces Efes Pils and Turkish Export Lager. Efes is also brewed at Istanbul.

There are three breweries at Istanbul. One brews, under licence, Löwenbräu. At Izmir, Turk Tuborg Brewery produces Tuborg Gold, Pilsner Special, Sade and Venus Light.

At Ankara is the Tekal Brewery.

Oceana

THERE ARE BUT two nations, Australia and New Zealand, in the vast area of Oceana that are sufficient in size and beer production to be included here. Oceana itself is an enormous region comprising all the many thousands of islands in the Pacific Ocean. As its name implies, the area is mostly ocean. Most of these islands are in chains or groups (many for administrative purposes), such as the French Marquesas, French Polynesia, the Solomons, the Bismarck Archipelago and the Carolines. A few could be regarded as somewhat substantial, such as Tahiti and Moorea, Samoa, Guam and Fiji. The Hawaiian Islands, obviously, is the western limits of the USA, and not a part of Oceana in this study. Excluding, then, Australia and New Zealand, the rest of Oceana produces a minute 945,000 hl of beer per year. Put in perspective, Oceana minus Australia and New Zealand produces 165,000 hl less beer than Jamaica and, taken in its entirety, ex-Czechoslovakia produces 210,000 hl more.

☛ Australia

Population (1990 est): 17,100,000; **density:** 2.2/sq km (5.8/sq mi); **distribution (1990):** 86% urban, 14% rural; **annual growth (1990):** 0.8%.

Per person annual beer consumption (1990) is 108.2 litres, down slightly from 111.0 litres in 1986. Production is 19,000,000 hl. This places her just behind The Netherlands on the world league list.

AUSTRALIANS ARE CRAZY about their Lager, which they think is the best in the world. In this respect, they are very similar to Americans who give double-thumbs-up to their North American Lagers. When it comes to beer, nationalism runs deep. Australia always ranks in the top five beer drinking nations, with Belgium, the Czech Republic, Germany and Luxembourg. Michael Jackson thinks Darwin (the Australian city, not the scientist), in the Northern Territory, ranks as the number one beer drinking city in the world, with an per-person rate of 230 litres per year. The national average is 108.2 litres per person.

It is Lager they drink now, but in Australia's early days as a British colony, they brewed and drank ales. The first brewer was John Boston. He set up shop in Sydney in 1794 when Captain John Hunter, RN, and governor (1795–1800) sought a brewer to switch the unruly exiles from their addiction to spirits, especially gin and rum. Evidently barley and hops weren't grown then because Mr Boston malted maize and used the leaves and stalks of Cape Gooseberry plants to flavour his beer. The resultant beer was far from satisfactory as the convicts decided to stick with their spirits.

The ensuing governor, Philip Gridley King (1800–1806), sent overseas for hops, but the plants arrived dead. If anything, he was persistent—he had hop seeds imported, and a brewery built. His next problem was finding a brewer. One, Thomas Rushton stepped forward. He brewed 12,000 gallons of both strong- and table beer.

Cash was scarce back then. What to do? One enterprising publican, Dan Cooper, advertised that he would take absolutely anything in payment for his beer at his pub: "property, land, houses, grain, cattle, sheep, pigs, poultry, eggs, cheese, butter, kangaroo skins, seal skins, wood, coal, hemp, shoes, soap and cedar logs".

In 1835 Toohey's Standard Brewery was founded at Sydney. By 1900, there ware 21 breweries in Sydney. In Melbourne, the Carlton Brewery was established in 1864. Carlton is now one of the largest brewers in Australia, operating as Carlton and United.

Fosters Lager is the most popular Australian brand in the USA (and round the world). Ironically, it was the two Foster brothers from New York, who opened their brewery, called Gambrinus, in Melbourne in 1885, who set all this in motion. Today, it is a powerhouse.

Tasmania grows 60% of Australia's hops and a majority of her barley. It is also home to the Cascade Brewery, which has longest unbroken brewing history in Australia. It was founded in 1824.

Australia is a very regulated nation of only 16m souls, perhaps a carry-over from her days as a penal colony, or perhaps from her left-leaning population. Each state specifies what size glasses in which beer may be served. This varies from state-to-state, and can be confusing to travellers.

Beer is served nearly ice-cold, similar again to a common practise in the USA. At near-freezing temperatures, the taste of beer cannot be appreciated, nor should its deleterious affects on the stomach and digestion be overlooked.

Australia's breweries have undergone a consolidation the same as what happened in the USA and the UK. Over 90% of the market is DIVided between a group (Tooheys, Fourex, and Swan) controlled by Alan Bond (42%), and his rival, Fosters, controlled by John Elliott.

Australians have a choice of 125 local brands and about 50 imports, though most drinkers remain fiercely loyal to their home-state brands, eg Fosters in Victoria; Tooheys in New South Wales; Fosters and Reschedules in Queensland; Castlebar Fourex and Power Bitter in South Australia; Coopers and West End in South Australia; SWAn in West Australia; Boa's and Cascade on Tasmania.

☞ New Zealand

Population (1991 est): 3,500,000; **density:** 13/sq km (34/sq mi); **annual growth (1991):** 0.9%.

Annual beer production is 3,700,000hl. Per person annual beer consumption is 110.8 litres, placing her between Ireland and Britain. New Zealanders seem to have slacked off just a

bit—consumption was 121.0 litres in 1986.

New Zealanders annually consume 110.8 litres of beer per person, placing them in the First Division. They certainly can't be accused of being slouches.

NEW ZEALAND'S BREWING traditions goes back to one of the world's most famous naval seamen, Captain Cook, RN. He was from Yorkshire, one of Englan d's great brewing counties.

When he landed on the South Island in 1773, he almost immediately proceeded to brew a beer composed of "the small branches of the spruce and tea plants by boiling them for three or four hours". He then added molasses and yeast and waited a few days until he had what he considered a passable beer.

New Zealand developed quite differently than did Australia. Immigrants wished to create a new society opposite that of what they viewed as the intemperate and squalid conditions in the Britain they were leaving. The temperance movement was established before serious settlement of the country began in the 1840s. The movement was directed by the Protestants, mainly from Scotland and Wales.

The battled between drinkers and prohibitionist continued until after the first world war when prohibitionists forced the government to referendum on the issue. At first count, the prohibitionists won, but the four out of five returning soldiers voted "for" alcohol. The prohibitionists lost 51–49%.

Prohibitionists won in the USA BECause they put pressure directly on Congress to take the decision, rather than trust the issue to referendum. In other respects the parallels between the countries are similar.

The result of the fight against the prohibitionists was that the breweries consolidated into three groups, which exist to this day.

The first is New Zealand Breweries, which controls 60% of the local market. It has breweries on both the North- and the South Islands. Some of its brands are Lion Red, Lion Brown, Lion Super, Mild and a Double Stout.

The second is the Leopard Brewery. It has a very small estate of tied houses, so it turned its attention to the export market. It forged links with Heineken, which has a strong presence in the area via its former colonies, especially Indonesia. Heineken supplies the brewery with yeast. Through Heineken it has links to Whitbread and, thusly, England. Leopard beer is exported throughout the Pacific Islands, and to Great Britain and North America.

The third brewing group is Dominion Breweries. It controls around 35% of the market. It has four breweries. It has also bought up and closed three others. Between it and New Zealand breweries controlling about 95% of the market, one can easily appreciate the decision Leopard Brewery took to follow the "export or die" path.

Dominion's best-selling brand is its Bitter. It also brews the Scottish Tennants under licence.

Lager brewing arrived in NEW Zealand in 1900, when Moss Davis, owner of the Captain Cook Brewery brought Conrad Breutsch, a Swiss brewer to the country to introduce it. Many of the beers brewed on the island still show his influence. Though they are copper-coloured like Ales, they are fermented with lager yeast.

Beer's future

FROM THE BEER-DRINKER'S perspective the increasing number of micro-brewers and pub-brewers should mean better, fresher, beer in more and more styles, than is normally available. This rates a Double Thumbs Up!

There is a brewing revelation occurring. The number of micro- and pub-breweries is almost exploding, not only in traditional beer-drinking countries such as Great Britain, Canada, Germany, the United States, Denmark, and The Netherlands, but in most of Africa, Latin America and Asia. As with all commercial activity, the most important prerequisites are long periods of peace, a market economy and a capital pool. Brewers, such as Youngs of London are seriously looking at the Chinese market as well as the rest of Asia for opportunities. Beer is going international—in a big way. Coupled with this is the lovely-to-behold trend of re-introducing ale brewing in places where it has been dormant for 125 (or more) years. As Real Ale lovers, and active home-brewers, we are overjoyed.

Again, from the beer drinker's perspective, the continuing rise in excise on beer, especially in Great Britain and the United States rates a Double Thumbs Down, British beer drinkers, for example, pay more in excise duty on beer than the rest of the ec combined. The government collected over 3.154bn ECUS (European Currency Units, a form of money used in trade) in 1991. German was second at 8.04m ECUS (just over a quarter of what the British pay). No wonder more and more people are taking up that ancient and noble human activity—home-brewing. Studies now indicate that imposing ever-higher tax on beer (and tobacco) is now having negative results, yet governments continue to impose outrageous "sin" taxes. Any one who thinks drinking beer is a sin is truly sick.

Growth or shrinkage?

THE QUESTION OF whether the brewing industry grows or shrinks in future may be answered several ways. The answer depends on the policies of government on a national, region or state or even local level. Tax policy plays an important role. Raise excise high enough and people who have only marginal discretionary spending many cut out or eliminate alcohol from their budgets. Recession, depression and boom periods affect ion, but these are cyclical. War, civil or otherwise affect consumption. Religious fervour, especially in Muslim lands can have the same effect, witness Iran. Globally, the consumption, and therefore the production of beer should increase into the foreseeable future.

Brewing is now Big Business, and international in scope. This is the realm of the HCBS. They continue to merge and forge links amongst themselves, looking for openings in countries where consumption is low (read Africa and Asia, especially China). There simply aren't that many small breweries left in the world for the HCBS to buy and then close, though this does still happen occasionally. Yes, any brewer can send a few palates abroad on a regular basis, but it takes a certain production capacity (beyond that which brew-pubs and micro-breweries possess) to enter the export business with a strong move to the hoop.

The bigger brewing gets, the more economic power it draws to itself and, consequently, the more political juice it accumulates, and the more lobbyists they can hire. This is important in the battle against neo-prohibitionists and environmentalists who are beginning to smell blood around the brewing body. Ken Don, head-brewer at Youngs & Co's Brewery (London), said they are doing all they can reasonably do now to be environmentally responsible, and are investigating ways to be even more so. There are some long-term savings to be gained from some schemes. Brew-pubs and micro-breweries hardly have the resources to hire lobbyists. To illustrate: New York state charged the same annual fee for a brewing licence, regardless the size of the brewery. Anheuser-Busch paid the same as the Woodstock Brewery (NY). For three years the small breweries in the state tried by themselves to get this changed in the state legislature—to no avail. They were told it was impossible. Finally, they scratched up $5,000 to pay a lobbyist, and his lobbyist son. Wouldn't you know it, but within days, the law was changed.

Everybody should gain from the reduction in the licence fee, often an impediment to people wanting to start a brewery, especially on a small scale. The result should be an increase in the number of brew-pubs and micro-breweries.

Whilst beer sales for the HCBS have been as flat as stale lager, independent breweries have been experiencing moderate growth. We suspect most future growth will come from this market. Much of the growth of the independents has been at the expense of imported brands (speaking from a USA perspective). Local brewers can always beat any imported beer on freshness. In future, much of the growth will be at the expense of the HCBS, but several things will have to happen to allow the independents to reach, say, a 25–50% market share. Perhaps this is expecting much, but it can happen. First, many hundreds if not thousands of brew-pubs will have to open in practically every county of every state; hundreds of micro-breweries will have to open in every region. This then will permit access to any one who wants to try craft beers. Distribution (of the breweries and their product), at present, is too haphazard. Second, a national beer-drinkers' consumers group, similar to CAMRA in the UK, is needed to spread the word about craft real beer. At present no organization exists, though there is a growing number of speciality magazines and papers devoted to the subject. Word of mouth is a too-slow process, though it is doing a good job. Much of the growth so far has been due to this. There is so much yet to be done. What of "Beer Drinker's of America", you ask? They do a fine job lobbying (with high-profile advocates) against higher excise tax on beer and against neo-prohibitionists, but they do nothing of note to promote real beer or educate the public about it. Three, the working press need to be educated about the differences amongst beers; between quality beer and fizzy yellow water, and style differences. Four, women need to be brought back into the fold. Yes, women drink plenty of beer, but what style do they most-often drink? "Light" fizzy yellow water. Why? Because so many are on perpetual diets. Until women, too, learn the benefits of real beer, they will stay their course. There is a carry-over effect on men because women still do the majority of shopping, and what they bring home is what their men drink. It is often said that women are much more health-conscious than are men. If this is so, then surely by pointing out to them the added health benefits of drinking real beer, uncontaminated by adjuncts and chemicals, can only stimulate interest (and sales). Until the last century, when brewing began to become big business, women were the family brewers, the brewers at brew-pubs (though they weren't called brew-pubs then. They were called ale houses.). That's when men, seeing opportunities, muscled them out of the way.

One final item (actually there are two, but they walk hand-in-hand), which will hold growth in consumption down is the ever-increasing penalties for drunk-driving and the lowering of limits on what constitutes being "drunk". These are led by neo-prohibitionists and politicians looking to score votes.

Anti-alcohol forces

A NOT SMALL influence on the upward pressure on excise is the neo-prohibitionists. In every society there is always a small group who love to interfere and tinker (social experimenters) with the lives of others (who mostly want to be left alone to get on with their lives). They feel important and powerful doing this. Unfortunately, like worshippers of false Messiahs, many people fall for their words of sin, tragedy and woe. Their argument is that since alcoholism costs billions of dollars in health costs each year, then drinkers of any alcohol should be taxed (to death) to pay these bills. This is the same tired argument they used in the years leading up to Prohibition. Though the USA never had a true Patrician Class, neo-prohibitionists act as if they are of this class, looking down at beer-drinkers.

"I've come down from the upper class,

To mend your rotten ways.

My father was a man of power,

Whom every one obeyed."

Jethro Tull—Thick as a Brick

Another scheme they have succeeded in getting the government, media and much of the public to believe is their definition of alcoholism and, therefore, who "needs help" (treatment). People who drink alone have an alcohol problem because they are "anti-social". People who drink more than occasionally have a problem because they are "habitual" drinkers. People who get drunk have a problem because they "obviously" are using alcohol to mask a "much deeper" problem (after all, no one in their right mind likes to feel hung-over, and since the result of getting drunk is a hangover, this again signifies the drunk has a problem). They have so widened their definition of who and what constitutes a "problem drinker" that almost any one who has more than a celebratory glass of champagne at New Years or at a wedding is considered one.

Their scare tactics have convinced many sane

and "normal" drinkers they have a serious problem and need help. Often their viewpoints have been incorporated into official state policy. For example, many state mandate that people convicted of drunk driving attend Alcoholics Anonymous (a group that never lets go, once they "have" you). A person convicted of drunk driving can be said to have made a big mistake in judgement driving an auto in that condition, but it does not follow that he has a problem with alcohol. What skews justice is that the system allows a "way out" for a person arrested for drunk driving. Defence lawyers argue that alcohol "clouded" their client's judgement, rather than have their client stand up and simply admit he made a mistake in judgement—that he should have called a cab, or waited until he'd sobered up before driving. This saves the client from having to face the fact he made a mistake (in his mind he can remain guilt-free), and the courts and prosecutor's office can mark up another statistic caused by evil alcohol. This neatly places the blame elsewhere than where it often belongs.

Beer-drinkers won a major point this year (1993) when the courts in the USA stopped federal government agencies from (effectively) lobbying for these neo-prohibitionists. It is against the law.

Chapter 4
Beer Styles

THERE ARE JUST two classifications of beer—ales and lagers. Within each classification, there are many different styles of beer, ranging from ultra-pale nondescript North American lagers who's brewers refer to as "Pilseners" to the blackest of stouts. Fred Eckhardt, a noted American beer writer, has identified 38 styles and a further 42 sub-styles. In this section we will list and describe all of them (and others), and give commercial examples of each .(where appropriate and possible) Description of each will be drawn from Michael Jackson's *World Guide to Beer*, and his *Pocket Guide to Beer*, Fred Eckhardt's *The Essentials of Beer Style*, Roger Protz's *The European Beer Almanac*, Dietrich Höllhuber and Wolfgang Kaul's *Die Biere Deutschlands*, other sources, and from our own experiences. We will skip the laborious and boring task of identifying who said what, when and where about each style, except in cases of major discrepancy. Alcohol content will be percent by volume (instead of by weight) and displayed, as an example, 4.5% ABV in every instance. Hop bittering units are expressed in International Bittering Units (IBUS)

A brief reminder: the determining factor that traditionally places a particular beer in one category or the other is the yeast type used. Whilst there are many strains of yeast, they are divided into top fermenting and bottom fermenting types. Top fermenting yeasts are ale yeasts. Bottom fermenting yeasts are lager yeasts. To keep which is which straight in mind, think of top as above and bottom as lower. The first letter of above and ale match; the first letter of lower and lager match.

Another distinguishing characteristic between ale and lager yeast is the temperature at which they are active. Ale yeasts ferment best at temperatures above 55°F, whilst lager yeasts continue to work down to about 32°F (0°C). It is easy to guess what type beer is in the barrels when one examines photographs of cold-looking beer storage cellars.

Finally, there are three beer styles, hybrids really, two of which are genuinely American. Developed in the late 19th century, they use lager yeast (normally), but are fermented at ale temperatures then lagered at cold temperatures. This is a style that is tricky to brew because lager yeasts impart off-flavours when fermented at warm temperatures, a problem home-brewers know all-to-well. It is also the reason why they don't often attempt lager brewing unless they have a beer-dedicated refrigerator or live in Northern regions where they can brew lagers over the winter.

There has been on-going debates about styles amongst brewers, beer judges and others in the industry, notably writers. The debate has centred around a core of issues (questions, really): how loose or tight should style parameters be?; should they be flexible or rigid?; how to define styles?; should brewers be called to task if they label a brand a certain style when it certainly is not?—or should we even care?; are there too many style designations, and if so how could they be pared; should exceptions be made for a single brand that is unique?—give it its own style designation, or should it be tossed in to the closest-appropriate one?.

For some, simply to determine if a beer *drinks* good (or not) is enough. Notice we did not mention the *taste* of the beer. There is a difference between drinking beer (as to quench a thirst) and tasting beer (to enjoy it), and here we do not bring inebriation into this). Others feel good if they know to which category a beer belongs.

It is human nature to categorize practically everything. It is that upon which science is built. Every specie, every element, every atom and particle in this universe that has been discovered has been studied and described and categorized. It is a way of man.

Why should it be any different when it applies to beer? It shouldn't, but there are practical limits beyond which categorization becomes pedantic and even down-right stupid. It is not the purpose of this book to delve into these discussions, but to illustrate but a single point: two brewers set out to brew the same beer—style isn't important. They use the exact same recipe: the amounts of the same variety hops; they boil the wort for the same length of time; they use the same yeast strain; and they use the same amounts of pale malt, but with this difference—they use different suppliers. One's barley is malted to a slightly darker colour than that of the other maltster. This results in a perceptibly, but only slightly, darker beer that tastes just a wee bit sweeter. Should both still be classified in the same style? Of course. What if, instead of using the darker grain, that brewer used a different hop? One that gave the beer a more floral aroma? The two would probably still be grouped together. But what if the different hops made that beer much more hoppy to the palate, as is the difference between a Continental Light Lager and a Continental Pilsner? Here the two have to be separated.

Some differences between styles ale subtle and narrow, and others are gulfs apart. Stout developed from Porter. It was at first called Stout Porter, meaning strong Porter. Then roasted unmalted barley was introduced into the recipe, which changed the taste somewhat (and darkened the colour still further). The two co-existed for a while, then Porter went down the road to oblivion whilst Stout prospered. Now, Porter is back, by trying to regain its identity. It is still defining itself, or, more accurately, the brewers are.

The Confederation of Belgian Brewers appears to consider almost every brand to be a unique style, and we wouldn't want to put ourselves through the enormous effort to learn, define and profile each of those styles. That is a bit much. *D'accord?*

The style guide, which follows, is meant to give the reader a sense of the scope of styles brewers produce. Some styles are extremely old, dating almost to man's earliest attempts at brewing. Others are new (relatively). Still others are making a comeback after being abandoned by brewers for decades or longer. New styles will develop. It is bound to happen as more curious people take up brewing. Perhaps the next new style will be the result of an accidental discovery, or perhaps the result of a carefully thoughtout effort. We do not care how it happens, just so long as the result is delicious, and made from quality ingredients. We do not want more ersatz, chemical-laden beer.

We encourage readers to seek and try beers of the different styles: the written word seldom does justice to actual experience.

Ales: Top-fermented beer

Aged Beers

Old Brown/Belgian Brown Ales

Oud Bruin or Old Brown Ales of Belgium are an interesting lot. They are loved or hated with equal passion because of their distinctly sour taste and, often, aroma. This is by design, not the result of something gone very wrong during the fermenting or lagering stage—though originally it was. Some enterprising and inquisitive brewer, somewhere in brewing's unrecorded past, as loathe as any man of commerce to throw away something of potential value, probably tried to recover a barrel of old beer gone sour. Perhaps he mixed it with young beer, tried the result, and found he liked it. Then he tried it on customers and found they did too. *Voila!* A new beer style was born.

The trick was in replicating the discovery but, in time, that was worked out too. Today Belgian Oud Bruin brewers would never think of trading their antiquated brewery equipment for new modern stainless steel plant.

They leave conditions exactly as they have been for decades, fearing any change would effect the wild yeasts and bacteria that make Oud Bruin possible. Their brewing practises are the similar to those described in brewing books that are centuries-old. They are the most traditional of all brewers.

Belgium is very strict with their beer classifications, especially for excise tax reasons, so the specifications for each type of beer is sharply defined. Similarities between brands can be hard to find because each brewer has his own recipes. There has been no great movement towards a centre or common ground like what happened with mass-produced American lagers and "Lites". A recent count revealed 34 different brands of Oud Bruin.

Colour ranges from red to brown to almost black. Alcohol content is ABV 4.8–5.2%. Bitterness ranges between 15–25IBUS. Aromas—there can be many, and are induced from the bacteria, micro-organisms and yeasts: malty and sweet, acidic, port and sherry wine-like, floral and fruity. Oud Bruins will not have a hoppy aroma. Almost all Belgian beer styles are very lightly hopped. Two and three year old hops are often used because their aromatic properties have evaporated, though their bittering and preservative ones remain. Sazz, Goldings and Styrian hops which are low-bittering, but not overly aromatic are preferred.

Unlike their British cousins, Belgian Brown Ales often are aged a long time after they come out of the finishing tanks. In the case of Liefman's Goudenband, it has 3–12 month's bottle-maturation. If it is kept cool (but not refrigerated) and in a dark place, it will improve with age and reach its peak in, say, two years.

Commercial examples are Liefman's Goudenband (the base of their Kriek beer), a beer Michael Jackson called "surely the world's finest brown ale", Gouden Carolus, Felix Speciaal Oudenarde and Rodenbach.

Profile: Goudenband

ABV 5.2, OG 1052, BITTERNESS 20IBUS

Ingredients: pale, chocolate and crystal malts, torrefied barley, maize and caramel sugar, Czech Sazz and Whitbread Goldings Variety hops

Nose: fruity and peppery hops aroma

Palate: sweet fruit and chocolate in mouth, dry and pleasantly sour finish

OLD RED

This Belgian style is one of the finest and most exquisite beers in the world. It is exemplified by Rodenbach's Belgian Red Ale.

The Brouwerij Rodenbach at Roeselare in the southwest of Flanders is undoubtedly a Belgian national treasure, even if not officially declared so. There are more than 300 oak casks standing higher than 20 feet on site. Four coopers are on staff to maintain them. The beer is fermented at least 18 months in the casks.

Rodenbach Red Ale is brewed using four malts, one pale summer malt, two- and six-row winter malts and Vienna crystal malt, which imparts the red cast to the beer. Brewers Gold and some Kent Goldings hops are used. Several yeasts are used, plus those that have taken up residence in the oak tuns. These impart the unique freshness and sourness to this world-class beer.

Michael Jackson calls this beer, "The world's most refreshing beer." Tim Webb says of it, "One of the world's classic beers, and the finest example of an old Flemish red ale."

Profile: Rodenbach Red Ale

ABV 5.1, OG 1047.5, BITTERNESS 14IBUS

Ingredients: pale malts, caramunich malt (Vienna malt, maize grits, Brewers Gold and Kent Goldings hops

Nose: Very strong sour and fruit

Palate: ripe fruit; prolonged bitter and sour finish

Holy Beers

Trappiste, Abbey & Belgian Strong Beer

Trappiste:

There are five Trappist monasteries in Belgium and one in the Netherlands that can, by law, use the name "Trappiste" in their beer descriptions. The monasteries are:

1: Chimay (Abbaye de Notre-Dame-de-Scourmont, in the French border province of Hainout. It was founded in 1850.

2. Orval (Villiers-devant-Orval) is in Luxembourg Province near the border with France. It was founded in 1070.

3. Rochefort (Abbeye Notre Dame de St Rémy) is near Dinant in Namur Province.

4. St Sixtus (Abbeye de St Sixte) is at Westvleteren in West Flanders Province. It was founded in 1831.

5. Westmalle (Notre Dame du Sacré-Coeur) in Antwerp Province. It was founded in 1836.

6. Trappistenbierbrouwerij De Schaapskooi (Abdij Koningshoeven) is near Tilburg in North Trabant Provence of The Netherlands. It was founded in 1884.

Affligem, Lesse, Maredsous and Tangerloo are other Belgian monastic orders that have ceased brewing their own beers, but have licensed their names to commercial breweries.

Trappiste beers are usually strong, from 6–10% ABV, and use candi sugar (glucose chips or dextrose) in their formulation. They are always bottle-conditioned, and their colour ranges from bronze to deep brown. Following ancient traditions some brands get flavoured and/or scented with spices such as coriander, cumin and ginger.

These beers are really a sub-set of the category, though each is distinctive of the others due to the various yeast strains and bacteria (there are usually several in each beer) that are in these beers. In one aspect of their brewing process, these are closest to beer as it was originally made thousands of years ago: once the wort has been boiled, the beer is cooled and left exposed to the air until it picks up air-borne yeasts and bacteria until fermentation begins. The area around Brussels, by whatever quirk of nature, is ideal for this process. This is the complete opposite of the sterile laboratory conditions in which modern lager brewers operate. Anheuser-Busch's brewers shudder at the condition of Belgian breweries of this type.

Commercial examples: Chimay Red (ABV 7%), Chimay White (ABV 8%), Chimay Blue, (ABV 9%), and Chimay Gold (the bottled version, called Grande Réserve), from the Abbaye Notre-Dame de Scourmont. These are called the "Burgundies of Belgium"; and Orval (ABV 6%) brewed at the Brasserie d'Orval, Abbaye Notre Dame d'Orval. Others are Westmalle, Westvleteren and Rochefort.

Abbey Beer

The English word "abbey" (Flemish: abdij; French: abbaye; German: abtei) should be used to describe any beer brewed in a Trappist style, but not at one of the six monasteries.

Too often the use of the word Abbey on beer labels has been misused by commercial brewers to create a false status to their brands. This is not always the case. There are several Abbey beers that are delicious.

Commercial examples are Cuvée de l'Ermitage, Leffe Radieuse, Maredsous and St Idesbald Abdij.

Dubbel and Trippel

These terms are commonly used, often by commercial brewers with little regard to the truth. Dubbels (double) are commonly dark, medium-strong, sweet and mellow. They date from the Middle Ages, but their range of original extract is now restricted to OG 1063–1070. Tripels (triple) are often pale, very strong, full-bodied, well-rounded and bitter.

Dubbels have ABV 6–7.5%, and bitterness of 18–25IBUs. The colour range is dark amber to brown. Their aromas are sweet and malty with a very faint hoppy note. They are never hoppy-tasting. Their bodies can be full, but some are a bit thin.

Commercial examples are Bornem, Grimbergen Dubbel, Leffe Brune and Westmalle Dubbel.

Trippels originated at the Westmalle Abbey. They are the easiest of Belgian styles to classify because they have a very narrow profile. They are just a little darker than a Pilsener, but their aromas range from neutral to estery to malty to sweet; sometimes with a very peppery Goldings hop-aroma, if any hops are present at all. Taste is almost always very neutral, but with generous mouth-feel. The finish is

quite sweet with alcoholic warming, but very little alcoholic taste. Some may have a bitter aftertaste imparted by the yeast. Alcohol content is ABV 7–10%. Bitterness is 20–25IBUs.

It is said that Trippels got their name from the fact that they are three times the strength of Specials, which are really the weakest pale ales in the brewery's product line.

Commercial examples are Affligem, Augustin, Brugse Tripel, Corsendonk Agnus and Grimbergen.

These styles are some of the most enjoyable beers to drink, though they are an acquired taste. It is a big jump from a Pilsener, especially American pseudo-pilsners.

Pale Beers

Special

This category, in Belgium, has different parameters than the British one of the same name. In the former country, Special generally applies to the weakest pale ale on a brewery's list. This is confusing to an unknowing drinker, especially when it is found on a label.

Altbier

Düsseldorf is the traditional home of Altbier (but not the only place Altbier is brewed in Deutschland). To paraphrase the Lord's Prayer, give us this day our daily beer, for this is how Düsseldorfers take their Altbier. The word "Altbier" is the German term for a top-fermented beer. Classic examples of this style are dark-copper to rich-brown coloured, use only pure single-cell yeast strains, are cold conditioned for three to eight weeks and are ABV 4.0–5.0%.

Only by hasty examination can they be compared with British ales. They are as similar as dissimilar. An Englishman would argue that their ales have more individuality, and a German might retort that their Altbiers are cleaner and smoother. Altbiers have little of the acidity and fruitiness of British ales. Rather, they have a much cleaner palate, and a complex, well-balanced and intricate blend of hop bitterness and malty body. Altbier is traditionally dispensed from the cask (wooden) as are British Real Ales.

Two or three German malts (Munich and Vienna) may be used in Altbier brewing. Wheat often is 10–15% of it's make-up. The Pinkus brewery at Münster uses about 40% wheat. The same goes for its hops, with Spalt hops being traditionally preferred. Hop IBUs range from the mid 20s to the 50s.

Commercial examples are Pinkus Alt, Rhenania Alt, Weihenstephen Alt from Germany, and Widmer Alt from the United States.

Kölsch

This is the hometown drink of the metropolitan area of Köln (Cologne), Germany, hence its name. The German capital, Bonn, is included in this area, which is in the industrial northeast. Like Altbier, Kölsch is an ale. They make up a minuscule portion of the entire beer production of Germany. If this style is brewed elsewhere in Germany, under German law, the word Kölsch must be proceeded by the name of the city of origin.

Kölsch is a very pale, golden, highly-hopped beer with an ABV range of 4.3–5.0%, OG 1045–47. It is slightly lactic tasting, too.

Bitterness is 16–34IBUs. This style uses Vienna, Pilsener, Bayerisch and caramel malts and, up to 20%, wheat malt. Normally, the hops used are Hallertauer, Perle and/or Spalt.

In Germany, Kölsch must, by law, be filtered, unless it is labelled as Unfiltered. Lagering is for 14–40 days.

Since Grolsch Brewery, of the Netherlands, has taken over Küppers, Köln's largest brewery, there is a possibility that Kölsch might be exported to a wider area than it is at present. At the least, it should become more popular in the Netherlands.

Pils Ale

This is a unique style some Dutch breweries are developing. It is like a Pilsener-style lager, but it is brewed with ale yeast. These are comparable to Kölsch, but are not like a typical Pilsener. Most are a bit darker than one would expect to see in a light-coloured Pilsener. Contrarily, they are not like Pale Ales. So, what to do? Come up with a new category. Voila! This category is a cousin to American Steam Beers and to cream ales.

The Abdij Koningshoeven, 't IJ Brouwerij, Raaf Bierbrouwerij and Us Heit Bierbrou-werij, all in the Netherlands brew this style beer.

Bitter

In England, Bitter (never Bitters when referring to one, as in "I'll have a Bitters, please.") is the draught equivalent of Pale Ale. As the name implies, they are well-hopped. Colour ranges from bronze to deep copper. Some acidity in the finish is to be expected. Ordinary Bitters have an alcohol range of ABV 3.5–4.0%. They are not normally highly-carbonated.

Bitter accounts for, in English pubs, about 80% of draught beer sales.

From the Big Lamp Brewery at Newcastle upon Tyne comes an excellent example.

Profile: Big Lamp Bitter

OG 1040

Ingredients: pale malt, crystal malt and brewer's sugar. Fuggles and English and Styrian

Goldings hops.

Nose: Delicate and light malt and hops.

Palate: Well-rounded malt and hops balance. It has a deep dry finish and some notes of orange-peel. Plenty of hops and fruit character in a wonderfully balanced beer.

Best or Special Bitter

Special Bitter is mid-octane Bitter with ABV 4.0–4.8%. They tend to be medium-bodied, hoppy and dry.

The Larkin Brewery Ltd of Chiddingstone, Edenbridge in Kent has a superb Best Bitter.

Profile: Larkin Best Bitter

OG 1045, ABV 4.7%, BITTERNESS 45IBUS.

Ingredients: pale malt and crystal malt with some chocolate malt for colour. Fuggles, East Kent Goldings, Progress and Whitbread Goldings Variety hops.

Nose: Malty sweetness and delicious Kent Goldings hops.

Palate: Malt and tart fruit in the mouth, followed by an intense hop and fruit finish. A deliciously strong beer with an enormous hop character.

Extra Special Bitter

These are high-octane—ABV 5.5–6.5%, about double the strength of standard Mild. They are also highly attenuated, giving more alcohol than their Original Gravities would suggest.

In comparison to Bitter and to Best Bitter, Extra Special Bitter is maltier and sweeter.

I don't know of any beer in this class better than Fuller's ESB. It has won numerous awards and medals from CAMRA, national and international competitions. It is available in America, both bottled and on draught. When in good condition, it has a big creamy head. Steady as you go.

Profile: Fuller's ESB

OG 1054, ABV 5.5%, BITTERNESS 35IBUS

Nose: a blast of malt, hops and marmalade.

Palate: the initial attack is strong with malt and fruit with hop undertones. This it finishes with a strong Goldings hops character. There are mild hints of gooseberry, lemon and orange, and some tannin-imparted astringency.

A pile-driver of a beer.

Pale Ale

These have a colour range from amber to copper, and are brewed with pale malts and very hard water. Pale, in this usage, does not mean its obvious definition but, rather, pale in comparison to Brown Ale, Porter and Stout. The OGs of these are 1043–53 with a typical ABV 3.4–5.2%. Pale Ales are, often, not as highly attenuated as are Bitters, so they tend to be a bit heavier than the latter.

Bullion, Fuggles and Goldings hops are most frequently used. Bitterness range of 19–45IBUS is typical.

One must note there is a distinction between Pale Ales as a broad classification of ales and Pale Ale as a bottled beer name. The term Pale Ale is often used by brewers to label their best bitters, especially if they are bottled.

Good commercial examples are Anchor Liberty Ale and Sierra Nevada Pale Ale (American), and Bass Pale Ale, Ind Coope's Double Diamond and Samuel Smith Pale Ale (Britain).

Profile: Double Diamond

OG 1053, ABV 5.2%, BITTERNESS 35IBUS

Ingredients: pale, crystal and chocolate malts, high-maltose brewer's sugar; Galena and Target hops.

Nose: hops and rich fruit, and a hints of sulphur.

Palate: malty up front, then a big finish with excellent hop character. Refreshing.

The bottle recipe is used as the basis for their cask-conditioned ale which took the Champion Beer of Britain award at the Great British Beer Festival in 1990.

It is available in both bottle and keg in North America.

India Pale Ale (IPA)

Traditionally, a strong Pale Ale that was brewed for British Empire troops stationed in India, from the 18th century until 1945, when India gained independence. It was originally formulated by Mark Hodgson, a London brewer, sometime between 1790 and 1800. His IPA enabled him to dominate the export market to India up to about 1830. He was exporting 9,000 barrels per year by 1807 and this rose to 41,000 barrels per year by 1817.

Meanwhile, Burton brewers saw their Baltic export market collapse due to Emperor Bonaparte's conquest of that area. Britain and France were at war. The brewers sought new markets. As a result, Allsopp, a Burton brewer, asked Job Goodhead, their head-brewer and malter, if he could replicate Mr Hodgson's beer. His first effort was brewed in a teapot. He was successful. Within a year, Allsopp and Bass were both mounting a challenge to their rival, Mr Hodgson.

The Burton IPA variant was a pale, sparkling ale. It was heavily hopped and highly-conditioned. The beer had to be strong and hoppy to survive the long sea-journey there, which could take as long as six months under sail. Aesthetic reasons also were an influence in deciding on a pale colour.

Today it is a pale imitation of its former self, implying a premium (maybe) Pale Ale. Even the colour has lightened considerable to, in some instances, nearly as light as Blonde or Golden Ales. Some brewers try to capitalize on the recognition of the term IPA, and label their beers as such, when in reality they are nothing more than a common Bitter or Pale Ale.

Profile: Bridport IPA

OG 1031, ABV 3.2%, BITTERNESS 20IBUS

Nose: rich hops and malt aromas.

Palate: Very malty in the mouth followed by a balanced hop, fruit and nut aftertaste and an intense dry finish.

This was the unanimous choice from amongst ten British ales at a tasting put on by the Guild of British Beer Writers.

Notice the decline from a 1979 Ballantines Old India Pale Ale at OG 1076 and ABV 7.7%.

Oh, how the once mighty have fallen. It is almost senseless to keep the category except for sentimental historical purposes, and the fact, already mentioned, that brewers are increasingly using the term.

A story about a unique IPA

On 31 July 1993, at The White Horse at Parson's Green, London, a special Burton-brewed IPA was unveiled. This event was the culmination and result of a seminar Mark Dorber, cellar manager at The White Horse, organized in July 1990 seminar were four Burton brewers and several beer journalists. Springing from their discussions on modern Burton ale, the idea emerged to try to recreate a late 1800s ipa. In April 1993, a call to Gus Gutherie, technical director of Bass brewery, received a go-ahead to reproduce a classic IPA. Tom Dawson, a retired Bass brewer agreed to act as consultant. To formulate this joint effort, Mr Dawson consulted Bass's brewing ledgers back to the 1880s.

The White Horse IPA was brewed in the Bass Brewery Museums brew-house that dates from 1920. It is a lovely example of a tower-type plant that was an experimental plant that was used at Cape Hill. It was transported in the late 1970s to the Bass Brewery and installed in an old engine-house, which is now within the confines of the Museum. The plant has a five-barrel capacity. Two brews were necessary to fulfil a White Horse beer festival order of "at least six-hogsheads".

At joint team made up of young Bass brewers and cellarmen from The White Horse assembled at 6.00am on Saturday, 19 June 1993 at the brewery. Twenty-nine hours, two brews and a clean-up later they were done. Then it was up to the yeast to do its work, and the brewers to be patient.

Profile: White Horse IPA

ABV 7.0%, OG 1064, BITTERNESS 85IBUS

Ingredients: Halcyon malt 90%, brewers sugar 10%, Progress whole hops in Copper, Kent Goldings for dry hopping.

Nose: strong hops overpowers all else

Palate: long-lasting hops. Note the bittering units at 85, which is most appropriate for a strong Stout.

Colour: 18

Note 1: lovely big white head

Note 2: because the Progress hops used had a higher than normal alpha acid content (7% versus a more normal 5%) the bittering units imparted were 40% more than what was intended in Mr Dawson's recipe. Compounding this just a bit was the fact that originally 11 barrels were planned, but the final result was under ten. They were, in fact, looking for a bittering rate of about 55.

Note 3: the OG at 1064 would normally indicate an ABV of about 6.2–6.4%. The 7.0% ABV is quite remarkable.

Strong Pale Ales

It is nearly impossible to properly classify all the beers that fall in to this category, so it has been broken in two, Strong Golden and Strong

Strong Golden

The world-classic beer of this category is Moortgat Brewery's *Duvel*, which means Devil. When they changed (in 1970) its colour from deep brown to straw, they created a whole new category. Sometimes it is incorrectly taken as a strong Pilsener. Duvel's triumph has prompted other brewers to make beers in this style, which is singularly Belgian.

Highly aromatic Saaz and Styrian hops gives it its zesty bouquet, a distinctive yeast gives in a delicate fruitiness, and to achieve the light colour, only the most lightly-malted barley is used.

It throws such a big foamy head upon opening, that a special extra-wide-mouthed glass is used to contain it.

If you are expecting to taste a pilsener based on its colour, you will probably be disappointed. It's as if you went to an ice cream parlour and ordered a dark type without checking the name. You expect a chocolate something, but instead it tastes like watermelon. You happen to love watermelon as much as chocolate, but your senses and prejudices deceive you. You need to give this beer a chance and appreciate it for what it is.

Profile: Duvel

OG 1070, ABV 8.5%, BITTERNESS 30IBUS

Ingredients: pale malt and brewer's sugar for bottle conditioning; Saaz and Styrian hops.

Nose: beautiful hop and fruit aroma.

Palate: at first it is like ripe pears that gives way to fruitiness and, finally, a hop bitterness.

Strong Pale Ale

These beers are dark gold to copper to amber coloured with an alcohol range of OG 1065–1090.

The following profile is from Frobes Ales made at the Oulton Broad Brewery at Lowestoft in Suffolk.

Profile: Merrie Monarch

OG 1072, ABV 8.0%

Ingredients: pale and crystal malt, an assortment of hops

Nose: a nice balance of hops, nuts and malt

Palate: Smooth with definite alcoholic warming. Starts and finishes malty with good hops balance, but adds fruit to finish.

Extra-strong Pale Ale

Extra Strong ales are classified, here, as all Pale Ales with an ABV > 9%. The profiles of beer in this category are rather broad. Virtually each beer could have its own unique category. Abbey beers are not included in this category or the Extra Strong Dark Ales category. Abbey beers stand alone.

Profile: Thomas Hardy's Ale

This bottle-conditioned ale is one of the finest in the world. Each batch is different-tasting from the previous one, and each years beer changes throughout its life. The quotes below are from Thomas Hardy, the great English author, after whom the beer is named. Each bottle is numbered. They are best laid down, and consumed at least three years after bottling date. They last upwards to 25 years.

OG 1125, ABV 12%, BITTERNESS 75IBUS

Nose: "Brisk as a volcano"

Palate: "Full in body; piquant, yet without a twang; free from streakiness"

Comments: "Luminous as an autumn sunset...the most beautiful colour that the eye of an artist in beer could desire".

Dark Ale

Mild Ale

In Britain, Mild Ale is a low-alcohol dark brown beer, though some are copper-coloured. Alcohol content ranges ABV 3.0–3.6%. They are light to medium-bodied, malty, sweet and lightly hopped. Mild Ales are a true "session" beer meant to be drunk in great amounts. Though they may be bottled, they are at its best as a cask-conditioned draughts.

In England, Mild Ale has a blue-collar/ working man's image.

A typical example might be the Mild Ale from Adnams & Company.

Profile: Adnams Mild

OG 1034, ABV 3.2, BITTERNESS 20IBUS.

Ingredients: pale ale malt, crystal malt, brewer's sugar (for priming), Fuggles and Goldings hops.

Nose: Light malt and hops.

Palate: rich soft malt with a gentle finish, and good chewy malt and hops undertones.

Brown Ales-British

This is one of the broadest categories, by style definition, of all the beer styles. They range in colour from amber to deep brown (though not black). Their taste is mild to assertive. English Bullion, Fuggles and Goldings hops are used. Alcohol content is ABV 3.0–4.5%.

There are actually two distinct types of this style. The first could be called Southern English Brown. This type is mild, sweet and very dark. OG 1031–41 but, more typically, OG 1030–35.

The second is the Northern English Brown. This is dryer-tasting, red-brown coloured, and are a little stronger, with Samuel Smith Nut Brown Ale weighing in at OG 1049. Typical range is OG 1044–50.

As with many ales, their alcohol content has fallen during this century. There are references to brown ales with OGs at 1055 and 60IBUS bittering.

Commercial examples are Newcastle Brown Ale, Samuel Smith Nut Brown Ale and Vaux Double Maxim.

Porter/Entire

Porter is the style beer that led directly to the growth of commercial brewing in London in the 1700s. Prior to then, almost all brewing was done by the pubs themselves. Because Porter has a long maturing process, much longer than pub-brewers could afford to match, they gradually lost ground to the newly-formed commercial brewers. Porter was so popular that controlling Porter production led to dominance of the brewing market. This was in London where Porter was popular, but in the countryside it was a different story where regular ales were still preferred. It wasn't until efficient cooling systems were developed that the inhibition warm weather had on ale brewing was lifted, thus allowing commercial brewers outside London to move into the market of providing quality beer during those months. Gradually commercial brewers improved their techniques and equipment until, finally, they were able to provide beer pub-brewers could not match in price, consistency and quality. Pub-brewers gave up.

In the late 1800s there was a middle-class revolt against Porter, and the shift was on to Pale Ales. Lighter-coloured ale was in, Porter was out. It went into decline and, by the first world war, it had all but disappeared.

Today Porter is having a revival on both sides of the Atlantic. It's growth has been triggered by growing interest by the drinking public in darker speciality beers. Most Porters are brewed by micro-breweries, such as Sierra Nevada, and brew-pubs. One can not be sure if these are in the same mould as original Porters because present-day brewers are working from very old recipes, the original Porter yeasts have been lost, and the brown malts that used to go in to Porter are no longer made, being too difficult and costly. Sad but true.

This profile will, obviously, be a thoroughly modern one. It is not narrowly defined. Superficially Porter looks like Stout. Indeed, Stout developed from Porter, and was originally called Stout Porter. Whilst Stout should be black, traditional Porter should never be darker than a deep dark brown with hints of red because it should not contain roasted bar-

ley and black grains which give Stout its black colour and distinct flavour profile.

Porter should, above all, have a full-bodied malty flavour with enough alcohol to give it the desired amount of balance and warmth. Low original gravity beers quickly get out of balance with the hops bitterness and roasted malt flavours standing out too much. Hop aroma should not be overdone. There should be grainy and malty notes and, possibly, some ester-based hints of fruit, and burnt pungent aromas from the roast malt used.

Alcohol content range is ABV 4.5–6.0%, OG 1045–1060, bitterness 25–45IBUs

Commercial examples are Burton Porter, Pimlico Porter, Pitfield London Porter and Samuel Smith Taddy Porter (all British). Some North American Porters are Anchor Porter, Sierra Nevada Porter, Catamount, Labatts and Yuenglings Pottsville Porter. The last could/should more accurately be classified a Continental Dark because in it fermented with lager yeast, but the brewer calls it a Porter, so a Porter it is.

A last note on Porter. There has actually been a recent cleave in the Porter style. On one hand there are the traditional Porters, as described above, with which some brewers are staying. On the other, there is a, what we call, Modern Porter. This latter style is characterized as: being very dark to black, like Stout; and, perhaps, a weaker Stout, but without the roasted barley used in Stout, and less hop bittering, say, 38IBUs instead of 60IBUs.

Again, because this is a re-emerging style, some brewers are introducing beers with "ball park" Porter/Stout characteristics and branding them Porters.

Profile: Larkin Porter Ale

OG 1052, ABV 5.5, BITTERNESS 59IBUS

Ingredients: pale, crystal and chocolate malts. Fuggles East Kent Goldings, Progress and Whitbread Goldings Variety hops.

Nose: very hoppy with a lovely baking chocolate aroma.

Palate: at first a perfect balance of malt and hops, bitter-sweet, followed by a finish of fruit and chocolate. Very delicious and complex.

Scotch Ale

Scotch ales usually have a malty character. They are brewed, in Scotland in four styles: Light (ABV 3.0%), Heavy (ABV 4.0%), Export (4.5% ABV) and Strong (ABV 7.0–10.0%).

"Scotch Ale", used as a term, implies a very dark, thick, creamy, malty ale with a high alcohol content. It is now produced in Belgium, where it has gain high status, and in France, with an alcohol content of ABV 7–8%. It's introduction in these two countries is thought to been during the first world war when it was brewed for British servicemen. There are now more Scotch Ales brewed in Belgium than in Scotland, where it has fallen out of favour. One brand, Gordon's Highland Scotch is brewed in Edinburgh. It is available in Belgium but, strangely, not in Edinburgh. Go figure.

Commercial examples are Belhaven, Traquair House Ale and McEwen's Scotch Ale.

Profile: Traquair House Ale

OG 1075, ABV 7.0%, BITTERNESS 35IBUS

Ingredients: pale ale and crystal malts, East Kent Goldings and Red Sell hops.

Nose: dark chocolate, hops, malt, fruit and spices. Stunning.

Palate: at first a strong attack of malt and hops changing to an intense bitter finish. Chocolate and pineapple clearly evident. Outrageous.

Stouts

As stated previously, Porter gave birth to Stout. This was a case where the son surpassed, then overwhelmed the father.

Stout contains highly roasted grains and roasted unmalted grain, which traditional Porter doesn't. Stout is much darker (in some cases black) than Porter. Some modern Porters are made with the same grains as Stout, but in lesser amounts. The two styles tend to somewhat overlap (the naming habits of different brewers tend to fog the issue). One could say that the father (Porter) got to see his son (Stout) grow into a strong healthy man, but never got to see his first-born grandson, a near spitting image of himself (modern Porters). One can almost imagine writing this in a biblical style of who begat whom, but I will avoid the temptation!

By the mid-nineteenth century, Stout had become Ireland's national beer. Stout and Ireland are as associative as Lager and Germany or Pale Ale and England. The Stout from Guinness is world famous.

There are four main Stout styles: Dry Stout, Sweet Stout, Double Stout and Imperial Stout. In the British Isles, Dry Stout's OG is 1040–1046, ABV 4%. This is a profile for Draught Guinness. In North America it is a little more. A more common brand of Guinness is its bottled Extra Stout, which has an ABV 5.4%, OG 1055.

In some tropical countries it reaches ABV 8%. Hopping rate is 55–62IBUS. It is always best on draught, though Guinness has made a lovely bottle-conditioned version which, sadly, they have decided to discontinue. CAMRA is fighting the decision, but bottle-conditioned Guinness Stout's days appear to be numbered.

Other commercial examples of a Dry Stout are Sierra Nevada Stout (USA), Sheaf Stout (Australia), Beamish Irish Stout and Murphy's Stout.

Profile: Beamish Stout

ABV 4.2%, OG 1039, BITTERNESS 38–44 IBUS

Ingredients: pale and stout malt, malted wheat, roast barley, wheat syrup,. Hallertauer, Irish Northdown and Perle hops for bittering. Styrian Goldings hops for aroma.

Nose: rich aroma of Goldings hops and roast malt.

Palate: roast barley, chocolate and hops in the mouth, a bitter finish with some fruit and hops notes, and a slight astringency (usually induced by the grains).

It is not as dry as either Guinness or Murphys. It is creamy and smooth.

Both Beamish and Murphys are now owned by international brewers, so they should become more available to the rest of the world. A bit of marketing muscle should do the trick.

Sweet Stout or English Milk Stout usually contains lactose (milk sugar, hence its name). Sweet Stout is much lower in gravity and, therefore, alcohol content than Dry Stout —OG 1044–48, ABV 3.7–3.8%. Colour is a very dark amber. Commercial examples are Mackeson Stout (UK), Louwaege Stout and Bios brewery's Wilson Mild Stout (both Belgian).

There is a sub-category of Sweet Stout called Oatmeal Stout that, as its name states, uses some oats or flaked oats in its recipe. The main commercial example of this is Samuel Smith Oatmeal Stout.

Imperial Stouts, so named because they were brewed for some of the Crown Heads of Europe, have Barleywine proportions (OG >1074). Indeed, they have Barleywine taste characteristics that do not resemble Stout's. Here, again, it is a matter of what the brewer decides to name his beers. There is a citation of an Imperial Stout with an OG 1094, and a Russian Imperial Stout with an OG 1105, and a bitterness of 140 IBUS (estimated). (Both are enormous by present-day beer standards, even by Stout standards. It is not a beer one would ordinarily find stocked on the local beer merchant's shelves!). A commercial example is Samuel Smith Imperial Stout.

We will call attention, here ,to the very high hop bittering rates used in these beers, both Porters and Stouts. High hop bittering rates are essential to make these beers drinkable. With rates similar to Pilseners or Pales Ales, Porters and Stouts would be so out-of-balance to the malt/sweet side of the field as to be sickeningly sweet. Conversely, an American Lager with the bittering rate of a Stout would be even more undrinkable, even to lovers of hoppy tasting beer.

Bière de Garde

These are French beers from the North of that country along its border zone with Flanders. Farmers in that area typically brewed beer for themselves and their workers. The term, Bière de Garde, was originally applied to strong, amber- or copper-coloured beer. They are conditioned in corked champagne-style wire-wrapped bottles, after spending a long time maturing in casks. It is filtered, but not pasteurised. Modern Bière de Gardes range in alcohol content ABV 5.5–6.5%. They are a blend of pale and dark malts in the mash.

Jenlain by the Duyck Brewery, founded by Felix Duyck, a Flemish farmer, is a classic example. It is an all-malt beer, and takes its name from the village, Jenlain: population 1,000.

Profile: Jenlain

ABV 6.3%, BITTERNESS 25IBUS

Ingredients: Flemish hops, French Beauce, Brie and Gratinais malts and spring water.

Nose: malty, fruity and peppery hop.

Palate: exuberant full malty mouthfeel followed by a bitter-sweet finish with hints of licorice. There is an superb balance between hops and malt with lovely fruity overtones the yeast imparts.

Old Ale

Contrary to its name, Old Ales are not beers that have gone stale. Rather, they are beers that are brewed to high alcoholic strengths not normally seen today, especially in North America. Unfortunately for competition and for choice, many of the several states that all, in the United States, regulate the beer industry, insist on having any beer stronger than, say, 5% labelled "Malt Liquor", a name sure to ostracise within the majority culture any quality beer labelled as such. Malt Liquor suffers from the same Blue Collar (or much worse) image in the United States as do Milds in Great Britain.

Old Ales, in Britain, have an OG range 1050–1065, putting them in the medium-strong class. A good example would be Old Peculiar, brewed by T&R Theakston Ltd, of Yorkshire.

Remember that just because the label says "Old" somewhere on it, that does not necessarily mean that its contents are an Old Ale.

The following is definitely one, from the British Oak Brewery at Dudley in the West Midlands.

Profile: Old Jones

OG 1060, ABV 5.5%

Ingredients: Target pale malt, black, crystal and wheat malts; Challenger and Fuggles bittering hops and Goldings aromatic hops.

Nose: enormously malty; ripe fruit with strong hop aromas each fighting the others for prominence.

Palate: starts heavy and winey followed by a gigantic finish of raisins/prunes, baking chocolate and hops.

Strong Mild

This is an original English style with parameters similar to Old Ale. These are malty and moderately strong. They are not highly attenuated.

The following profile is the winner in its category at the 1993 Great British Beer Festival. It is brewed in a remodelled hotel brewery, and is named for the brewer's grandmother.

Profile: Sarah Hughes Mild

ABV 5.5%, OG 1058

Ingredients: Pale and dark crystal malt. Fuggles and Goldings hops.

Nose: Lovely rich aromas of malt and ripe fruit.

Palate: Starts with strong malt and hops, and finishes intensely dry with ripe fruit and some tannins.

Note: This example has a beautiful brown colour, and a strength reminiscent of Milds brewed in the 1800s.

Barleywine

This is a sub-style of Strong Ales. It is a matter of choice as to what a brewery names beers of this profile. Beers in this category are malty, obviously strong, indicated by good alcoholic warming at the back of the mouth.

Youngs Ram Brewery , London, produces one of the finest Barleywines, named Old Nick with ABV 7.3%, OG 1084.

Old Nick has superb aromas of nuts, hops and fruit. Malt is predominant throughout, with good hops to balance all that malt, and hints of nuts.

BREWED AND BOTTLED BY YOUNG & CO'S BREWERY PLC.

THE RAM BREWERY, LONDON, ENGLAND

12 fl.oz.
355 ml.

A TRADITIONAL ENGLISH ALE BREWED BY
YOUNG'S

SERVE AT
50°-55°F.

Seasonal Beers

In many European countries and Great Britain, brewing seasonal beers is a long-lived tradition. The Belgians are lucky in that their brewers brewed special beers for all the seasons, whilst in Great Britain their speciality beer season was at Christmas and the winter. It was a tradition that nearly died, but it has been reviving itself during the past twenty years or so, coincidental with their renewed interest in Real Ales (thanks to the efforts of

CAMRA). We have noticed an up-swing in advertisements in *What's Brewing* the past few years. Both the Dutch and the Germans brew strong special lagers. The Dutch have taken a page, too, from the Belgians by introducing several seasonal ale styles. One, Grolsch Autumn Amber, is new to North America.

Bok Ales

Like their Pils Ales, the Dutch have taken to brewing Bok Ales, an other hybrid. Unlike their lager cousins, the German Bocks and Maibocks, these Bok Ales are top-fermented. They cannot be compared directly with Bocks (which are Lagers) nor to Brown Ales (regular or strong). Therefore, Tim Webb, the writer of the *Good Beer Guide to Belgium and Holland, The Best Bars and All the Breweries*, has created this new category. We agree.

Two good examples of this style are Arcen's Oerbock, ABV 6.5%, described as "Smooth, subtle, sienna-coloured, all-year-round, Bokbier", and 'T IJ's IJ Bockbier , ABV 6.5%, which is described as "Lively, fruity, dark reddish-brown Bok. Improves with age".

Christmas Ale/Winter Warmers

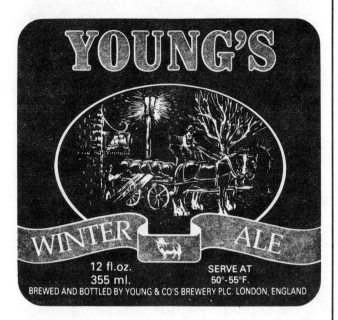

This style has exploded in popularity, even in the United States, as more and more breweries, especially the micros, have started to introduce them. They tend to be dark and strong; some are spiced as well.

The brands imported in to the USA seem to be severely rationed out to distributors. The distributors do the same with their accounts. The owners of our local buy every case of Samuel Smith Winter Warmer on which they can get their hands. They carefully ration it amongst their patrons. Being a Regular helps, especially knowing when the First Day Arrival will occur! The same treatment is accorded Sierra Nevada's Celebration Ale.

The Christmas Ales of Flanders are somewhat comparable with British Barley Wines. Others are Scotch Ale-derived.

The Dutch, it seems, have no tradition of winter beers. However, brewers, being businessmen, have not let the Belgian success with the Christmas Ales go unnoticed and, therefore, are beginning to introduce their own variations. Traditions have to start somewhere. If you don't have your own, borrow them from someone else and modify them!

The Arcen Brewery (again) has an excellent straw-coloured example of this new Dutch style called Arcener Winterbier.

A world-class example of the Belgian Christmas beer has to be the highly recommended *Stille Nacht* (Silent Night) from De Dolle Brouwers at Esen-Duiksmuide. It is described as "Delightfully subtle, sweet and deceptively powerful amber brew." ABV 8.5%.

A British example from George Bateman & Son Ltd at Skegness in Lincolnshire:

Profile: Winter Warmer

OG 1058, ABV 6.2

Ingredients: pale malt, roasted barley, wheat and Brewer's sugar; Goldings hops.

Nose: intricate blend of delicious malt and roasted grains with exquisite hops aromas.

Palate: Sets off sweet, nutty and malty, then finishes hoppy and suggestive of dry biscuits. Well-rounded and complex.

Saison

These are brewed during the spring, when it is still cool in the North or France and Walloonia in Belgium, for summertime consumption. They are remarkably refreshing, as they should be, since they are meant for warm-weather relief. They are very well attenuated and have a high hop-rate to preserve them. Alcohol range is ABV 4.5–8.0%. Colour ranges from amber- to copper- to medium brown-coloured, with a very big head that leaves good lacing down the side of the glass. Taste varies, with the body ranging from firm to completely thin. The best Saisons have a lovely balanced palate of sweet fruitiness and refreshing sourness, and a clean mellow finish. Saisons are most often naturally conditioned in corked wine bottles (0.75–1.0l).

The most popular beer of this style is Saison Regal from the Brasserie du Bocq at Purnode, Belgium. It is described as a "pleasant, light-brown ale with a huge hop punch that does not last". The most recent citation lists ABV 6.1%, which seems to have been increased from ABV 5.6% mentioned in an earlier citation. Kent Goldings, Hallertauer and Saaz hops are used. It spends a month in secondary fermentation tasks maturing.

A world-class Saison is from Brasserie Dupont at Tourpes-Leuze, Hainaut Province, Belgium. It is the golden-coloured Vielle Provision Saison Dupont. It is refreshingly dry with herbal and hoppy notes. ABV 6.5%.

Some brewers have begun to produce Saisons year-round, causing them to begin to lose their seasonal identity.

Other Seasonal Beers

Though many beers are brewed for a Season such as Christmas / new year's, Lent / Easter, autumn harvest, &c, beers in this category need not be brewed only for a particular season, but I would like to include, here, special events, also. This might encompass Anniversary Beers, Birthday Beers, Centennial events, The-President-Comes-To-Town Beer, and so on. Hell, a brewer could brew a special batch for the birth of his first son: throw it in here. Let this be a Catch-all category, with Ale and Lager sub-categories.

North American Real Ales

This style group twins the British originals. For every British style, there is a North American version. Original Gravities match, and the big differences are in the aromas and tastes the hops and yeasts impart. Being brewed in North America, many of the brewers use North American equivalents of traditional Fuggles and Kent Goldings hops, though other British hops are not readily available in North America, so domestic hops are substituted.

Micro-brewers and brew-pubs have led the way with these beers Except for an all-malt brew from Millers, none of the HCBs have entered this market. These small brewers are doing much to re-educate north Americans to the pleasures of Real Ales. Some of these brews exceed (in taste and freshness) their imported British counterparts. Sierra Nevada's Porter comes instantly to mind. It has been called the best in the world, by more than one beer writer.

Since the beers in this class closely match those from Britain much more closely than do Real North American Lagers match their European counterparts, there is no reason to break this section down further as we did for the Lagers. Refer to the generic styles listed above to check each style's parameters.

Fruit Beer

Frambozen, Kriek & Peche

The three flavoured lambics produced now are *Kriek* (cherry), *Framboise* (raspberry) and *Peche* (peach). Both the Lindemans and the Liefmans breweries (amongst others) produce these beers. There is another Framboise brewed by Brasserie Cantillon called Rosé de Gambinus. Brasserie Cantillon is the only gueuze brewery in the Brussels area. Gueuze is a blend of lambic beer and a combination of malted barley and wheat grain. The brewery does make a Kriek also, as well as a full range of beers with Gueuze as their base.

The alcohol content varies a bit: from ABV 3.9% in Lindemans Framboise to 7.8% in Liefmans Kriek, but there seems to be some discrepancies between Fred Eckhardt's figures and those from other sources.

Here, for example, is a tasting profile of Liefmans Frambozenbier.

Profile: Frambozenbier

OG 1053, ABV 5.2%

Ingredients: Pale and crystal malt and chocolate malts, torrefied barley, corn and caramel sugar. Czech Sazz and English Whitbread Goldings hops. Nineteen units of bittering. Ale yeast.

Nose: Powerful fruit and hops aroma.

Palate: Raspberry fruit in the mouth with a long-lasting sweet-sour finish.

Other Fruit Beers

This is a realm more of homebrewers or very small speciality micro-brewers, than of large breweries, for these are truly speciality beers with very little commercial demand (though demand can always be created). The Belgian brewer, Keersmaeker, does produce a lovely fruit beer called Mort Subite Cassis. Black currents are use. The aroma is massive, the palate is of bitter-sweet fruit, and the finish is lingering

Homebrewers, who are more able to experiment than are brewers, try practically every type (especially berry) fruit in their beers. Some are better than others, with citrus fruit lending themselves poorly to beer making. Blueberries, blackberries, strawberries and currents, amongst others have been used.

As beer judges, we've had plenty of opportunities to sample these beers. Some have been exceptional, such as Cherry Stouts. Properly brewed, Cherry Stouts are as pleasurable as any beer you will ever drink. Others, we almost wish we had never tried (yet one must remain open-minded). We distinctly remember (or, should we say, we will never forget?) someone in the home-brew club we belong to giving us a sample of his Lemon Lager. It never advanced up our scale of "We'll Have Another List" (a make-or-break criterion).

This category is very hard to judge because there are virtually no commercial examples against which to judge these beers. Working in a near vacuum, one is forced to be more subjective than objective: does it smell agreeable? Does the stated fruit appear at all? Is it in balance? Are there still beer-like qualities such as a head and carbonation? Or has it turned out to be more like a wine-cooler?

A commercial example from Belgium of a fruit beer is St Louis Cassis Kir Royal, Blackberry Pale Ale. ABV 5.0%.

Spiced (&c) Beers

In several countries, the United States and Belgium included, spiced beers are being re-introduced.

Essences, herbs, spices and other flavourings have long been used to flavour and/or preserve beer, especially in the times before the wide-spread use of hops for the same purposes. For simplicity's sake, we will use the term Spiced Beers to encompass all that fall into this category.

Some narrow-minded beer experts don't even consider Spiced Beers to be truly beers, or ersatz, at best. This is too harsh a judgment, especially when one considers these are styles that date back centuries. One can, perhaps, sympathise with German brewers, who are limited by their *Reinheitsgebot*, to using only barley malt, hops yeast and water in their brews.

The beer categories best suited for spicing are higher-gravity Brown Ales and Pale Ales, and sweet-tasting ales, all of which tend to be fairly complex in the first place.

The list of spices going in to beers in this category are almost innumerable. A short list:

all-spice, chocolate/cocoa, cinnamon, cloves, coffee, coriander, cumin, curaco, ginger, jalapeño pepper, licorice, molasses, nutmeg, peppermint, spruce and tea.

Here again, homebrewers are at advantage over commercial brewers. It is much less expensive to chuck out a five-gallon batch gone wrong than a 20-barrel test batch at a brewery.

Commercial examples are few and far between except, of course, in Belgium. Many spiced beers are brewed for Christmas/new year's, and should probably be better off classified in the Seasonal Beers category.

The Brouwerij Huyghe at Melle, Belgium is making a reputation for itself by selling several beers in this category. Two of their better ones are La Guillotine (ABV 9.0%) and Delirium Tremens (ABV 9.0%). On the flip side, their Minty, bright green and peppermint flavoured, has been described by one writer as "possibly the worst beer in the world".

The example we'll profile is from De Kluis Brouwerij van Hoegaarden at the brewing town of Hoegaarden. The brewery is part of the Interbrew group (Stella Artois). Though it is part of an HCB, Hoegaaden beers are generally excellent.

Profile: De Ferboden Frucht

ABV 9.0%,

Ingredients: malt, Challenger and Styrian hops, coriander

Nose: herbal hoppy and spicy

Palate: sets out mellow and fruity, then finishes dry with subtle hop, orange and vanilla accents.

Wheat beers

Wheat has been used in brewing for centuries. It is not as versatile and more limiting than barley, but has useful purposes, the most useful being that it aids in head retention and head size. The Germans and the Belgians have done the most to promote Wheat Beer as a style unto itself, with concentrations running upwards to 75%. American brewers, also, are introducing more wheat beers.

The four major categories are North German Wheats, Bayerisch Wheats, Belgian Wits, and New American Wheats.

Besides the fact that they share several styles within their group, they can also be divided by whether or not they are filtered, or have the yeast still in bottle. We will not distinguish, as sub-categories, between those that have yeast and those that do not. I will leave it that, in Germany, it is again fashionable to drink one's Wheat beer with the yeast (*mit hefe*). It is considered "Green" and health-minded to do so. It certainly keeps the digestive system flowing.

Berliner Weisse

Called the *Champagne du Nord* by French soldiers during the Napoleonic Wars, Berliner Weisse is an extremely dry, sharp, tart and refreshing beer. It is an ideal hot-summer-days beer. The tartness comes from a healthy dose of lactobacillus combined with its yeast and a high (67–75%) wheat content, not from hops. In fact, the hopping rate of these beers is very low—4–15 IBUS. Too, they have a very low alcohol content—ABV 2.5–3.7%, which has been scaled down from the 4.4% they were at the end of the last century. The colour is very pale, and they are clear, if you are careful not to pour out the yeast sediment with the beer.

To be a "Berliner" Weisse, the beer must be brewed in the city of Berlin. It has been noted as a style as far back as 1572, but it rose to popularity at the end of the 1800s when Berlin was an Imperial city. The style has also been called Champagne of the Spree (the Spree, a river that flows through Berlin). The term Champagne should really be reserved for wheat beers, especially Berliner Weisse, but has been misappropriated by light-coloured lager brewers. C'est la vie.

They are most often and best served in wide-mouthed glasses because they are very frothy. A shot or dash of sweetened fruit (raspberry being the favourite) or woodruff syrup is traditionally added. Or the inside of the glass may be first coated with syrup and then the beer poured into it.

The two great Berlin breweries that make Weissebier are Kindl and Schultheiss.

Profile: Kindl Weisse

ABV 3.1%, OG 1030, BITTERNESS 4IBUS

Ingredients: Wheat malt (75%) and pale malt, lactobacillus

Nose: has an evenness of aromatic fruit and sourness about it.

Palate: instantly sharp and dry; finishes with acidic and sour. The shot of fruit syrup help those not too keen on this type of palate.

North German Weisse

This is a category for Weissebier not brewed in Berlin. Not much of a difference her, except that the alcohol content goes as high as ABV 5.0%. Wheat content is 35–75%. These are not necessarily as sour and tart as are their Berliner cousins.

Graetzerbier

These beers, too, have low alcohol content, OG 1030–34, but are much more highly hopped, 50IBUS, than Berliner Weisse. Graetzerbier is made up of two-thirds highly-roasted wheat malt and one-third pale barley malt.

Weizen

This is a South German/Bavarian style that differs considerably from North German and Belgian styles. South Germany encompasses Bayern and Baden-Württemberg. The heads are big and creamy in both styles. Carbonation is very high, and therefore a slow steady pour is necessary. Weizenbier usually use different, distinctive yeast strains that impart a blend of apples and citrus fruit in the aroma and a clove-like taste. Wheat content ranges from 40–70% and barley malt, similar to North German Weissebier, but they also include, in some brands, dark and roasted wheat and barley malts. The hop-rate is low, intruding only slightly into the profile. The majority are pale to very pale coloured. This last item does not apply to Dunkelweizen and Weizenbock beers. Alcohol content ranges ABV 4.5–5.7%. Bitterness is usually 13–19IBUS.

The first profile is from the Brauerei Ayinger at Aying, Bayern.

Profile: Bräu Weisse

ABV 5.1%, OG 1049, BITTERNESS 15IBUS

Ingredients: pale and wheat malt, Hallertauer, Hersbrücker and Spalt hops

Nose: Lovely aroma of apples, cloves and esters

Palate: Extremely refreshing and invigorating. It has a sparkling wine effervescence. Tart. Finishes with fruit tastes that linger.

Dunkelweizenbier

These are darker coloured variations of normal Weizenbier. All the other parameters are very close or unchanged.

Steinweizen

Here is a rare and unusual style: a German wheat beer brewed by use of super-heated stones. See Steinbier for further description of the process used by the Rauchenfels Brauerei.

The one example we have has a low abv 3.5%. Aromas and palate characteristics are burnt and smoky grain. The finish is big, as would be expected and spicy, with phenolic notes.

Weizenbock

Bockbier, a lager, is, in Germany, defined as having an OG of at least 1066, ABV 6.6%. The ABV range is 6.25 to 6.9%. Weizenbockbier is brewed to the Bockbier requirements, but r mains an ale. They are considerably darker than the normally light-coloured weizenbier. The amount of wheat ranges from 40–60%.

The following example is from Privatbrauerei Erdinger Weissbräu, Werner Brombach GmbH at Erding, Bayern.

Profile: Pinkantus Weizenbock

ABV 7.3%, OG 1071

Ingredients: pale and wheat malt, Hallertauer hops

Nose: excellent balance between malt and ripe fruit aromas

Palate: starts off with wheat grain and tart fruit, then finishes bitter-sweet; hint of fruit, too. Alcoholic warming present and expected of a beer of this gravity.

Weizen-Doppelbock

As Doppelbockbier is to Bockbier, so Weizen-Doppelbock is to Weizenbock. The alcohol range is ABV 7.2–7.5%. Weizen-Doppelbock may be light- or dark-coloured (though most are light), with a pronounced barley-malt and wheat-malt aroma and mild hops bittering. Both styles may come clear or they may have yeast in the bottle.

Witbier

This style was well-defined well over 100 years ago but, like Porter, it all but disappeared. The last of 30 original brewers closed in 1954. It was re-introduced in 1966 by Pierre Celis, who bought the De Kluis Brouwerij in Hoegaarden. Then, in 1978, with two Dutch partners, he bought an old factory that used to produce lemonade. He converted it into a brewery. There was an unfortunate brewery fire in 1985 that would have cost around $10m to rebuild. Their insurance wasn't sufficient. Interbrew, the largest Belgian brewery, backed him in his rebuilding efforts. Eventually M Celis sold the brewery to Interbrew, but they retained his services with a contract that eventually expired in 1990. Interbrew now controls 73% of that country's beer market. Hoegaarden Witbier has declined from the world-class beer it was before the takeover, but it still is excellent. There are 14 other Belgian brewers now producing Witbier—quite a turnabout in 37 years.

For those curious about the fate of M Celis, not to worry. He moved to the United States, and opened the Celis Brewery on a seven-acre site in Austin, Texas. He now produces a Grand Cru, White, Pale Bock and a Golden, all bearing his name. Are you wondering why he chose Austin? The water at Hoegaarden is remarkably limey. It is an important ingredient in the styles of beers he brewed there. Austin, as you might now have guessed, has similar water.

Life has a strange way of casting ironies about. M Celis is now back in Belgium, with Christine, his daughter, who is president of his firm, selling his White Beer, under contract to his native countrymen. It was she who encouraged him to do this. The 40% duty levied by the EU on American beer prohibits him exporting his White Beer from Texas.

Witbier was originally meant to be bottled or casked within four or five days after completion of primary fermentation, and consumed within two weeks. If not, it went quickly acidic and sour. During cool weather months, it could last, perhaps, four or five weeks.

Witbier is pronounced wheat beer, but means White Beer. In French the name is *Bière blanche*. The name derives from its clearly evident milky haze. This is because the particles in suspension are too light-weight to settle out, as happens in most other beers. The haze is from reflected light off the particles.

Witbier's main characteristics are that they are white (no, not like milk) cloudy, and highly carbonated, which produces a dense enormous head. When on, they are a refreshing drink.

As with most Belgian brews, hops play a minor role. Brewers use hops aged one to three years, aiming for their preservative properties, not their bittering or aromatic ones.

The beer we profile below, Hoegaarden Wit or Witte van Hoegaarden has led the resurgence of this style. Because spices are used in this beer, it could be classified a Spice Ale, but we will leave it here because the Witbier category normally is kept in the Wheat Beer group.

Profile: Hoegaarden Wit

ABV 5.0, BITTERNESS 16.5IBUS

Ingredients: unmalted wheat (45%), unmalted oats (5%), barley malt (50%), coriander, curacao and hops.

Nose: very spicy

Palate: malt with spices, orange and coriander scents. Finishes light and dry. Refreshing. The palate turns honeyish with age.

North American Witbier

We have taken the liberty of starting a new style. The honour of this style should go to M Celis because in a very short time he has done much to introduce this delicious style to North America. Though it is brewed in Texas, it is brewed by a Belgian. We thought much about including his White Beer in the Wit Style, but the use of American Cascade and Willamette hops (the later a Fuggle variety) begs for a new style to be named.

In time more North American micro-breweries and regional breweries will begin brewing beers to this style, when they see the increasing popularity of Wits, and the continuously improving tastes of North American beer drinkers. The more people turn to quality beer, the more of them brewers will bring to market.

Profile: Celis White

ABV 4.9%, OG 1048, BITTERNESS 12–15IBUS

Ingredients: unmalted wheat (50%), barley malt (50%), coriander, curacao, and Cascade, Saaz and Willamette hops.

Nose: fruity aroma

Palate: refreshing fruity flavour, spicy and tart, balanced with a natural sweetness.

North American wheat

This is a newly developing style that is diverging from the taste profiles of German Weizenbier. The divergence is due, in the main because different wheat strains are grown in America that in Europe. Additionally, North

American brewers feel no constraints to match European wheat beers. Instead, they are experimenting and developing their own styles. At present, the style is in its infancy so there are no set parameters, but we can give you some sample characteristics. Original gravities seem to be staying in the 1040–50 range; alcohol content ABV 4.0–5.0; bitterness 15–20IBUs; colours range from gold to dark.

Some commercial examples are August Schell Weiss, Pyramid Wheaten, Pyramid Dark Wheaten Ale and Widmer Weizen.

Profile: Sam Adams Wheat

OG 1042, ABV 4.4%

Ingredients: Malted wheat, Klages/Harrington malt, Saaz, Hallertauer and Tettnanger hops

Nose: Clove aroma and spicy

Palate: Clean tasting and refreshing

Wild Beers/Lambic

These beers are the only ones of their kind in the world. They are composed of 40% unmalted wheat and 60% malted barley (this is a general parameter). They are fermented by spontaneous fermentation to air-borne yeasts and bacteria. The base Lambic is a component part of many Fruit Beers and has several versions. They could be included in the Wheat Beer category, but because of their unique fermentation method, they deserve and are acknowledged a category all their own. A pure Lambic has very low carbonation; *Vieux* (Old) *Lambic* from Brasserie Cantillon, cited as a perfect example of the style, has no carbonation. Nearly all the brewed Lambic is used to make *Gueuze* and Fruit Lambics. Some is sold as *Lambic Doux* (Sweet), *Lambic Vieux* or *Faro*. If a *Lambic* less than six months old, it is often labelled as *Jong* (Young) or *Vos* (Fox) *Lambic*.

Lambic wort is usually boiled a minimum of three hours. Sometimes it is boiled and then simmered overnight, quite in contrast with normal one to two hour boils given other beer worts. Aged hops two to three years old are exclusively used. The idea is to avoid hop aromas, but to extract their presevative or antiseptic components.

Lambics are brewed in and around (out to about 20km) Brussels. The area where the proper air-borne yeasts and bacteria exist is limited to this region. There is no complicated explanation. It is simply a quirk of nature. That is not to say that somewhere else in the world similar conditions do not exist. It's simply that no other brewers have experimented: failure is expensive, and the taste of these beers are so very different from ales and lagers that enticing drinkers to accept Lambic beers would be long-term and difficult.

Note that many Lambics are aged two years or so. Vieux Lambic is aged for three years in cask and an other in bottle. It is pink-tinted Sherry-coloured and has nearly no carbon dioxide.

Faro (also called Faro-Lambic)

These are young Lambics made from blending moderate-strength worts, or high-strength and low-strength worts and sweetened with candi sugar. They are sometimes coloured with caramel, and sometimes diluted with water. Usually they are less than one year old.

Brouwerij Lindemans at Sint-Pieters-Leeuw (Vlezenbeek) brews a Faro-Lambic that we will directly cite a description from the *Lambic* book by Jean-Xavier Guinard.

Profile: Lindemans Faro

"Faro-Lambic: (filtered) amber, sherry-like colour; high carbonation and low, unstable foam; mild lambic aromas (acetic acid and

Brettanomyces (a yeast strain) character that comes through as wet wool or warm bread) combined with woody, caramel, vanilla, raisin, prune, yeasty, cooked vegetables and olive aromas; slightly oxidized; quite sour (dissipates quickly, though) and sweet."

Yiiiiooowwww! Virtually any of the cited the aromas would, by itself, damn a Pilsener, and most would do in an Ale! Yet here are the Belgians banging Faro-Lambics down the hatch! They are an acquired taste.

The description above bears close resemblance to many homebrewed Ales I've judged at competitions as being "undrinkable due to contamination and poor handling". Too, we've talked with homebrewers who tried to brew Continental Darks or Brown Ales, found they'd "gone wrong", entered them as Belgian Lambics in competition—and won!

Gueuze

Gueuze is a blend of lambic beer of different ages which are bottle fermented. The best Gueuzes are an equal blend of one-, two- and three-year-old Lambics. They are coarsely filtered after blending and then bottled. In addition, they newly bottled Gueuze should be laid down for nine months spanning one summer (meaning a cool and a warm period). The temperature changes are necessary because the several yeasts and bacteria do their best work at different temperatures. Too high a temperature can damage traditional bottle-conditioned Gueuze because they are still alive. They have to be carefully handled and stored. Owing to hot weather in 1931, over 3m bottles of Gueuze were destroyed in Brussels.

Some brewers make their Gueuze in bulk, subject it to cold-filtration, flash-pasteurization and artificial carbonation before bottling.

Brewers of this style beers often use Gueuze, rather than Faro, as a base for other styles, especially Fruit Beers.

The name derives from the *Guezenstraet* or *rue des Gueux* in Brussels. In French, *Gueux* means Beggar.

Alcohol strength ranges ABV 5.0–5.5%.

The following profile is from the Brasserie Cantillon at Brussels. It is the last Brussels-based Gueuze brewery. It is also the home of the Gueuze Museum.

Profile: Rosé de Gambinus

ABV 5.0%

Ingredients: pale malt (65%), unmalted wheat (35%), three-year-old Kent Fuggles and Belgian Star hops

Nose: light aromas of cider and other fruit

Palate: Dry and refreshing; finishes with lovely fruit tastes

Mars

Mars means *March* in French. March signified the month in the brewing season when Mars brewing stopped. It was produced from the second mashings of the grains during the brewing process. The first (and stronger) wort was used to make Gueuze and the second, weaker runnings were used to make Faro and Mars.

Mars had an ABV of about 3.0%. We refer to Mars in the past tense because it is no longer made, modern brewing practices making it obsolete. Indeed, it is hard to find any lengthy printed references to it in modern brewing books. We've included it here since this book is, after all, a history of beer.

Other Beers

Tafelbier-Bière de Table

This is a style that is in danger of being replaced by NABLAB s (No Alcohol Beers-Low Alcohol Beers), which are heavily promoted and profitable for their brewers. Tafelbier is Flemish for Table Beer. In French it is called Bière de Table. Tafelbier is a sweet, low-alcohol beer. They are made with the second or last spargings of grains during in the mash tank. The result is a low-gravity wort, which in turn produces a low-alcohol beer: ≤ ABV 3.0%. In Belgium, they are classified as Category III beers with OGs of 1004–1016, and account for about 3.5% of total beer production.

Tafelbier is that with which Belgians and the French break their children in on to get them used to drinking beer. The French do the same with diluted wines.

This style is similar to the English Mild, but tends to be even less alcoholic. It is also in decline like Mild Beer.

Grand Cru and Cuvée

This is a slightly difficult style to pin down because it has been suggested that it is a marketing ploy, in similar manner as American Super Premium Lagers, such as Michelob, but this would be to slander these superior Belgian beers. Grand Cru, meaning Special Vintage are really the brewer's favourite or best beer. These were most often used for special occasions, such as weddings, victory celebrations, grand openings with the town mayor in attendance, &c. They were used much the way champagne is used in other countries.: as a special something not meant to be had everyday. Grand Crus were brewed in smaller quantities, or shorter brew lengths than regular brands.

Tim Webb, writing in the Good Beer Guide to Belgium and Holland says this about Grand Cru/Cuvée:

"The terms "cevée" and "grand cru" are frequently applied to a wide variety of beers in Belgium and the Netherlands. However, the terms are worse than useless to the consumer. They say nothing about the beer in the bottle except to imply that it will be expensive.

"Cuvée" is commonly used in the names of label beers, regular brewery ales, which are masquerading under a false name for a particular distributor. One Dutch bar owner told the Guide that "grand cru" means "big crutch" and is used either to suggest machismo or else because the beer is so puny that it needs extra support!

"The Guide uses neither term in classifying a beer's style."

A fairly strong indictment.

One can also look at these as either pumped up Old Ales or as Strong Ales. The brand from Rodenbach is a stronger Old Red Ale. Alcohol content is ≥ ABV 6.5%. Hoegaarden Gran Cru is listed as 7.5% ABV. Stropken Grand Cru has 6.75% ABV. A third, Zottegemse Grand Cru from the Crombé Brouwerij at Zottegem has 8.4% ABV. The last has been described as "surprisingly full, copper-coloured, bittersweet ale, with a saccharin backtaste."

It would be very easy to simply toss these into the Strong Ale category, but there is a problem: the labelling. We prefer to retain this category, but point out that these beers are, indeed, Strong Ales. Too, since many of these are aged for prolonged periods, it wouldn't do them justice to simply toss them into the general Strong Ale category, where, perhaps, they might get lost or marginalized.

Unlike Celis Wit, for which we made a new sub-style of the ever-increasingly popular wheat style, Celis Grand Cru stays put. Yes, even though it is brewed in America, the style remains uniquely Belgian. Should more North American brewers decide to brew Grand Crus (or variants), that will be the time to create an additional sub-style for them.

Profile: Celis Grand Cru

ABV 8.2%, OG 1078 BITTERNESS 20–25IBUS

Ingredients: Barley malt (80%), speciality malts (20%), Saaz and Cascade hops, dried orange peel and other spices.

Nose: rich ,warm and complex aromas.

Palate: subtle, creamy taste from a mixture of malts, slightly tart, with a very warming finish from the high alcohol level.

Dampfbier

This is an other speciality beer, like Steinbier, from German. It is likewise, undergoing a revival of sorts, though we don't reckon it will ever become hugely popular.

The style is very fruity, and the brand from Maisel Bräu has vanilla undertones. It is made using four malts, and hopped with Hallertauer. Alcohol content is about ABV 5.0%. Dampfbier is paler and with more a reddish cast than, say, an Altbier from Düßeldorf.

Like Anchor Brewery's Steam Beer, Maisel's Dampfbier name is registered and not meant to indicate a style, though it is in its own right. Unlike Anchor Steam Beer, Dampfbier is made with different production techniques and, too, has a different palate.

Steinbier

This style is very old in the making. One can just imagine some of the earliest German brewers super-heating stones (nowadays at 1,200°C) and placing them in the wort to bring it to the boil. The reason for using heated stones in this manner was because the style dates to before the advent of iron vessels. The ones made of wood could not be directly heated with fire, and this was the solution of these early brewers.

To continue, but in the present tense, the stones are then removed from the wort. Both are cooled and fermentation begins. The stones are then replaced in the wort and the yeast attacks the crystalized sugars that concentrated on the stones within seconds. A violent secondary fermentation quickly begins. It gradually subsides during the ensuing three weeks. What results is a light mouthwatering beer with definite smoked tones. It is smooth and somewhat dry.

The style nearly went extinct, but this very rare beer is undergoing a bit of a revival beginning in the 1980s. Sailer-Bräu, in the Schwabian town of Marktoberdorf near Coburg, brews a Steinbier simply named Rauchenfels Steinbier.

In Germany, this and Rauchbier are described variously as "new speciality beers" or "new Old Beers". Too, more marketing effort and money are being put into them.

Lager: Bottom-fermenting Beer

In every country except Great Britain, Lager is king. It is Number One, El Supremo, der Führer, the King. In a very short time, it displaced Ale as the most-brewed beer in the world.

Lager is different from Ale in several ways. First, a different yeast, a bottom- instead of top-fermenting type, is employed. Second, it is fermented at a lower temperature than Ale. Third, it is aged (or Lagered, hence its name) much longer, at a much colder temperature than is Ale. We are comparing here average Lagers and Ales such as a Pilsener and a Bitter. There are exceptions to every rule: Belgian Trappist Ales are aged for up to three years. Forth, because Lager beer should be kept cold right until it is served to the drinker, it has a longer "shelf-life" than does Ale. Cold temperatures help retard spoilage. Fourth, comparing the most commonly drunk Lagers to Ales, there is a colour difference. The average Pilsener is gold-coloured whilst Bitter or Mild is pale- to copper- to medium-brown-coloured. One advantage (or disadvantage) is the misperception about beer colour amongst people. It is commonly held that the darker the beer the stronger it is. This is not true. For example the Belgian Tripple is straw-coloured and has an average ABV 9.5%. The brown-coloured English Bitter has an average alcohol content of, say, ABV 4.2%. Taken farther, the average English Bitter has the same alcohol content range as American Light Lagers such as Miller Lite (ABV 4.2%) or Coors Light (ABV 4.4). For these wondering about calories, their main source is alcohol, so there is really no reason to drink bland light beers to save weight when for about the same calorie count one could drink delicious Ale.

There are two main groups of Lagers. The first is the traditional German Lagers, which are subject to the *Reinheitsgebot,* the Beer Purity Laws. These require German beer to be made from only malted barley, hops yeast and water (malted wheat is permitted). Unmalted raw, and roasted grains are not permitted, as are all other adjuncts. Thus, German beer is the "purest". The second group are the Lagers made elsewhere but Germany. Most all other countries have lax or no brewing laws to speak of. Practically anything goes: the use of corn, rice, brewing sugars, and other cost-cutting adjuncts; preservatives other than hops (in East Germany, before unification, it has been reported, brewers were forced by authorities to use cow bile, as a cheaper substitute for hops!); chemical treatments to get essentially dead beer to appear as if it were a German Lager; &c.

National brewers in the United States are in the second category. Because they use non-traditional brewing practices, they oppose all efforts to force them to divulge ingredients on container labels (there entire container probably hasn't enough room on it to list all the chemicals added).

Their efforts have been so successful that government regulations and law ban traditional-minded brewers from listing the healthful properties of the beer they brew. These brewing interests have no desire to divulge what they put in their beer, else they would be exposed as marketers of inferior product. The health-conscious would definitely have second thoughts about drinking their fizz-water.

We will omit all specific tasting profiles of North American beers that fall in to the styles: North American Standard and Premium, NAB-LABS, North American Malt Liquors and Japanese-style Dry Beer, as we do not endorse them. We will give category description only.

California Common Beer

This is the one true American-developed beer style. It was first brewed during the era of the Gold Rush (late 1800s) in the San Francisco bay area. The style spread all across the West Coast, to Alaska, Idaho, and as far east as Wisconsin state.

Like Pils Ale and Bok Ale, California Common Beer is a hybrid beer. The difference is that is brewed with Lager yeast, but at a warm (60–70°F). The two European styles use Ale yeast. Since we are using yeast-type as the determining factor of classification, California Common Beer is placed with Lagers.

Wide, shallow fermenting vessels are used, similar to some British and European fermenters, but quite in contrast with today's vertical cylindrical vessels.

We use the term California Common Beer instead of Steam Beer because that name is copyrighted by Anchor Steam Beer Brewery of San Francisco, California. Not only is the style unique to the United States, the Anchor Steam brand is its only commercially widespread example. It is interesting to note that the style is encouraged by the American Homebrewers Association.

The term Steam probably was used because it was the breweries source of power—a high-tech plant of its age.

The colour range of original California Common Beer was all over the place—light to dark. Now it seems to have settled on amber. They are medium in alcoholic strength, ABV 4.4–5.6%. In addition, they are hoppy beers, 30–45IBUS, both in aroma and in taste.

North American Lager

This is the big battleground ferociously fought on all fronts by Anheuser-Busch, Coors, Millers, Strohs, &c. It is these brewers, and others, who wiped out ale-brewing in North American starting in the mid-1800s. By the end of the first decade of the 20th century, ale brewers had all but been driven from the field. Prohibition finished them off, and almost all others.

We are going to take the liberty of breaking all these styles in two. The categories starting "North American" Whatever will contain all the mass-produced, chemical- and adjunct-laden fizz-water brands, no matter who brews them.

We propose, and list here, new categories we call "Real North American" Whatever. These categories will contain all lager brewed by micro-breweries and brew-pubs that do not adulterate their products. Should any HCB brew beers to this criterion they would be included here. It is not the source of the beer that counts, but, rather, its ingredients. As an example, Miller Brewing Company has introduced, in bottle form, an all-malt lager called Miller Reserve. This would be classified in our new category, and not as a North American Lager. At the moment, this beer is probably the best HCB-produced Lager in North America. It goes to show that these brewers have the ability and capability to brew excellent beers if they choose to. They, in the main, do not.

North American Light (low calorie beer)

Water is Zero on the colour scale. These are as close to zero as the brewers can make them.

Almost tasteless.

ABV 2.3–4.4, OG 1023–1040, BITTERNESS 7–19IBUS, COLOUR 0.5–2.0.

There are two ways these (we hesitate to use the word) beers are made. First, enzymes can be add to convert unfermentable dextrins to fermentable sugars. The second is to use plenty of water to dilute the wort even more.

North American NABLABS

No alcohol/low alcohol beers differ from their Light brothers. The former strives to remove as much unfermentable sugars as possible to reduce calories, not necessarily alcohol. The latter remove most of the alcohol. By the way, there is no such thing as a completely alcohol-free beer. These usually have < ABV 0.5%.

Some of the NABLABS might even be considered tasty because they retain some residual sweetness and hop charter.

Low alcohol beers have < ABV 1.6%.

Economy Beer

This category is for inexpensive brands, which are most-often sold in supermarkets, &c. These are often watered down versions of a company's regular brand. These, like their sires, are bland and characterless. Alcohol content ABV 3.2% or less, giving them some advantage in states that encourage this strength beer in the market.

There is great need in North America for a tasty economy beer in line with English Mild and Belgian Bière de table. In Germany, lagers of this alcoholic strength are not brewed.

Standard & Premium American

Lager

This is a catch-all category. Included are what HCBs call their Premium and Super Premium beers. These are marketing or advertising terms that bare no relation to reality. "Premium" beers are nothing but their standard beer. Super Premiums are (just barely) tarted up versions of their standard beers.

We have reviewed the style specifications for both Standard and for Premium Lager and, frankly, the differences are so slight as to make the claim of distinction a joke or a fraud.

Here are the differences. "You make the call."

The biggest dissimilarity (the others are so minimal as to be acceptable within one single category) is that Premium Lagers use fewer adjuncts than Standard Lagers, 30% versus up to 65%; rice adjunct instead of corn; a little bit of two-row barely malt instead of six-row. Rarely will the brewer use more hops (16 versus 14IBUs). The types of hops used are the same: Cluster, Cascades, Willamettes and, on occasion, Hallertauer (domestic or imported) and Saaz for aroma. Alcohol content is boosted (ABV 4.7% to 4.8%; OG 1044 to 1048 (Big deal!)).

To make specific the above comparison, we will give you a basic profile of Budweiser and Michelob. Budweiser: alcohol content ABV 4.7; OG 1044; bittering 10.5IBUs; colour 2.0. Now, Michelob: alcohol content ABV 4.8; OG 1048; bitterness 14IBUs; colour 2.0. Ahem...Knowing this, do you think paying a premium price for Michelob is worth it?

Japanese-style Dry Lager

This is a new style introduced by Asahi Brewing Company in 1987. Asahi was quickly followed by Kirin, Sapporo and Suntory. The Japanese quickly brought the product to North America, where it was almost immediately imitated by the HCBs there.

The term Dry is really a misnomer. It is a nice short word, ideal for Madison Avenue promotion. Dry, in this sense, means "not sweet", not "not wet". It was actually ported over from wine descriptions.

Leave it to the Japanese to genetically engineer a strain of yeast with a special enzyme that converts normally unfermentable dextrins into fermentable sugars, thus reducing the sweetness of the beer.

The alcohol content of these are similar to Regular and Premium Lagers: ABV 4.4–5.0%; OG 1040–44. Because the style is so highly-attenuated, alcohol content is a bit higher than the OGs would indicate. The colour (2.0–2.5) is about the same as other beer styles in this category. Bitterness is about 18IBUs. Bitterness is a little more apparent because the style is so lacking in malt sweetness to counter-balance it.

North American Malt Liquors

Here is another hybrid, a Lager fermented at ale temperatures, then lagered at 32–33°F for one to five weeks. This style has absolutely nothing to recommend itself, except as a vehicle to get stoned quickly and cheaply. It is best drunk (we don't recommend it) ice-cold (32–35°F) because as soon as it warms, it is bland, characterless, vinous swill. Besides, drinking any beverage at those temperatures is not a healthy thing to do. It is not good for the stomach.

ABV 5.6–8.1%; OG 1058–80, or more. The increase in alcohol content is often the result of adding dextrose (corn sugar or syrup) Bitterness is 5–14IBUs. The low number here is the absolute minimum allowable under law for it to be called a malt-beverage. Colour 1.0–4.0.

North American Bock & Double Bock

Like many North American beers, Bocks in this category seldom measure up to their European counterparts. Of course, there are exceptions.

In Germany the dividing line between regular Lagers and Bocks is alcohol content. Beer must be at least ABV 6.4%, OG 1064 to be classified as Bockbier in Germany. In North America, Bock beers have ABV 4.5–5.0%, and are often ordinary Lagers with caramel syrup added to darken them. Another piece of fiction.

North American Bock beers were first developed around the mid-1800s. Then, they were a seasonal beer, brewed and lagered through the winter, and released in the spring. Like many things relating to beer, Prohibition killed Bock beer in the USA. It enjoyed a brief spurt when Prohibition was repealed (December 1933), but not long afterwards production stopped due to declining sales. The "style" was revived in the 1970s by a few brewers, but has languished until recently. Rolling Rock introduced an ABV 5% Bock in September 1993 to great fanfare, but to derision from those who dislike pseudo-Bocks.

North American Dark Lager

These not-so-dark Lagers are virtually the same as the "Light" counterparts except for the colour. Some are simply darkened by with caramel syrup. Some might be darkened with a pinch of Münchener or black malt. The colour is not nearly as dark as German Dunkles. North Americans have been so propagandized by the HCBs that the majority now think that any beer not as light as champagne is "dark".

The taste in these beers is minimal, as is any hop character, aroma and bouquet.

Short and sweet: OG 1040–48, ABV 4.0–5.0%, BITTERNESS 9–15IBUS.

This style has nothing to recommend.

Now we come to some good stuff. Parameters of the fairly new beers, original gravities, alcohol content, hopping rates and type of hops employed are still being established by brewers.

Since the Samuel Adams brands have reached national distribution, we have decided to use some of their brands as benchmarks. This is not to say they are better than other micro-brewed brands—there are many tremendous beers out there brewed by other micros. The problem we face is trying to select beers to which North American drinkers have access. We, obviously, had to ignore this problem when selecting foreign beers, especially the Real Ales from England, and some of the Belgian and most of Dutch brands (they aren't imported).

You can expect variations in alcohol content, hopping rates and malts used by other North American micro-brewers from the figures cited here, but you will get an idea of these new styles. Too, compare these with their European cousins. These are often amber-coloured instead of pale as the European originals are.

Profile: Samuel Adams Boston Lager

ABV 4.8%; OG 1052; BITTERNESS 35 IBUS

Ingredients: Klages/Harrington and caramel 60° malts, Hallertauer and Tettnanger hops.

Nose: Floral hoppy aroma

Palate: somewhat sweet tasting; finishes with a complex dry mouthfeel

Note: Attenuation is somewhat low

Real North American Lager

This is a growing category, one that micro-brewers and pub-brewers have keenly taken to. Thank god. The first Lager from these brewers will, most often, be in this style. This is out of necessity. To get their Lager into pubs and restaurants they must offer a beer that is similar, at least in appearance, to that of the HCBs' Lagers. When drinkers are able to compare a Real Lager to the yellow fizzy water, Real Lager wins outright. This accounts for much of the growth micro-brewers and contract brewers have been experiencing. The success of Samuel Adams's Boston Lager is a fine example of this. If any HCB feels pressure from below, it is from these beers. One can hope this pressure will result in the HCBs to either scrap the use of adjuncts in their beers or to introduce all-malt brands. We would love to see the former. Heineken has recently done this, so there is no reason why North American HCBs cannot follow suit.

Alcohol content is >4.5% and frequently push up towards the lower limits of a German Bock. There does not seem to be any skimping on the malt here. Colour ranges from light to golden amber, and bitterness is comparable with quality Euro-Lagers, ie, 25–40 IBUs.

Profile: Hudson Lager

This is a beer from one of the new breed of micro-brewers. Whilst not yet widely available, Nat Collins, the owner, has produced several other interesting beers, such as Ichabod Crane Pumpkin Ale with an 8.3% ABV.

Several other styles are in the works, including an Ale, a Porter and a Stout.

ABV 5.3%, OG 1052, BITTERNESS 20IBUS

Ingredients: Munich (2-row), Hallertauer hops for bittering, Tettnanger for aroma.

Nose: Malt and floral hops

Palate: A refreshing balance of hops and malt. Smooth maltyness with a long, pleasant-finish of mild hops.

Continental Lagers

Of all the brewers in Europe, only the German ones are constrained by their beer purity laws. The disadvantage is that they cannot make cheaper beer by using cheaper ingredients. On the other hand, what better way to promote the fact that one's beers are pure and unadulterated. There are other brewers in Europe, other than the Germans, who adhere to the *Reinheitsgebot*. It is a strong selling point. Besides, their customers like the fact that "their" brewer is producing wholesome, all-natural beer.

Brewers in other countries never had such constraints and developed their own traditions and styles, but most shunned the use of chemical adjuncts especially in their cask-conditioned beers.

These beers arose from the development, in the mid-1800s, of bottom-fermenting, cold temperature working yeast strains. These yeasts developed from the long-time brewing practise, in certain regions of Europe such as the mountainous regions of Bayern, of storing beer in cold caves or caverns. By reuse of the yeast cultures from one batch to the next (after the discovery of yeast's function in fermentation), over time the yeast adapted to the cold environment.

Within about 60 years, Lager completely displaced Ale, except in Great Britain (as previously mentioned). It was in Europe that it got its start, at different sites, which developed their own singular styles. From Europe, lager-brewing was brought to North America by German immigrants.

Now we will examine the styles from which American lager styles except California Common Beer are derived.

Profile: Grolsch Premium Lager

ABV 5.0%, OG 1047, BITTERNESS 27IBUS

Ingredients: Pilsener malt from spring barley, small fraction of maize, Hallertauer and Sazz hops.

Nose: Floral hops, as can be expected from the use of noble Hallertauer, delicate and lovely.

Palate: Hoppy, some expected citric fruit notes, easy bitter-sweet finish. A very refreshing balance of malt and hops.

Note: Conditioned for 10 weeks. Unpasteurized in bottle. This is a beer that deserves every bit of the success it has attained. Some critics pooh pooh this beer, but they should know better.

Oud Bruin (The Netherlands)

Not to be confused with the Belgian Ale with the same name, this Lager is from the Netherlands. It is a low-alcohol beer with an ABV 2.0–3.5. At its upper end, the alcohol content is comparable with English Milds. It is a very sweet beer, and is classified in the Netherlands as a Tafelbier (Table beer). This is not a style one would make a special trip to the Netherlands to seek out and drink.

Some experts classify Oud Bruin all by itself in a category named Weak Lager. It seems a bit much to give a solitary beer its own category unless it is so singular that it fits nowhere else. This isn't.

No style profiles available.

German NABLABS

The Germans refer to and categorize these beers as *Einfachbier*, which translates as Simple beer. The root, *einfach*, can also be translated as elementary, easy, plain, ordinary homely and frugal. A name that would more-often show up on a container label would be *Alkoholfrei* (alcohol-free).

Alcohol content ranges ABV 0.5–1.5%, and their colour can be light or dark. They are watery or thin, mild, and are without pronounced character. This, to a German's palate. Compared with North American NABLABS, some of these German NABLABS might even be described as tasty.

Total production (1985) of German NABLABS is 0.1% of that country's output. Though we have no current figures, production is bound to increase somewhat, especially with Germany's much-stricter (than before) drunk driving laws.

To sum up the German attitude towards these beers, we'll quote Dietrich Höllhuber and Wolfgang Kaul, authors of *Die Biere Deutschlands* (The Beers of Germany): "Ask us not, how man came to this beer and how he tasted it!" (*"Fragen Sie uns nicht, wie man zu diesem Bier kommt und wie es schmeckt!"*).

Bière de Paris

These are similar in style to *Bière de Gardes*, but are not. Close, but no bière. They are a distinctly Parisienne style. Like *Bière de Gardes*, they come in wine bottles, but they are lagers instead of ales. A lager yeast strain developed because the beers were aged in very cold caves, which encouraged their development. The style, previously, was known as *brune de Paris* (Paris Brown).

People think of France as a nation of wine-drinkers. This is true, but the history of brewing in Paris dates to Roman times. At the time of the Revolution, there were twenty-eight active breweries in the city. The breweries were established in a section called *La Glacière* (The Ice-house).

This is a style unique to Paris and environs.

Parallel to the development of bottom-fermenting yeast in the caves of Bayern, a similar activity was occurring in the Paris region, where brewers stored their beer in icy caves.

The beers were strong and amber-coloured. That tradition continues. This example is lagered 60 days.

The following profile is brewed by Brasserie Nouvelle de Lutéce. *Lutetia* is the Roman name for Paris, and *Lutéce* is a corruption of it. It is now brewed near Douai.

Profile: Lutèce

ABV 6.4%, BITTERNESS 23IBUS

Ingredients: Munich, crystal and carapils amber malts, Saaz and Spalt hops.

Nose: fruit and malt aromas

Palate: malty; pleasant raisin and prune taste in mouth. Finishes with chocolate and licorice notes. Delicious.

Pilsner, Pilsener, Pils

This is one of the four main Lager styles. As its name suggests, Pilsener originated in Pilsen, in the Czech Republic. The brand that epitomizes the style is Pilsener Urquell. "Ur" in Germanic languages means "original". "Quell" translates as "the source". Pilsener is the lightest and hoppiest of all the lagers. This is the style beer Budweiser et al should be, and claim to be, but are not.

In Germany, the general parameters of Pils are as follows. Alcohol content (typical) ABV 4.8 (range in class ABV 4.8–5.7%); OG 1044–56; light to very light colour; foamy (white) head; fine hops bitterness; very fine hop aroma. Hop types used are Hallertauer, Northern Brewer, Spalt or Tettnanger. Water hardness ranges from 200–400ppm.

Pils falls within the German *vollbiere* (full beers) category. There are four German classes of Pilsner: *klassische Pilsener* (Classic Pilsener); *süddeutschen Pilsener* (South German Pilsener); *Sauerländer Pilstypus* (Sauerland Pilsener-type); and the *hanseatische Pilsenertyp* (Hanseatic Pilsener-type). It is the only style that is brewed in every German *länder* (states).

Klassische Pilsener has more stress on the hops. It is precisely crafted to be robust, have a full mouth-feel, and be well-rounded. A good German example of a Classic Pilsener is König Pilsener.

Süddeutschen Pilsener is more robust and has more aromatic malt aroma than the German norm for the style. An example is Braumeister Pils from Hacker-Pschorr in München.

Sauerländer Pilstypus is particularly light and delicate, but not very bitter at all. It is, often enough, easily identified because of its particularly light colour. Warsteiner Pils is a good example.

Hanseatische Pilsenertyp is particularly bitter, dry and sharp-tasting from the hops. This North German style is mostly found around Jever.

In comparison to Export Lager, Pils is a little less alcoholic, but much more finely hopped, is a bit slimmer or more delicate in taste, and has a brighter mouthfeel.

Profile: Pilsner Urquell

ABV 4.8%, OG 1048, BITTERNESS 40IBUS

Ingredients: Pale Pilsener malt, Saaz hops

Nose: Great big hops, honey and malt aroma

Palate: Very complex. Beautiful balance of malt and hops with hints of vanilla. Finish is fruity and hoppy with spice notes.

Dortmunder-Export

Export is a style that originated in Dortmund, and has now spread throughout most of Germany. Only beer brewed in Dortmund itself can be labelled Dortmunder. Others of the style are labelled Export or Dortmund-style. Unfortunately, this style has a blue-collar image in the Dortmund district, as Export is a favourite of the workers in this industrial area. The brewers, ever-conscious of their image, do very little to promote the style, preferring instead to concentrate on Pilsener.

German Export beers have bigger bodies than Pilseners, and are not as hoppy/dry. Export is not as sweet as Münchener Lager, so the style falls between the other two, but Export is stronger than both. In other countries, brewers use the term Export to indicate a premium beer. Alcohol content is ABV 5.25–5.5%.

As is often the case in Germany, different regions brew their beers to slightly different specifications. German Export is light-golden to dark in colour with a full mouth-feel. The South German type is malt dominant in aroma. The North German type is the opposite—hops dominant in aroma. Do you notice the trend here? The North Germans prefer much more hops in the beers than do the South Germans, who prefer malt over hops. This applies to both aroma and palate. Bitterness, 24–37IBUS, too, is between that of Pilseners and Müncheners. Hops used are Hallertauer, Northern Brewer, Spalt or Tettnang.

Dortmunder Actien Brauerei, the biggest of the seven Dortmund breweries brews an excellent Export.

Profile: DAB Original

ABV 5.0%, OG 1047, BITTERNESS 27–31IBUS

Ingredients: Pale malt, Hallertauer Northern Brewer hops

Nose: Malty with lemon-citric notes

Palate: Refreshing and malty with nice hop balance. Ends with very strong bitter taste mixed with lemon.

Münchener (Munich) Bayerisches

This style is said to have originated at Spaten Brauerei in München in the mid-1800s. Gabriel Sedlmayr was its head-brewer. The style is alternately called Munich or Bavarian since it has now spread throughout Bayern. It has two sub-categories, *Dunkles* (Darks) and *Helles* (Lights)

This style is the maltiest of the four major German lager styles. Mouth-feel is modest, hop aroma is mild, and it is mostly malt in the aroma.

One of the best examples of dunkelbier is from the Schloßbrauerei Kaltenerg, 8085 Geltendorf. The beer is named after Prince Luitpold's great-grandfather. It is lagered for about two months.

Dunkles (Darks) & Schwarzbier

Colour is dark-amber to brown; alcohol content is ABV 4.8–6.3%, OG 1048–1063; bitterness is 20–45IBUS. Carbonation is average or normal. The taste can best be described as malty and sweet with only mild hop bitterness. The body is thick to very thick, even oily. The style is very popular with students who also enjoy Hefe-Weizenbier.

Breweries in the North and West of Germany don't usually have Dunklesbier in their assortment. It is sometimes called *schwartzes Pils* (Black Pils) or *Schwarzbier* (Black Beer). The Mönchshof Brauerei at Kulmbach brews one of the best schwarzbiers. It is simply called "schwarzes Pils" that comes in an elegant black and gold Vichy 0.30l bottle. Michael Jackson reported in a Summer 1993 column in *zymurgy* that, sadly, this beer has been discontinued. He was appalled to learn this.

Mr Jackson did report on another schwarzbier brewed at Bad Köstritz, Thuringia, in the former GDR (East Germany). The brewery has been bought, in 1992, by Bitburger. Bad Köstritz is about 10km both from Gera and from Erfurt, Thuringia's capital. Their schwarzbier has an OG of 1048–50. Instead of being fermented out to 5.0% ABV, fermentation is halted by pasteurization, and the result is 3.5% ABV. Mr Jackson describes the beer as solid black with an "aroma of malt loaf, a slightly oily body, bitter chocolate and coffee and some roastiness in the finish".

Bad Köstritz was first mentioned as a brewing centre in the early 1500s. At the very end of the seventeenth century there is reference to a brewery in the castle of the local count. The present tradition is rooted in that brewery. Evidently this beer's fame was "international", if early advertising claims are to be believed. The present brewery was built in 1907. It was nationalized by the communist regime after their takeover. Thankfully, the wall and the regime fell.

Profile: König Ludwig

ABV 5.6, BITTERING 24–26IBUS

Ingredients: Pale and chocolate malts, Hallertauer hops

Nose: a rich blend of malt and chocolate

Palate: begins light with smooth maltyness; finishes dry with hints of coffee.

Hell (Light-coloured Lager)

This is the everyday German session beer. The colour is golden; alcohol content is ABV 4.5–5.5%, OG 1046–55; bitterness is 20–30IBUS.

Carbonation is average or normal. Helles doesn't reach as high up the alcohol content scales as do Dunkles, but otherwise the other parameters are about the same. This style developed in the early 20th century. Prior to then, Bavarian brewers produces mostly dark beers, but they notices the popularity of pale beers brewed elsewhere in Germany and the rest of Europe.

A great example of the style is from the Hacker-Pschorr Bräu GmbH, 8000 München 2. It was founded in 1417.

Profile: Münchener Hell

ABV 4.7%, OG 1045, BITTERNESS 20IBUS

Ingredients: Pale malt. Hallertauer and Tettnanger hops.

Nose: lovely gentle malt aroma

Palate: a real thirst quencher—balanced hops and malt up front; finishes malty.

Märzenbier

This style is very similar to the Wiener (Vienna) style, but it is not the same. Some writers lump them together along with Festbiers, but we do not. Märzen was developed before the advance of refrigeration as we know it today. Each March (März is March (the month) in German) brewers would brew an extra-strong beer to survive the long warm months of summer, until it was unveiled at the end of that season. Its last stocks were finished in October. It was brewed as the last batch of the winter brewing season (this before modern refrigeration made it possible to brew year-round).

Märzen is malty and the colour is deep golden or a rich saturated yellow with an alcohol content ABV 4.8–5.4%. Mouthfeel is full and the aroma is malty.

The profile below is brewed by Hacker-Pschorr Bräu GmbH. The ABV% is a little high for category, and the colour is a little more coppery than it should be for style, but this is still a lovely beer.

Profile: Oktoberfest Märzen

ABV 5.6, OG 1055, BITTERNESS 20IBUS

Ingredients: Pale malt. Hallertauer and Tettnanger hops

Nose: Rich malt aroma with soft hops in lovely balance.

Palate: Starts off soft malt in mouth. The finish is deep and dry with biscuity malt and spicy hops.

Wiener (Viennese)

This is the fourth of the classic German Lager styles, though its brewing has died out in Wien. The city, though, is still honoured by the use of its name in the English-speaking world.

Wienerbier is a close cousin of Märzen, but is a little stronger than its German relative. This style developed in Wien (Vienna), Austria. Strangely, this is a style hardly brewed in Wien any longer. Stranger still, Mexico is the largest producer of Wiener-style beer, and it is frequently brewed throughout Central and South Americas. Dos Equis (Two Xs) from Mexico is one of the remaining classics.

The style features medium-strong alcohol content; ABV 5.0–6.0%, OG 1050–1060. Colour range is amber-red or copper to medium brown. Bitterness is 22–35IBUS. Hoppiness in the aroma is light, and the palate is malty.

It is important to note that nowhere in our German references are any of the four classic German styles, except Pilsenser, referred to by their city's names. We, in the English-speaking world, are the ones who have given city-names to those styles.

Bock Beers

All Bock beer is in the German Starkbier (strong beer) class. The Starkbier class encompasses all lagers between ABV 6.25–12.5%; OG >1064. There are several Bockbier styles (See below for the others.)

The Germans describe Bockbier as being Light- or dark-coloured; filtered or with active yeast; little hop bitterness; very full-mouthed; and with strong to very strong malt in the palate.

Bockbier was first brewed in Einbeck, a Hanseatic city in Niedersachsen (Lower Saxony). Therefore, a Bockbier from there, Einbecker Ur-Bock gets to carry the "Ur" (Original) in its name. It is thought that "Bock" is a linguistic corruption of "Beck". Einbecker Ur-Bock is brewed by the Einbecker Brauhauses, the last commercial brewery in the city.

The town has a very long brewing history and rivalry with München. Martin Luther fortified himself during the Diet of Worms in the 1500s. München has tried to lay claim to Bockbier as one of their own styles ever since a North German duke married a southern nobelwoman. He brought with him several Fäßer (barrels) of Bockbier. Evidently it was a smashing success. Einbeck's height of brewing was in the 1600s. It seems the whole town consisted of brewers—about seven-hundred of them (We spelled it out so no one might think the number was a typo!). The Braumeister would take some of his apprentices or workers and go with the city-owned brew kettle house to house so each could brew their own beer. How's that for municipal services?

Einbeck, being a Hanseatic trading city brewed their beers strong to survive long journeys, much in the same way that traditional IPAs developed. It is believed that the first Bockbiere were top-fermented wheat beers of dark colour. Since the development of lager yeast, they are bottom-fermented and have developed into *Helles* and *Dunkles* styles.

Doppelbocks (Double Bocks)

These are the stronger brothers of Bocks. Alcohol content is ABV 7.2–7.5, OG >1074. Bitterness range is 25–40IBUs, but is overpowered by the malt. Colour can be *Helles* or *Dunkles*; very full-mouthed; it has a pronounced malt aroma. Grains used in Doppelbocks are pale Munich, dark Munich, black malt, carapils and dextrin. Hallertauer hops are used. Too, Doppelbocks may be considered the Lager-equivalent of Barleywine.

Doppelbocks can, quite often, be distinguished from Bocks by their label because the brand names usually end with *ator*, Doppelbock's traditional designator.

Profile: Paulaner Salvator

ABV 7.7, OG 1077, BITTERNESS 27IBUS

Nose: malt, malt and more malt

Palate: lip smacking smooth sweet malt with just enough hop balance, big mouth-feel; lingering malt finish.

Eisbock

"Eis" in German means "ice". What does ice have to do with beer? In this instance, ice is removed from the beer by freezing it. Because water has a higher boiling point than does alcohol, the beer is cooled until the water freezes. At that point it is separated from the beer. What remains is a very sweet-tasting beer with a higher alcohol content, and a very malty aroma. The main reason it is so sweet is that it is not balanced by bittering hops. One of the few examples is Kulmbacher Reichelbräus *Eisbock Bayerisch G'forns* (Bavarian Frozen).

Contrary to common thought, EKU Kulminator 28, also brewed at Kulmbach, is not an Eisbock. That beer is briefly frozen to precipitate yeast, but not to increase alcohol strength.

Reichelbräus Eisbock has an ABV of about 10%.

Maibock

This style is a super-premium Bock made for spring celebrations such as Maypole Day. They are released each year on 1 May.

Bokbier

This is a Bockbier derivative brewed in The Netherlands. It has changed enough from the original to warrant spelling *Bock* in Dutch, and giving it its own style.

In The Netherlands, the style developed originally as a dark beer, which was brewed once a year in June. It was released in October, and was available just in that month.

By 1970 the style had died out in The Netherlands, but beer drinkers took up its cause and it was re-introduced. By 1991 about 30 different brands were brewed. A few Dutch brewers are breaking away from the June-only brewing, and are now producing it year-round. The styles main differences to the German Bockbier is that the Dutch version is hopped to a greater extent, and is dryer, which is apparent in the palate, and they tend to all be brown-coloured.

The alcohol content of Bokbier is ABV 6.5–7.0%.

The oldest Dutch brewery, Koninklijke Brand Bierbrouwerij (established 1340), has an ABV 7.0% brand named Imperator.

Profile: Brand Imperator

ABV 7.0, OG 1072, BITTERNESS 22IBUs

Ingredients: Pale, chocolate and Münchener malts; Hallertauer, Hersbrücker and Perle hops

Nose: exquisite and malty with vanilla undertones

Palate: sets off a tad sweet and creamy and finishes with hops slightly dominant over the malt

Dubbelbok

The Doppelbock style has not yet fully developed in the Netherlands. We'll give it its own style listing here, and watch if it fills up.

Brand also has an ABV 7.5% Dubbelbok, simply called Brand Duppelbock (some brewers maintain the German spelling).

More than ten Dutch, and several Belgian brewers have taken to brewing Ale Boks, which are not to be confused with these Lagers.

Meibok

The Dutch version of the German style. Colour range is narrow, from amber to copper. Alcohol strength is stronger (ABV 7.0–7.5%) than is common Bock. *Meibok*s are sweeter with a more substantial character than the *Bokbiers* of early autumn. They also have a stronger finish. Some lump *Meibok*s with common *Bokbiers*, but the two styles are dissimilar enough to separate them.

A good example of this style is brewed by De Kroon's Bierbrouwerij at Oirschot. Their *Meibok* is amber-coloured, somewhat sweet and has an alcohol content ABV 7.0%.

About half the *Meibok*s produced are Ale Boks

(top-fermented). Each has its own style, and therefore its own listing.

Real North American Bock

This is a style we are waiting for to develop. There are a few from brew-pubs and micro-breweries producing it, but none with widespread distribution.

We suggest: this category should be very close to, if not matching, German parameters. Furthermore, for a beer to qualify for this category, it should meet these criteria, and not be included simply because the brewer decides to brand a beer a Bock because the name will spur sales.

We would love to see north American brewers, the HCBs included, flex their brewing muscles and bring to market real Bocks of Germanic strengths, and not the weakling examples introduced so far.

Real North American Dobble Bock

The new breweries are starting to turn out some excellent Double Bocks, though they may not all adhere to German brewing requirements for this category. If you like beers of this style, you'll have to do some hunting to find good ones. If your local brew-pub doesn't make a Bock, ask him to do so. If enough customers ask for something, the brewer is bound to respond positively. Again, some brewers take liberties for commercial reasons with the names they slap on their brands. One that doesn't is from Samuel Adams. Watch out! Each 12oz has 240 calories!

Profile: Samuel Adams Double Bock

OG 1081, ABV 7.5%

Ingredients: Klages/Harrington malt, Caramel malt 60°, Saaz, Hallertauer and Tettnanger hops

Nose: Very malty with hints of chocolate

Palate: Heavy malt flavour; smooth, very full-bodied; delicious

Strong Pils

This classification is for Pilseners brewed with ABV ≥ 7.0%. In Germany, the Bock style parameters kick in at ABV ≥ 6.5%, so this style is analogous with a blond Bock.

Amstel, a subsidiary, now, of Heineken, pro-

duces an ABV 7.0% beer of very ordinary character in this style.

Carlsberg of Copenhagen also brews a beer that fits this category. It is widely available throughout the world, and is a brand the brewery has been specially proud. Don't be put off by its Malt-Liquor designation in America. It bears no resemblance to the god-awful Malt-liquors from some of the HCBs.

Profile: Carlsberg Elephant Beer

ABV 7.5%, OG 1065, BITTERNESS 38IBUS

Ingredients: Pale malt and brewing sugar, Hallertauer hops.

Nose: fruity and moderate hoppiness, with grainy aromas.

Palate: Fruity combination of orange, tangerine, and lemon; dry, hoppy finish with alcohol apparent.

Rauchbier

This is a style from Bamberg and environs. The name means Smoked Beer. The malts are dried over Beechwood chips. During the process the smoke penetrates the malt, which then passes the flavour and odour to the beer during the brewing process. The alcohol content is ABV 5.0%. Colour range is dark to very dark. The smoked aroma is fine to very strong. Malt is still apparent in the aroma. Hop bitterness runs from delicate to robust. Mostly brands are lagered in barrels in the traditional manner.

Kaiserdom Rauchbier is an example. It has ABV 5.0%, OG 1051, bitterness 25IBUs. The Aecht Schlenkeria Rauchbier Märzen, brewed by Heller Bräu is considered the best example of this style.

Liquor-flavoured Lager

As we were finishing this manuscript, we came across an article Michael Jackson wrote about a "Hunt" in the Strasbourg section of Alsace. He described two beers which he now considers a sub-category of Smoked Beers or Rauchbiers. The Fischer Brewery (Pêcheur in French) and its subsidiary, Adelshoffen, have been brewing some speciality beers, two of which are beer with Scottish malt whisky added.

☛ The first brand is Adelscott. He describes it as a "malty beer, though very subtle in its supposedly-malted whisky-malt character. It has nonetheless inspired enough imitators in other countries to constitute a sub-category among smoked beers." Alcohol content is ABV 6.4%.

☛ The second brand is named Adelscott Noir; ABV 6.6%. Michael Jackson describes it as, "… indeed, an almost-black colour, with just a hint of cherry red when it is held up to the light, and a distinctively greyish head (that sounds unattractive, but it is actually n interesting colour).

"Adelscott Noir also has a dash more flavour. It is still only lightly peaty, but has its own grainy-smoky notes, especially at the back of the mouth."

☛ Kingston is another liquor-flavoured beer from the same brewery. This brand has white Martinique rum added. Again, Mr Jackson: "This beer, at a potent 7–9 per cent ABV, has a distinctively soft body, a lightly sweet palate, and a gently rummy aftertaste.

"It is not the most serious of beers, though I could see it selling well to young drinkers, and not only those of Caribbean ethnic origin."

Stout Lager

This is another new style, a bottom-fermented Stout of medium-strong alcohol content. The stronger style dark beers are re-appearing as public interest return after many year's absence. There are only a few brands in this style at the moment, but this situation should change for the better.

Many traditional top-fermented Stouts now have lower alcohol contents than these Lager Stouts. Compare Guinness Stout, ABV 5.1 to the Arcener Stout below. It is brewed by De Arsense Bierbrouwerij at Arcen.

Profile: Arcener Stout

ABV 6.5, BITTERNESS 27IBUS

Ingredients: Münchener, chocolate, pale and coloured malts and caramel; Hallertauer Northern Brewer and Hersbrücker Spät hops

Nose: Lovely malt and chocolate aromas

Palate: chocolate, coffee and malt; finishes dry and bitter

Speciality beers

An essay by Rob Haiber

Belgium, a special place for beer

SPECIALITY BEERS ARE to other beer styles as chocolate eclairs, Napoleons and strawberry cheese cakes are to ordinary deserts: *la creme de la creme.*

There are so many different ingredients brewers can add to beer. Rather than have a separate style for each ingredient, we (and others before us) have put them in to one. Commercial examples of most of these are not universally available or abundant in North America (this is changing for the better). To try these beers one must make the effort to seek them. Europe is the best starting place (a quality beer seller would be another, if you are lucky enought to live within a reasonable distance from one). There is nothing quite like tasting beer fresh from the brewery.

Historically, brewers have (before both the rise of hops as the bittering agent, and the commercialization of beer styles), used many ingredients to counterbalance malt's sweetness. Most fell by the wayside as drinkers' tastes changed, but others barely clung to life in small breweries. A few are enjoying abit of an upswing as the growing numbers of new microbrewers and brew-pubs try different recipes as a way of sparking customer interest, and to differentiate themselves from other brewers.

Surprisingly, to many, Belgium is the world's leading (almost only) producer of these styes. The country is somewhat obscure and out of the news in North American, but it has a long and distinguished history as a brewing nation. A history that goes hand-in-hand with their excellent cuisine. Belgians are very conscious of the fact that Jan Primus (corrupted to Gambrinus), the "King of Beer", was a thirteenth-century Flemish duke (Flanders being a part of Belgium). More recently his name has been borrowed by the Czechoslovaks and Germans for use on their bottle labels.

Besides their world-class specially beers, Belgium is also a producer of many conventional styles: Pilsener; Wheat; Mild; Bitter. Generically, they are in the ale category, brewed in the top-fermenting or warm method. Many are similar to English Ales, though usually stronger and drier. This is because until the 1980s, cafés were prohibited from serving spirits, so the brewers responded to demand for something strong, by brewing robust-strength beers. Business will always supply demand. Thankfully, that bit of government folly was overturned, but the strong beers remain.

You may ask why Belgian brewers chose cherries, raspberries and peaches to flavour their some of beers. A good question. The answer is that these beers are direct descendants of beers produced before the discovery of hops as a flavouring agent. Before this breakthrough, brewers used all manner of fruit, herbs and spices as ingredients to counterbalance malt's sweetness. Remember, too, that the origins of these beers pre-dates the discovers of yeast as the thing which ferments sugars, in the process creating alcohol. Yeasts have always existed on this planet since shortly after the land arose from the seas. Man just couldn't see the little buggers until he invented the microscope. Even then, it was quite a while from the microscope's invention to the discovery of yeast's role in making beer (scientists were looking elsewhere).

This brings us to another peculiarity of Belgian speciality beers: their method of fermentation. Brewers of long ago could not just nip round to their local brew-shop and buy a packet of yeast as one can today. So how did they get their wort to ferment? Most simply left it exposed to open air. It was a hit-or-miss situation because they were at the mercy of whatever blew in on the wind and happened to settle in the fermentation vats. In combination with yeast remaining in the wood of the barrels they conditioned the beer in, this was all it took to start wort fermenting.

Most Belgian speciality beers are sold only in bottle, not casks, though other Belgian beers are. Brewers bottle-condition their beers. This is good for the beer-drinker since bottled beer is more readily available than kegged beer because it is more easily stocked. To small specialty brewers, this is an advantge, otherwise they would be unable to bring their brands to the export market. Not much would reach that market if it weren't for the bottle.

Finally, in a world of interesting beers, Belgian speciality beers are the most unique group of them all.

Appendix of Brewing organisations

THE FOLLOWING IS a list of beer consumer groups working for the interests of beer-drinkers and breweries that provide high-quality beer. Some are still limited in nature, others have quite wide scope, but all are growing and spreading the word about quality beer.

CAMRA, PINT, OBP and SÖ are part of the European Beer Consumers Union. Other organizations from Denmark, Finland and France "may soon be joining", according to Andrew Sangster, our contact at CAMRA.

We wish them success and continued growth. We envision the time when every country has a similar organization.

☛ The Campaign for Real Ale Ltd (CAMRA), 34 Alma Road, St Albans, Herts, AL1 3BW. Tele: 0727 86 72 01, Fax: 0727 86 76 70

☛ Confédération des Brasseurs du Marché Commun (CBMC), 191–197 Boulevard du Souverain, bte 10, B–1160, Brussels, Belgium. Tele: (02) 6 72 23 92; Fax: (02) 6 60 94 02

☛ Deutscher-Brauer-Bund eV, Annaberger Str 28, Postfach 200 452 or 200 453; 5300 Bonn 2, Germany. Tele: (0228) 9 59 06-0; Fax: (0228) 9 59 06-16

☛ European Brewery Convention (EBC), Generalsekretariat, POB 510, NL–2380 BB Zoeterwoude, the Netherlands. Tele: (71) 45 60 47 or 45 66 74; Fax: (071) 41 00 13 or 41 50 77.

☛ De Objectieve Bierproevers (OBP), Postbus 32, 2600 Berchem 5, Belgium. Tele: (32) 03 280 13 30; Fax: (32) 03 230 18 88

☛ Prometie Informatie Tradtioneel Bier (PINT), Postbus 3757, 1001 AN Amsterdam, The Netherlands. Fax: (32) 010 212 21 62

☛ Svenska Ölfrämjandet (SÖ), Box 16244, 10325 Stockholm, Sweden. Tele: (46) 042 11 98 36; Fax: (46) 042 10 53 08

Appendix of Brewing Schools

Belgium

☛ Hogere School Voor Gistingsbedrijven CTL, Gent

☛ Instituut Voor Gistingsbedrijven to Brussel-COOVI

☛ Katholieke Industriele Hogeschool Oost–Vlaanderen St Lievens-Gent

☛ Katholieke Universiteit–Lueven

☛ Université do Louvain-La-Neuve–Sciences et Technologies Brassicoles

Write for information about these schools, and about Belgian beer to:

☛ Confederate der Brouwerijn van Belgie, Maison des Brasseurs, Grote Markt 10, Brussels, Belgium

Germany

☛ Doemens-Technikum, Stefansus Str 8, Postfach 1325, 8032 Gräfeling, Germany. Tele: (089) 8 58 05-0; Fax: (089) 8 58 05 26

☛ Hans Wilsdorf Schule Brauereiabteilung, Georg-Hagen-Str 35, 8650 Kulmbach, Germany. Tele: (8650) 77 47; Fax: (09221) 6 73 31

☛ Staatlische Brautechnische Prüf u Versuchsanstalt Weihenstephan, 8050 Freising-Weihenstephan, Germany. Tele: (08161) 7 10 or 71 33 31; Fax: (08161) 71 41 81

☛ Technische Universität München, Fakultät für Brauwesen, 8050 Freising-Weihenstephan, Germany. Tele: (08161) 71 32 59

☛ There are schools in virtually ever corner

of Germany. The ones listed are some of the main ones (or more accessible).

United States

☞ The Institute for Brewing Studies, POB 1510, Boulder, CO 80306-1679.

☞ The Siebel Institute of Technology Inc, 4049 West Peterson Ave, Chicago, IL 60646. Tele: 312.463.3400

☞ The University of California at Davis.

United Kingdom

☞ Brewlab, The Life Science Building, University of Sunderland, Chester Road, Sunderland, SR1 3SD. Tele: 091.515.2535

Appendix of Brewing Publications

☞ All About Beer, 1627 Marion Ave, Durham, NC 27705. Tele: 919.490.0589; Fax: 919.490.0865. Subscription prices: $20.00 for six issues, USA and her Possessions; $30.00, Canada & Mexico; $45.00, all other countries

☞ Ale Street News, POB 5339, Bergenfield, NJ 07621. Tele: 201.387.1818. $14.96 for one year (six issues)

☞ American Brewer & Beer, the Magazine, pob 9877, Berkeley, CA 94709. Subscription tele: 800.646.2701.

☞ Barley Corn, POB 2328, Falls Church, VA 22042. Tele: 703.573.8970. $15.00 for one year

☞ Brewers Digest, 4049 West Peterson Ave, Chicago , IL 60646. Tele: 312.463.3400. $25.00 per year

☞ Brewing Techniques, POB 3222, Eugene, OR 97403. Tele: 503.687.2993; Fax: 503.687.8534; Toll Free: 800.427.2993. $30.00 per year

☞ Southwest Brewing News, 11405 Eveningstar Drive, Austin, TX 78739. Tele: 512.467.2225. $12.00 for one year (six issues). Circ @35k. Distribution in AZ, AK, CO, KS, LA, NM and OK.

☞ The Celebrator, Box 375, Hayward, CA 94543. $14.95 for one year (six issues)

☞ The New Brewer, (the magazine for micro- and pub-brewers) POB 1679, Boulder, CO 80306-1679. Tele: 303.447.0816; Fax: 303.447.2825.

☞ What's Brewing, 34 Alma Road, St Albans, Herts, AL1 3BW. Tele: 727 86 72 01, Fax: 727 84 87 95. Monthly, with membership (US$25.00). VISA charge accepted.

☞ Yankee Brew News, POB 8053, JFK Station, Boston, MA 02114. $7.95, published quarterly (possibly going to bi-monthly in 1994. Circulation 35,000. Distributed in New England. Tele: 617.522.2182; Fax: 617.361.6106; ComputerServe: 70571,3252.

☞ zymurgy, POB 1510, Boulder, CO 80306. Tele: 303.447.0816; Fax: 303.447.2825

Appendix of Brewing Statistics

Some Facts

The United States brews the most beer in the world. She is followed, in order, by Germany, Britain, ex-Soviet Union, Japan, the ex-Czechoslovakia, France, Mexico, Canada, Australia, Spain, Belgium, Poland, Brazil, The Nederlands, ex-Yugoslavia, Columbia, Denmark and Italy.

The top twenty beer-drinking nations are (first to last): Germany, Belgium, the ex-Czechoslovakia, Australia, New Zealand, Luxembourg, Denmark, Ireland, Britain, Austria, Canada, The United States, The Nederlands, Switzerland, Hungary, Sweden, Finland, Bulgaria, Venezuela, and the ex-Soviet Union.

The ten biggest brewers in the world are: Anheuser-Bush (USA), Heineken (The Nederlands), Miller (USA), Kirin (Japan), Coors (US), Stroh (USA), Heileman (USA), Bass (UK), Allied (Skol) (UK) and Carling (Canada). The Allied breweries have just merged with the Carlsberg brewers of Denmark, so its position might be even larger than Bass's. All these large breweries are on a acquisitions and mergers binge so their positions might have changed since this list was put together.

Market shares of the top six breweries in the United States are:

1. Anheuser-Busch	45.7%
2. Miller	22.1%
3. Coors	10.2%
4. Stroh	7.0%
5. Heileman	5.0%
6. Pabst	3.8%

In the United States, there are some significant regional breweries. We'll list the top ten and their 1991 or 1992 taxable production (in US barrels).

1. Latrobe Brewing Co (PA)	840,000
2. Hudepehl-Schoenling (OH)	515,000
3. Evansville Brewing Co (IN)	330,000
4. DG Yuengling & Son (PA)	210,810
5. FX Matt Brewing Co (NY)	206,000
6. Minnesota Brewing Co (MN)	175,000
7. Jacob Leinenkugel Co WI)	165,000
8. Joseph Huber Brewing (WI)	134,500
9. Anchor Brewing Co (CA)	82,653
10. Sierra Nevada Brewing (CA)	68,039

There are many "contract" brewers in the United States. This is often the least expensive way to enter the market, what with brew plant being extremely expensive.

By far the run-away leader of the contract brewers is the Boston Beer Company, with a 22.6% share of this category. They have gained national prominence due to the excellence of their Samuel Adams brands, which have won numerous brewing awards.

The top five contract brewers are (US barrels):

1. Boston Beer Co (MA)	273,000
2. Pete's Brewing Co (CA)	35,700
3. William & Scott Co (CA)	15,000
4. Brandevor (WA)	11,000
5. Brooklyn Brewery (NY)	9,200

AMERICA IS HOME to some of the world's largest brewing firms. Unfortunately their size does not translate into a good product. Most all large brewers in this country "cut" their beer by using corn andor/ rice in their formulas. You can easily tell which are which by looking at the label. If it says, say, "choicest grains" instead of "all barley malt" or words to that effect, it is not quality beer you're holding in your hands. Thankfully there is a growing number of micro-breweries in the US who are brewing delicious beers in the traditional manner.

Of all countries, Belgium brews the most distinctive and varied types of beers. Besides brewing traditional lagers and ales, they also brew fruit beers, wheat beers, Scottish ales, Lambics and some incredible Abbey Beers.

Britain and Ireland are the homes of traditional ales, porters and stouts. These styles are again becomming popular in the United States. Their lagers, however, leave much to be desired.

France, in its northern provinces, is also a beer brewing region of some note. The beers from there are often called country ales, haute tradition beer or bière de garde. Further to the East, in Alsace near the German frontier, the French brew lagers much as their neighbours do, but without the *Reinheitsgebot* restrictions.

Germany is the homeland of lagers, brewed in several different styles, the principal ones are Münchener, Dortmunder and Pilsener, though Pilsener-style beer had its origins in Pilsn in what is now the Czech Republic. Wheat beer, both filtered and unfiltered are also a major style of beer there. They are gaining popularity in the USA. One distinctive feature of many, but not all wheat beers is a clove-like aroma.

The Nederlands brew mostly lagers, though they have some interesting styles that are only distributed in the home market.

Appendix of Beer Contents

Beer Contents

The following is a list of the contents of one-litre of Vollbier (full beer, such as a German Exportbier). Except for alcohol content and calories, the United States government refuses to let brewers put this information on beer labels or packaging. This is one instance where the government definitely does not want the public informed—for fear it will drink more beer.

☛ Base substances:

Carbohydrates: 38–40gm

Protein: 3–5gm

Alcohol: 35–43gm

Carbonic acid: 4–5gm

Water: 840–880gm

☛ Vitamins

B–1, Thiamin: 0.04mg

B–2, Riboflavin: 0.3–0.4mg

B–6, Pyridoxin: 0.47–0.82mg

H, Biotin: 0.005mg

Niacin: 6.3–8.8mg

Folic Acid: 0.8mg

Pantothenic Acid: 0.9–1.1mg

☛ Elements

Sulphur: 0.5–0.6mg

Potassium: 0.42–0.57mg

Phosphorous: 0.12–0.16mg

Chlorine: 0.11mg

Calcium: 0.06–0.09mg

Magnesium: 0.05mg

BIBLIOGRAPHY

☛ *Die Biere Deutschlands*, Dietrich Höllhuber and Wolfgang Kaul, Verlag Hans Karl, Nürnberg, Bundes Republik Deutschland, 1988

☛ *Das Grosse Lexicon vom Bier und Seinen Brauereien*, several authors, Scripta Verlags-Gesellschaft, 7000 Stuttgart, Bundes Republik Deutschland, no date

☛ *Brew Your Own Real Ale at Home*, Graham Wheeler and Roger Protz, CAMRA Books, St Albans, England, 1993

☛ *Everyday Life in Babylonia and Assyria*, HWF Saggs, Dorset Press, New York, 1965

☛ *History oy Prussia*, HW Koch, Dorset Press, New York, 1978

☛ *History of the Art of War, Vol II The Barbarian Invasions*, Hans Delbrück (1848–1929), Translated from the German, and copyright (1975) held by Walter Renfroe Jr, University of Nebraska Press, Lincoln and London by arrangement Greenwood Press, Inc.

☛ *Sumerian Economic Texts, from the Drehem Archive*. Summerian and Akkadian Cuneform Texts in the Collection of the World Heritage Museum of the University of Illinois. Vol II. By Shin T Kang. 1972

☛ *The Essentials of Beer Styles, a Catalogue of Beer Styles for Brewers and Beer Enthusiasts*, Fred Eckhardt, Fred Eckhardt Associates, USA, 1989

☛ *The Simon and Schuster Pocket Guide to Beer, the Connoisseur's Companion to the Fine Beers of the World*, Michael Jackson, Mitchell Beazley Publishers, London, England, 1986

☛ *The European Beer Almanac*, Roger Protz, Lochar Publishing Ltd, Moffat, England, 1991

☛ *The Real Ale Drinker's Almanac*, Roger Protz, Lochar Publishing Ltd, Moffat, England, 1991

☛ *Belgian Ale*, Classic Beer Styles Series, Vol 6, Pierre Rajotte, Brewers Publications, Bolder, CO, 1992

☛ *Lambic*, Classic Beer Styles Series, Vol 3, Jean-Xavier Guinard, Brewers Publications, Bolder, CO, 1990

☛ *Porter*, Classic Beer Styles Series, Vol 5, Terry Foster, Brewers Publications, Bolder, CO, 1992

☛ *Home Brewing*, The CAMRA Guide, Graham Wheeler, Alma Books Ltd, St Albans, England, 1990

☛ *Steiner's Guide to American Hops*, copyright by S S Steiner Inc

☛ *The Structures of Everyday Life, Civilization & Capitalism 15th–18th Century, Vol 1* by Fernand Braudel. Harper & Row, Publishers. Copyright 1979.

☛ *The Encyclopædia Brittanica*, 1950 edition, copyright by Encyclopædia Brittanica Inc

☛ *The New Grolier Multimedia Encyclopedia* (on CD-ROM), copyright 1991 & 1992 by Grolier Inc, and copyright 1987–1992 by Online Computer Systems Inc

☛ *The Good Beer Guide to Belgium and Holland*, compiled by Tim Webb, Alma Books Ltd, St Albans, England, 1992

☛ *The Great British Beer Book*, Roger Protz, Impact Books, London, England, 1987

DEFINITIONS

We have combined some foreign language words with the English beer and beer-related words/ terms in this glossary section to educate readers. English words are designated with an (E), French with an (F), German words with a (G), &c.

Abbey beer (E): Any top- or bottom-fermented beer brewed under licence from a monastery, or by a brewery located near an abbey, or that has retained its original name and style of a particular abbey.

Aca: A type of maize beer brewed since, at least, 200BC in Peru.

Acidic (E): Describes a biting, sour or pungent aroma or flavour in beer that is reminiscent of acetic acid or vinegar.

Adam's water/wine (E): slang for water.

Additive (E): Any natural or synthetic chemical deliberately added to beer during production, packaging or storing for a specific reason.

Adjunct (E): Any unmalted cereal grain or fermentable ingredient that is substituted for barley malt and added to the mash for the purpose of reducing costs. Oats, wheat, corn, tapioca flour, flaked corn and rice, invert sugar and glucose are used in this manner. They tend to produce a paler, lighter-bodied and less-malty beer. Wheat is used to produce a distinctive style beer, and is usually acceptable to beer purists as an "acceptable" adjunct or, often, it is not considered one.

Aftertaste (E): The taste sensations that linger after beer has been swallowed.

Aftersmell (E): The sensation that lingers in the nasal passages after beer has been swallowed.

Alcohol (E), Alkohol (G): a colourless, volatile, pungent liquid (C_2H_5OH); grain alcohol; the intoxicating ingredient in distilled and fermented liquors.

Ale (E): a generic name for top-fermented beers, Ale is the predominant style in the United Kingdom. It is enjoying a rebirth in North America, led by the increase in micro-breweries, brew-pubs and home-brewing. Sub-categories of Ale include Abbey beers, Alt, Barley Wine, Bitter, Brown Ale, Kölsch, Mild, Pale Ale, Porter, Stout and others.

Ale-house (E): In England, a public-house where Ale is sold. Records indicate that as early as the 1300s, licenses were being issued to operate ale-houses.

Ale wife (E): from Medieval England, a female who brewed Ale, or who ran a tavern. **Syn:** Breweress; Brewster

Ale yeast (E): Top-fermenting yeast

Alkoholgehalt (G): Alcohol content

Alpha acid (E): The hop resin humulon. A measure of the main bittering substance present in hops.

Altbier (G): literally "Old beer". A dark beer that is top fermented (an ale). This is one of the original beer styles before the advent of lager yeasts. Lagers have largely replaced Altbier as the preferred style of beer in Germany. Alts are very similar to traditional English ales. Altbier is still brewed in Düßeldorf, Ißum, Korschenbroich, Krefeld, Münster and several other cities in the German states of Rheinland-Pfalz. Alcohol strength is ABV 4.3–5.0%.

Amber (beer) (E): describes a colour range of beer (both Ales and Lagers) between pale and dark. The description Amber beer should not be understood to be synonymous with Copper-coloured beer, which has much more red (usually imparted by a different barley malt) in its hue. There is a difference.

Amylase: Two enzymes, alpha amylase and

beta amylase responsible for the conversion of starch into sugars during the mash stage of brewing. They are often collectively referred to as diatase.

Anaerobic (E): occurring in the absence of oxygen

Anaerobic fermentation(E): a term to describe the phase of fermentation when the yeast, having used all the dissolved oxygen in the wort, switches to anaerobic respiration. It is during this stage that alcohol is produced. During the aerobic stage, the yeast culture is rapidly reproducing (pant…pant…heavy breathing!).

Armstrong rake (E): a rotating arm fitted to the bottom of the mash tun. It thoroughly mixes the grist and liquor. It is also used to loosen a set mash. Often called a "porcupine".

Aroma (E & G): description of the natural odours of beer produced by the ingredients. **See Bouquet**

Aroma(tic) hops (E): synonym for Finishing Hops.

Astringency (E): one of the many tastes that may be present in beer. It is caused by high levels of tannins, phenols and aldehydes, which cause the mouth and lips to pucker and tingle.

Astringent (E): description of a harsh, mouth-puckering sensation sometimes found in beer.

Attenuation: The drop in specific gravity of wort during the process of fermentation caused by yeast activity. The greater the attenuation, the less sweet a beer tends to be, and the greater the amount of alcohol that is produced.

Autolysis: When yeast cells die, they are digested by their own enzyme system.

Back: Alternative pronunciation, "buck". Brewers term for a holding vessel. Entemologically related to "bucket".

Bacteria (E): unicellular micro-oganisms that do not have chlorophyll. They recreate swiftly via simple fission. They are classified by their shapes, and weather or not they live by aerobic- or anaerobic respiration. Bacteria is what causes spoilage in foodstuffs (and diseases). They may be killed by disinfectants.

Barley-corn or Barleycorn (E): a single grain of barley.

Barley-wine or Barleywine (E): a synonym for Strong Ale. (OG 1065–1120 or more). They require a longtime to age, ranging from six-months to several years. Some Barleywines are fermented with a combination of yeasts, including Champagne yeast, which is better able to cope with the high-alcohol environment than is ale yeast.

The word derives from the ancient Egyptians and Greeks who called strong beer "wine made from barley".

Barrel: A 36gal cask. Brewer's standard unit of measure.

Beer/Bier (E) (G): the generic word for all beverages made from fermented grains. All Ales and Lagers are beer.

Beer engine (E): In England, the hand-pump device for drawing beer from the cask to the spigot.

Beta acid: Lupulon, a hop resin.

Bierarten (G): Beer varieties in top/bottom fermented brews.

Bierausstoss (G): Annual output of beer in Germany or of a brewery.

Biergattungen (G): Beer types classified by alcohol content, usually by volume, though in some countries, by weight.

Biersoten (G): Selection of brands a brewer has on offer. Popular brands of beer such as Pils, Export, Alt, Kölsch, Weizenbier, Bock.

Beim Bier sitzen (G): To sit over one's beer.

Etwas wie saures Bier ausbieten (G): Get rid of something with difficulty; to have something hanging on one's hands.

Bierartig (G): Beery

Bier vom Fass (G): Beer on tap or draft (drought) beer.

Bierbauch (G): Beer belly

Bierbrauer (G): Brewer

Bierdeckel (G): 22 Beer mat

Brauerei (G): Brewery

Bierbruder (G): Beer brother (literally). Heavy drinker

Bier eifer (G): Excessive zeal

Bier eifrig (G): Most studious

Bieressig (G): Malt vinegar

Bierfass (G): Beer barrel

Bierfilz (G): Table mat

Biergarten (G): Outdoor restaurant

Bierhahn (G): Beer tap; spigot

Bierhalle (G): Beer hall

Bierheber (G): Beer engine; beer pump

Bierhefe (G): Brewer's yeast

Bieridee (G): Beer idea (literally) Here means crazy idea

Bierkanne (G): Beer tankard

Bierkarren (G): Brewer's dray

Bierkneipe (G): Alehouse or pub

Biercomment (G): Student's beer ritual

Bierkrug (G): Beer mug, pot

Bierkutcher (G): Brewer's drayman

Bierlokal (G): Local tavern

Bierreise (G): Pub crawl

Bier schwengel (G): Beer engine

Bierseidel (G): Mug or glass

Bierstein (G): Drinking vessel decorated with proverbs. It usually has a special lid to keep its contents cool.

Biertonne (G): Beer barrel: pot-bellied person

Bierwirtschaft (G): Beer joint

Bierzapfer (G): Tapster

Bierzeitzung (G): Student burlesque

Bierzipfel (G): Pendant on watch chai

Bockbier (G): A bottom fermented beer, with 16–17% alcohol content (unreduced wort) or 6.25–6.9% by volume. Dark and Light styles.

Bottom (working) fermentation: Refers to fermentation by yeast which works towards the bottom of the fermentation vessel. This is typical of lager yeasts.

Brauen (G): To brew beer

Burtonising: Brewer's expression for a water treatment where the brewer tries to replicate the water at Burton-upon-Trent, which is considered the best because of its hardness, for producing Bitter/Pale Ale.

Cane sugar (E): Sucrose from sugarcane

Canstatter Wasen (G): An annual festival held in the Autumn in the Canstatt district of Stuttgart (Baden-Württemberg), Germany. The king of Württemberg started the event in 1818, originally as an agricultural one, but it has grown to be the rival of the better-known Oktoberfest in München, Bayern. The two lands are rivals.

Caramel (E): The result of heating dextrose or saccharose with an acid or alkali. Its use is to colour and to flavour beer. **Syn:** burnt sugar

Caramel malt: Malt made from sugar-rich barley that is fully modified. It is lightly steeped, kiln-dried, re-steeped and, again, heat-dried at 150–170°F (65.2–76.7°C) for one to two hours. This converts the starches in the grain to sugars. The temperature is then increased to 250°F (120°C). The grain is frequently checked for colour until it is correct—it is made in a colour range from pale to dark. It is used in amounts (12–15%) to add aroma, sweetness and darker colour to beer. **Syn:** crystal malt.

Cara-pils: European name for pale Caramel Malt (Crystal Malt).

Carbohydrate: Compounds composed of carbon, hydrogen and oxygen (with two hydrogen atoms for every oxygen atom). Celluloses, starches and sugars are carbohydrates.

Carbonated beer: usually refers to beer that has been artificially injected with carbon dioxide rather than occurring by priming or kraeuzening. Beer that has been primed with sugar when bottled is most often called "bottle-conditioned".

Carbonation: The process of dissolving or injecting carbon dioxide in a liquid to create effervescence. Beer may be injected with carbon dioxide, kraeuzened with young beer, or have priming sugar added at the bottling stage to created a secondary fermentation, which produces carbon dioxide.

Carbon dioxide: the inert gas which causes effervescence in beer. Formula: CO_2.

Carnaval de Binche: A festival dating from the 14th century that is held at Binche, Belgium on Shrove Sunday, Monday and Tuesday.

Carrageen or Carragheen: Synonym for Irish Moss.

Cascade hops: A variety grown in Washington state; contains 5.0–6.5% alpha acids and 5.0–6.0% beta acids.

Cask-conditioned beer: Beer, almost always Ale, that is conditioned in casks, formerly made of wood. Hence the term, "Beer from the wood". The casks, now steel, are delivered to pubs where they must spend two or three days in the cool (56°F (13°C)) cellars whilst they fall bright and carbonate before being placed on offer.

Cassava beer: Synonym for Manioc beer.

Cellarman: 1. The person, at a brewery, responsible for the beer whilst it is in storage. 2. In a pub, the person responsible for all preparatory activities associated with offering the beer for consumption. In Britain, cellarmen undergo training organized by the breweries to ensure proper preparation of their beers to drinkers. It is a skilled job.

Centrifugation: A method of clarifying beer by removing suspended solids by centrifugal force. It is used to strain and to clarify wort during the cooling phase, and finished beer before racking.

Cereal(E): any of the known wild or cultivated grasses (Gramineae) such as barley, corn, millet, oats, rice, rye, sorghum and wheat; with edible starchy seeds.

To malt a cereal, seed is wet down until it sprouts; then dried for further processing.

Cerevisia (L): Latin name for a beer made of barley, buckwheat, maize, millet, oats and rye, made by the Gauls. Pliny the Elder (23-79AD) mentions, in his *Natural History*, this beverage as the national drink of Gaul.

Julius Caesar is said to have preferred cerevisia to wine. There are references to Cerevisia being brewed back to around 400BC.

Cerevisia humulina: Cerevisia flavoured with hops. It is mentioned in 768 AD in the charter of Abbey St Denis.

Cervesa (S): beer, in Spanish

Champagne du Nord (F): name given by French troops in the early 1800s to Berliner style wheat beer.

Champagne of the Spree: name for Berliner Weiss. Spree is a river which flows through Berlin.

Cheesy: describes a smell or taste in beer caused by Isovaleric acid, which occurs when isoamyl alcohol is oxidized.

Chill haze: A hazy condition in beer caused by suspended protein and tannin molecules, that become noticeable when beer is chilled too quickly, at too low a temperature, and for too long. The condition is apparent around the freezing point, 32°F (0°C), and disappears by 68°F (20°C). The condition lessens as the beer warms.

Chiu: a wheat beer made during the Hans Dynasty (200 BC) in China. The name became the generic name for beer in that country.

Chondrus crispus: The scientific name for Irish Moss, a beer clarifier made from red seaweed.

Chung beer: A Tibetan style made from a local barley strain called chim.

Cidery: A taste or odour in beer reminiscent of apple cider. Usually considered a negative characteristic, especially in Lager.

Citric: A taste or odour in beer reminiscent of citric fruit such as grapefruit, lemon, lime and pineapple. Usually considered a negative char-

acteristic, especially in Lager, except in the minutest amounts.

Clean: Describes beer with no off-flavours or aromas.

Cloudy: A condition of beer that has unsettled particulate matter. **Syn:** hazy.

Cluster: A hop variety cultivated in the USA containing 5.5–8.0% alpha acids, and 4.5–5.5% beta acids.

Cold break: A phase of the brewing process after the boil, when the temperature of the wort is quickly reduced, thus causing the precipitation of protein chains and tannins. These settle to the bottom of the vessel, and the wort is separated from it. This is not an optional act of clarification, but, rather, a side benefit of a necessary action.

Comet hops: a very bitter variety grown in Washington state. Alpha acid content is 9.5–10.5%.

Commercial brewers (E): The reference, here, is to enormous national and international breweries such as Anheuser-Busch, Miller, Stella Artois, Heineken, Sapporo, Allied-Carlsberg, &c, not the regional and local micro-breweries.

Conditioning: Maturation of beer after it leaves the fermenter.

Copper: Synonym for a brew-kettle.

Copper finings: A substance, usually Irish Moss, added to the copper during the latter stages of the boil (after the last 15–30min) to aid the protein break, and improve the stability and clarity of the finished beer; as opposed to other finings added during he maturation stage.

Corn sugar: Sugar that is converted from corn starch by refining. **Syn:** glucose; dextrose.

Cream: The foam on beer.

Creamy: 1. Used to describe a thick and long-lasting head on beer. 2. Used to describe a full-bodied beer that has a rich and smooth texture.

DAB: The abbreviation of Dortmunder Aktien Brauerei. It is used on their bottle labels.

Das Gebräu (G): The brewery

Der Brauer (G): The brewer

Devil's Chapel: Medieval English term for an ale house.

Dextrins: The name given to non-fermentable or slowly fermentable sugars that remain in the wort after fermentation. Dextrins provide body and residual sweetness.

Diacetyl: A volatile compound produced by yeast during fermentation that produces a butterscotch flavour in beer.

Diätbier (G): Diet beer

Dolo: An unfiltered unhopped beer made in Africa from millet.

Doppelbock (G): In Germany, a lager brewed to at least ABV 7.5%. These are very easy to distinguish because the brand names always end in ator, eg, Maximator, Optimator and Salvator.

Dortmunder: A style of beer placed between Münchener and Pilsener. Darker than a Pilsener, but less malty than a Münchener. ABV @ 5.2%.

Downy mildew: A fungus, *Pseudoperonospora humuli,* that attacks hops. It was first observed in Japan in 1905 and in the USA in 1909.

Draught beer (spelt Draft beer in the USA): Beer served from casks or kegs rather than bottles or cans. It is best consumed within a week of brewing; one month maximum. **Syn:** Tap beer.

Dregs: The sediment at the bottom of a vessel.

Drop bright (E): is the stage in the conditioning process when yeast and other colloidals drop from suspention in the beer, leaving it bright (clear).

Dropping (E): is the method of transferring a liquid, by means of gravity, into another vessel underneath the first one.

Dry hopping: The practise of adding dry hops to the secondary fermenter or to the cask to add additional aroma, but not bitterness to finished beer.

Dry hops : Aromatic hops used to dry hop.

Dry malt: Malt in powdered form rather than as a syrup.

Dry Stout: Irish style Stout. It has more bitterness and alcohol than English Sweet Stout.

Dunkelbier (G): Dark beer

Dunnebier (G): Small beer

Easter Ale (E): a special Ale brewed for Easter festivities, in early England.

East Kent Goldings (E): an English hop variety with about a 6.5% alpha acid content.

EBU: European Bittering Unit; synonym for IBU, International Bittering Unit.

Effervescence: The fizz in beer caused by dissolved carbon dioxide gas coming out of solution.

Eisbock (G): the strongest Bockbier. This beer is made by bringing it the water's freezing point and then removing the resultant ice, thereby increasing the alcohol content of the remaining beer.

Entire (E): the original name for Porter.

Eroica: an Idaho- and Washington-grown hop variety with 10.5–11.5% Alpha Acid. Definitely a bittering hop.

Esters (E): volatile (easily evaporated) compounds that contribute to the fruity aromas and flavours of some beers. In some beer styles, these aromas and flavours are positive, in others, negative. They are formed during fermentation.

Estery (E): a term used to describe odours and flavours that are flowery, fruity or vegetal: apple, banana, pear, strawberry, &c.

Export (E & G): (on beer label): signifies a high-quality beer, usually with more alcohol; suitable for export. In Germany, a name for Dortmunder-style beer. In Belgium, the previous name (before 1974) for Category 1 beer. In Britain, a synonym for India Pale Ale, which was, obviously, exported to that country. Rarely used in the usa because it "might confuse" beer drinkers (If it is Export, what is it doing being on offer here, and if it was imported, why is it called Export?)

Enzyme (E): is any of various organic substances that are produced in plant and animal cells, and cause changes in other substances by catalytic (either speeding up or slowing down a chemical reaction) action; as pepsin is a digestive enzyme.

Faro: also called Faro-lambic. A Belgian beer made up of equal parts of high- and low-gravity beer. The mix is then sweetened with sugar and coloured with caramel. It is a near-extinct style.

Fermentation (E): put simply, the changes which take place when a saccharine (sugar) is exposed to the action of several fungi known commonly as yeast. The sugar is converted into carbonic acid (CO_2) and alcohol.

Festbier (G): in Germany, any special beer brewed for any special occasion or holiday.

Fining (E): the process of clarifying beer through the addition of fining agents.

Finings (E): Mineral or organic substances added to beer to clarify it. Finings cause impurities, yeast and other suspended matter to precipitate to the bottom of the fermenter or clearing tank, where it is separated from the beer. Some common fining agents are Bentonite, casein, charcoal, egg albumin, gelatin, Irish Moss, Isinglass, and wood chips.

Firkin (E): A beer cask with a capacity of about 41 litres (one-quarter barrel / 9 Imperial gallons).

Flash pasteurization (E): a procedure whereby the beer is pasteurized at a higher temperature, 160–175 °F (71–79°C), but for a shorter time (under one minute) than normal pasteurization.

Flat (E): said of a beer that has lost its carbonation.

Frambozenbier/Framboise: a lambic flavoured with raspberries.

Fructose (E): a sugar found in some fruit and in honey. It is 173% as sweet as sucrose, making it the sweetest of all sugars.

Frühjahrsbierfest (G): an annual München beer festival held on St Joseph's Day, 19 March.

Fruity (E): a term used to describe estery beers. Fruitiness can be a plus in some beer styles, a fault in others.

Fuggle (E): an English hop variety with a Alpha Acid content of 4.0–6.0%. This is one of the classic English hops.

Full-bodied (E): a term to describe a beer that is abundantly mouth-filling as opposed to beer that is thin and watery.

Galena (E): a Idaho- and Washington-grown variety of hop that is very bitter, with an alpha acid content of 12.5–13.5%.

Gassy (E): Said of beer with too much carbon dioxide gas.

Gerste (G): Barley

Gerstegraupen (G): Pearl barley or Scotch barley

Gerstekorn (G): Barley corn

Gerstensaft (G): Beer

Gerstenkorn (G): Barley kernel or seed

Gersteschleim (G): Barley water

Gerstezucker (G): Barley sugar

Glucose (E): A sugar formed in the wort by the yeast from maltose maltriose.

Goldings: An English hop, one of the most famous, with an alpha acid content of 2.8–5.0%. Some have stated alpha acid content of up to 8.0%, but this is wrong.

Goods: In brewerspeak, grist becomes goods when it is mixed with water in the mash tun.

Goudalier (F): Medieval north French name for a beer merchant.

Goût de jeune (F) (young taste): Phrase describing the rather unpleasant taste and odour of green beer.

Grains: Brewerspeak for spent goods.

Granny (E): Name given, in England, to a blend of Mild and old Ale.

Green beer (E): Fermented beer before it has been lagered or matured. If the wort is unhopped, at this stage it can be distilled into Scotch whisky.

Grist: The milled malt and adjuncts (if any)

load waiting to be put in the mash tun.

Gruit (other spellings: grut, gruyt, grug and gruz): A mixture of herbs and spices, used in Europe before being displaced by hops as the flavouring and bittering agent in beer. Gruit was made from aniseed, wild rosemary, caraway seed, coriander, cinnamon, coriander, ginger, juniper berries, milfoil, nutmeg, sweet gale and yarrow.

Gushing beer (E): Beer that is over-carbonated and foams out of the bottle when opened. It can be caused by bacterial contamination or over-priming. **Syn:** Wild beer.

Gyle: A particular batch of beer or brew; a charge of the mash tun.

Hag: Beer produced about 2000BC in Egypt. Also spelt: hek; hak.

Half and half: In Britain, a blend of two types of beer, eg, Ale and Porter; Ale and Stout; Bitter and Mild.

Hallertauer hops: A variety from the Hallertau region of Bayern containing 5.0–8.0% alpha acids.

Harsh: Term to describe beer that is overly astringent.

Head Brewer: Name for a Master Brewer.

Heavy beer: High-gravity beer.

Hefe (G): Yeast

Hefepilz (G): Yeast fungus

Hefig (G): Barmy, yeasty, yeast-like

Helles Bier (G): Light Beer

Hersbrücker (hops) (G): A German variety, also grown in Washington state, with an alpha acid content of around 5.0–6.5%.

High-gravity beer: Beer with a wort gravity of > OG 1047.

Hogshead: a 54gal cask.

Honey wine: Synonym for mead or pyment. Since this is not a product "from the vine", it is not a wine, but the term continues to be used.

Hopback: The vessel into which the wort is run after boiling. This allows the hops to settle and form a bed through which unwanted trub is filtered out.

Hop mould: The fungus Sphaerotheca macularis, that attacks hops. **Syn:** red mould; white mould; powdery mildew.

Hopfen (G): Hops used in beer

Hopfen und malz (G): Hops and malt

An ihm ist hopfen und malz vorloren (G): Literally, 'On him, hops and malt are lost'. Signifies a hopeless case.

Hopfenbau (G): Hop culture

Hopfebauer (G): Hop farmer (grower)

Hopfenernte (G): Hop picking

Hopfenstange (G): Hop pole. Also slang for a lanky person.

Hoppy: Said of beer that has predominant hop aromas and or taste characteristics.

Hops: Humulus lupulus, a perennial climbing vine.

Hot break: The coagulation and precipitation of proteins during the boiling stage of beer production.

Humlonaria: The name of the hop gardens at the Abbey St Denis (768AD).

Hydrometer: a clear glass or plastic instrument, consisting of a thin stem attached to a weighted float. Usually, inside the stem is a paper graduated into different scales (eg, original gravity, Balling, Plato) to read the specific gravity of liquids (as compared to water).

IBU (E): abbreviation for International Bittering Unit. **Syn:** EBU.

Imiak: the name of a home-brewed malt beer brewed in Greenland.

Imperial Russian Stout (E): an even higher-octane Russian Stout. It was brewed for the Russian Imperial Court until the 1917 communist coup d'etat).

IPA (E): the abbreviation for India Pale Ale. This is a style that has lost its meaning. It is a name some brewers give their Bitter Ales, but have no resemblance in alcohol strength to original IPAs.

Irish Moss: *Chondrus crispus*, a red seaweed, used to help clarify beer. It is usually added during the last 30min of the boil.

Isinglass: Fish gelatin processed from the swim bladders of sturgeon, carp, cod and ling, used to clarify beer.

Island Grog (E): a drink prepared adding 4oz powdered sugar and a shot of white rum to 12oz of Pilsenerbier. The concoction is heated to just short of boiling and then served hot.

Jetting machine (E): a machine used to automatically wash beer bottles.

Jungbukett (G): Unpleasant-smelling young beer.

Kaffir beer: A beer, fermented naturally by wild yeasts, made to different recipes in Sub-Saharan Africa. It was first brewed commercially in Salisbury, Rhodesia, in 1908. The beer is neither filtered or hopped.

Kaoliang beer: A style, made in China during the Song Dynasty (960–1278AD), from sorghum. Kaoliang is a Chinese word for sorghum, which is farmed in Sechouan Province.

Kiesel: a style of beer made in the Russian Republic and other Central European nations from rye and oats.

Kilderkin: An 18-gallon cask.

Klosterbräu (G): Abbey-brewed beer. Also, an Abbey brewery itself.

Kölschbier (G): A very pale ale brewed in the Bonn-Köln (Cologne) area of Germany. It is very hoppy with an ABV 4.6%.

Korma: also Corma and Kurmi; a beer brewed in ancient Egypt that was flavoured with ginger.

Kraeusen (G & E): the head of foam (often called "cauliflower" or "rocky") that forms on the surface of fermenting beer. It reaches its peak in four to seven days.

Kraeusening (E): a way of conditioning beer by adding a volume (15–20% of the total) of young, fermenting beer to fully-fermented beer that is lagering to make a second fermentation and natural carbonation.

Kulminator (G): one of the strongest beers in the world with ABV 13.2%. It is brewed at Kulmbach, (Nord Bayern) Germany.

Kupferstube (G): a copper-coloured lager brewed at Nürnberg (in Franconia), Germany. The roasted malts used helps impart the colour.

Kurunnu: in ancient Babylonia, a beer made from Spelt, an early type of wheat.

Lace (E): refers to the pattern the head of beer leaves down the inside of a glass as the level of beer is decreased by drinking. It is always taken as a good sign, and noted by beer judges.

Lactose (E): a non-fermentable sugar found in milk that is sometimes added to Porter, Stout and Brown Ale to add body and sweetness. Hence the milk can an the label of Mackeson's Stout.

Lagerbier; Lager beer (G&E): any of several bottom-fermenting beers. The style was founded in the 1840s, and is now the number one style of beer brewed worldwide. The exception is Great Britain where ale brewing predominates.

Lagering (E): the storing of beer. This applies to both Ales and Lagers, though it is where Lager beer took its name. The storage period can be anywhere from several weeks to a few years. It is synonymous with aging. The method originated in the Bayerische Alp in the 15th century where cold caverns were used for the purpose. Any prolonged period of storage may be referred to as lagering.

Last running(s) (E): the last and weakest of the wort that is filtered through the straining tank or its equivalents. The last runnings are used to make Schankbier (Germany) or Bière de table (France).

Lauter tun (E): A large tank which has a (false) slotted bottom and a drain spigot. The hot wort is strained down through the grains that settle on the false bottom. The grain act as a filter, removing precipitated protein and other particulate matter.

Lautering (E): from the German *lauter*, to clarify; the process of straining the sweet wort from the grains in the wort.

Lees (E): The sediment of bacteria, yeast and other solid matter that precipitates to the bottom of fermenting and storage vessels.

Li: A rice beer made in China circa 200BC, (Han Dynasty).

Light-and-Mild (E): In Great Britain, a 50/50 mix of Pale Ale and Mild Ale.

Light beer (E): 1. In America and Europe, a light-coloured beer, usually a Lager, as opposed to an Ale. **2.** In America, a low-calorie beer containing no dextrins, and having between 90 and 160 calories per 12oz. **3.** In America (and spreading to Europe), a low-alcohol beer containing ABV 2.8–4.0%.

Light-struck (E): a term used to describe the aroma and taste of a beer left exposed to sunlight too long. More common in clear- and green-bottled beers. Sunlight causes chemical reactions of hydrogen sulphide and other compounds of sulphur with isohumulones to form phenyl mercaptan. The latter is the cause of the skunky odour and taste. **Syn:** Sun-struck

Liquor: Brewerspeak for brewing water.

Loose hops (E): harvested, but untreated hop leaves that have been separated from the cones. **Syn:** Whole hops

Luda or ludi: a beer of ancient Ossetia in the Caucasus mountain region of Europe. The Ossetians are credited with having built, in Tappakallah, the largest (600l) beer tank in antiquity. It dates to 600 BC.

Maischbottich (G): mash tun

Maische (G): the mash.

Maichen (G): vt. mash.

Malt /Malz (E & G): processed barley grain. It is first steeped in water, then germinated by being spread across a floor, or in special boxes, or in rotating drums. Later, the grain is kiln-dried to convert the insoluble starch in it to soluble sugars. Malt is qualified by its protein content which preferably should be below 12.8%, its starch content, which should be as high as possible, and its germinative power, which should be greater than 98%.

Malt tannins: Tannins from the husks of barley malt.

Malzbier (G): An aromatic, dark, low alcohol

(ABV 0.5–1.5%). sweet beer It was initially brewed for children and nursing mother's, but now it is enjoyed by many.

Malzdarre (G): malt kiln

Malzer (G): Maltster

Malzerei (G): Malt house

Märzenbier (G): A style beer that was originally, before modern refrigeration, brewed in March. It was strong enough to survive the warm summer. Today Märzenbiers have an ABV of around 4.5%.

Wienbier (Vienna beer) and Märzenbier are enough similar that the terms are often used interchangeably.

Maturation (E): The aging process for beer, which improves its quality. During maturation, yeast settle out, and the beer acquires mellower, smoother characteristics than would otherwise be the case. Lagers are stored at near zero Fahrenheit. Ales are stored at 40–45°F (4.4–7.2°C).

Mealie beer: A South African style brewed from maize or millet.

Mellow: A word used to describe a smooth, sweet soft-tasting beer.

Metallic: A word used to describe beer with an undesirable taste of metal.

Méthod Champegnoise (F): A technique of secondary fermentation in the bottle, used primarily in Belgium and France; after the method of conditioning champagne.

Mild (E): A word used to describe a smooth, well-balanced beer that lacks roughness and excessive bitterness.

Mild Ale: Meaning "not bitter". A light- to medium-bodied ale in Britain, as compared to Bitter. It is usually dark brown, lightly hopped, and therefore sweet, with a low ABV of 3.0–3.6%.

Mother-in-Law: An equal mixture of Bitter and Stout.

Münchenerbier (G): An other of the great European Lager styles, brewed since the mid-19th century at Munich in Bavaria. Originally a dark beer, it has been surplanted by the Helles style first introduced in 1928 by the Paulaner-brauerei.

Natural conditioning: A secondary fermentation which happens in the maturation tank. At this stage the beer still has live yeast cells.

Nidaba: The Babylonian goddess of beer.

Nin Ka Si: The Sumerian goddess of beer. Also spelt as one word.

Nog: A strong East Anglian beer.

Northern Brewer hops: Grown in Kent, England, Oregon and Washington state. Alpha acid content of between 8.5 and 11.0%.

Nose: A word used to describe the overall aroma, bouquet and fragrance of a beer.

Nugget hops: A high bittering variety grown in Oregon. Alpha acid content of 9.5–13.0%.

Oatmeal: ground oats

Obergärig (G): top-fermented beer; ale

Off-flavour: Synonymous with aged, oxidized and stale flavours.

Off-scent: Grassy, musty, sour and stale scents (as appropriate for style) in beer.

OG: Original Gravity (abbreviation for)

Old Boy: An 18th century English name for Strong Ale.

Ordre du Houblon: An order founded in 1409 by the duke of Burgundy, Jean Sans Peur. It honoured those brewers who used hops in their beers.

Pa-e-bi: The official brewer of the royal court ant family in Mesopotamia (3000BC).

Pale Ale: The bottled version of Bitter. Original gravity of Pale Ale is (roughly) 1043–1053.

Parti-gyle: Applies when an entire range of beers are made from the same recipe, or from the same mash, the only difference being the amount of water added to the fermentation vessel.

P'ei: A style of beer popular in China during the Tang Dynasty (618–907AD).

Perle hops (G): A variety grown in Germany with an alpha acid content of 7.0–8.5%, and in Oregon with an alpha acid content of 9.0–11.0%. The latter is definitely a bittering variety.

Pilsener (bier): An other of the classic European styles. This originated in the Czech Republic (Bohemian) city of Plzen. Pilsener Urquell is the original type and the brewery copyrighted the name in 1898. Alcohol volume is around 5.0%. It is highly hopped and very light-coloured. **Also:** Pilsner, Pils.

Pin: A 4.5gal cask.

Pitching: The act of adding the yeast to the wort in the fermentation vessel

Pito beer: A style brewed in Nigeria from malted sorghum.

Pivo (CZ): Czech for Beer.

Piwo: Polish and Russian for Beer.

Pombé beer: A style made in Guinea from millet.

Poperinge hops: A variety from Flanders.

Poperinge Hoppefeesten: A festival held every third year at Poperinge, Belgium.

Porter beer: A bitter, very dark, moderately alcoholic ale first brewed in 1730 by a Mr Harwood at London.

Precipitation: A process where proteins and other impurities coagulate and sink in the brewing vessel, fermenting tanks and conditioning tanks.

Pricked beer: Beer that has turned sour or vinegary.

Priming: The process of adding, just before bottling, fermentable sugars, eg, maltose, corn sugar or corn syrup, to induce a secondary fermentation in the bottle or cask.

Provisie: A Belgian Brown Ale, aged from between two to twenty-five years. It is brewed in Oudenaarde. ABV is around 6.0%.

Rack, vt (E): To move, most often by hoses or metal lines, beer from one brew vessel to another. This is a necessity, but an added side result is that unwanted sediment is left behind at the bottom of the first vessel.

Racking back: The tank in which green beer is held for a brief period before it is transferred to barrels.

Real Ale: Beer that has been naturally conditioned in a cask, compared to pasteurized, filtered keg beer. It is best served at cellar temperature (56°F), NOT at room temperature as is often thought.

Rousing (E): The act of thoroughly stirring or agitating beer in a fermentation tank to aid fermentation by increasing the amount of oxygen in the wort, which encourages rapid yeast reproduction.

Run off (E): The act of emptying a vessel, most usually the mash tun.

Russ (G): name in German for a mix of Weizenbier and Lemonade.

Rye: the grain *Secale cereale*.

Sazz hops: A variety grown in the Bohemia, Czech Republic. Alpha acid content is 6.5–8.6%. It is one of the most ideal hops for brewing Pilsener.

Sahti beer: A style brewed in Suomi-Finland from barley and rye malts. It is flavoured with juniper berries as well as hops. It is strained through straw to clarify. ABV can range as high as 12.5%.

Saint Arnuf (F): The patron saint of brewers. He was born in Chateau d'Lay-Saint-Christophe north of Nancy in 580 AD. Also spelt: Arnou, Arnoul; Arnould; Arnold; Arnoldus.

Schankbier (G): thin beer (ABV 0.5–2.6%). In some regards it is comparable with Bière de table.

Scotch Ale: Originally of Scottish origin, but now also brewed in Belgium and France. Traditionally, Scotch Ales are very strong, ABV 7.0–8.0%, dark brown, and very malty.

Secondary fermentation: The slower stage of fermentation carried out after the beer has been racked from the primary fermentation tank. This second fermentation lasts from a few weeks to many months or even years depending on the style and strength of the beer.

Shandy (E): a ladies' drink that is a mix of ale and lemonade, ginger or ginger ale in England. It is sometimes called a Lemon Shandy.

Shive: A wood bung with a penetrable centre core, which is fitted to beer casks. A porous wood peg, called a spile, is driven through the centre to vent the cask.

Shu beer: A millet-based style brewed in China during the Han Dynasty (200 BC).

Sikaru: This might possibly be the oldest name man has given to beer. It was used in Mesopotamia 8000–4000 BC. The ancients in this region brewed sixteen styles of beer, ranging from light to dark. Some were made with barley, some with spelt, and some from a combination of the two. The name continued in use until about 562 BC.

Skimming: The act of removing excess yeast from the surface of the wort during fermentation.

Small beer: A diluted, weak beer. This beer used to be made from the last washing of the grains. The resultant runoff was captured and made into beer the same as the strong first running.

Sor: The Hungarian word for Beer.

Sparging (E): The act of flushing any remaining sugars from the goods in the mash tun.

Spatenwasser (water) (G): World famous water from the Spatenbrauerei's artesian wells.

Special beers: All beers produced by spontaneous fermentation with wild yeast.

Speltz (G), Spelt (E): Triticum spelta, a primitive variety of wheat. It is grown to some extent in Germany and Switzerland. It is intermediate between barley and wheat.

Spund (G): bung, plug, spigot

Spunden , spünden (G): to bung (casks)

Square: A rectangular vessel.

Stammkneipe (G): Favourite drinking place

Stammgast (G): Regular customer/patron

Stammlocal (G): a habitual watering hole; favourite pub.

Stammtisch (G): A table in a drinking establishment reserved for regulars or cronies

Starch (E): is a white, tasteless odourless food substance found in potatoes, cereals, yams, peas, and many other foods: it is a granular solid; chemically a complex carbohydrate ($C_6 H_{10} O_5$).

Starkbier (G): Strong beer: (ABV 5.1–10.0%)

Sterile beer (E): beer which has no living organisms because they have been either destroyed or filtered out.

Stillage (E): A structure, usually of brick, metal or wood, which supports the casks in the cellar of a pub.

Styrian Goldings hops: A variety grown in the ex-Yugoslavia. Alpha acid content is 6.0–8.0%.

Sucellus (L): The name the ancient Gauls gave their god of brewing.

Sugar (E): any of a class of sweet, soluble, crystalline carbohydrates, as the disaccharides (sucrose, lactose, and maltose) and monosaccharides (glucose and fructose).

Sweet wort: The wort from the mash tun before it has been boiled.

Talisman hops (E): a hop variety grown in Washington state. It contains 7.5–9.0% alpha acid, ranking it is a bittering hop.

Talla beer: An Ethiopian style brewed with roasted barley, maize and/or millet. It is flavoured with twigs and leaves of a native tree.

Tango: French; a mixture of pale beer and Grenadine syrup.

Tankard (E): a beer-drinking vessel used since the Middle Ages in Northern Europe. Tankards are usually tall and have a hinged lid (sometimes removable), and a single handle.

Tannin (Tannic Acid) (E): any one of a group of organic compounds found in grains and other plants, hops included. The tannins in hops help in the precipitation of protein during both the Hot Break and Cold Break of the wort. Tannin is mostly found in the brachts and stigs of hop cones. It imparts an astringent taste to beer. On the other hand, tannin from barley grain, which is found in the husks, constitutes the majority of tannin in wort. Chemically they are different from hop tannin.

Taproom (E): a separate room in a tavern where beer is served.

Target hops (Wye) (E): Developed by Wye College, in Kent, England, this variety has a high Alpha Acid content (10–11%), and is resistant to most powdery mildew strains and verticillum wilt. Today it is Britain's most important hop. It accounts for nearly 35% of that country's total hop crop.

Tavern (E), Taverne (G): Prior to 1635, in England, taverns were owned by vintners who were allowed, by law, to serve only wine. After that date, the sale of beer, food and tobacco was permitted. In more recent times, a place where only beer was sold, and women were not permitted.

Tettnanger hops (G): a Southern German variety grown in the Bodensee region. It contains 7.0–8.0% alpha acids, and it is used as both a boil hop and an aromatic hop. A North American version is grown in Idaho, Oregon and Washington states. The North American varieties have 4.0–6.5% alpha acids.

Thin (E): a description of a beer lacking sufficient body or fullness of palate.

T'ien tsiou: a Chinese beer made from millet that dates to 2000BC. It is a green or young beer not completely clarified or fermented. Tsiou is the clarified, fully-fermented version

Trub (E): the particulate matter in wort. It is composed of long protein chains, hop oils and tannins, which precipitate during the Hot and the Cold Breaks. It includes yeast that settle out during fermentation. The wort is separated from it between primary and secondary fermentation, and again between secondary and packaging.

Tun (E): a large vessel (usually metal) for holding liquids.

Tunnel pasteurization (E): a technique for pasteurizing bottled and canned beer by passing the containers through a machine that sprays hot water on them (60°C for 20min). Then cold water is used to cool them. Two thousand to six thousand bottles or cans are passed through the machine per hour.

"Two penny" (E): a small beer sold in 18th century England for two pennies per pint.

Ullage: The space at the top of a bottle, cask or keg between the beer and the top of the vessel. **Syn:** headspace.

Untergärig (G): Bottom fermented beer

Ur-(G): A prefix meaning Original.

Urtyp (G): Original Type, designating the source of a beer style, eg, Ur-Bock would designate Einbeck as the source of the Bockbier style.

Vat: Synonym for Tun. A large vessel for holding liquids.

Venting: The act of releasing excess carbon dioxide from a cask of beer prior to serving.

Vienna beer: An amber-coloured Lager first brewed in Vienna. It is made distinctive because of the unique malts from that region. Now the style is brewed in Mexico and South America, though the style is being revived in its homeland. It is similar to Märzenbier.

Vollbier (G): Full beer (ABV 3.0–4.5%). One of the three legal styles of beer in Germany.

v/v (always lowercase): Alcohol content by volume. Abbreviation for volume per volume, ie, the percentage volume of alcohol in the total volume of beer.

Weeping barrel: Term for a leaking wooden barrel or cask.

Weissbier (G): A generic term for Wheat Beer. Also spelt Weisse Bier.

Weizenbock (G): A wheat beer of Bock strength, ie, ABV < 6.25%.

Weize Oktoberfesten: In Belgium, a beer festival held since 1956. It runs from 30 September to 15 October.

Wild yeast (E): any air-borne yeast; any yeast other than that introduced by the brewer.

Willamette hops (E): a variety of the English Fuggles hop, with a slightly higher alpha acid (5–6%) content, and yield per hectare. It is grown in Oregon.

Wort: The state of beer just before the yeast has been added and fermentation begins. At this stage, it has been boiled and hops have been added.

w/v (always lowercase): Alcohol content by weight. Abbreviation for weight per volume.

Yeast (E): a white, tan or yellow, frothy substance consisting of a mass of minute fungi which germinate and multiply in the presence of starch or sugar, and form alcohol and carbon dioxide, and many chemical compounds, during a process of fermentation, induced by an enzyme: used in making beer, wine and as a leavening (rising) agent in baking; any of a family of fungi, Saccharomyceta-ceae, that form yeast. It is available in dried form from several makers, and often used by homebrewers.

Yeast bite(E): a sour, bitter taste in beer caused by yeast. Not to be confused with hops bitterness.

Yorkshire Stone Square (E): a 36hl capacity open fermentation tank. Originally it was made of stone, and later, particularly, of slate. The stone square is unique to the town of Tadcaster, Yorkshire, home of Samuel Smiths Brewery.

Zitos: Beer, in modern Greek.

Zuckerpilz (G): sugar fungus, a name given, around 1837, to yeast by Herren Kützing and Schwann.

Zymology (Gr): the science of the study of fermentation.

Zythos (Gr): an ancient Greek name for Barley Wine, borrowed from the Egyptians.

Zythum (Gr): a Pharonic Egyptian name for Barley Wine or beer. It was brewed in the Nile river delta.

African Beer Production—1991

(In ,000 hectolitres) One hectolitre = 26.42 US gallons

Republic of South Africa	22,500
Nigeria	8,386
Cameroun	3,965
Kenya	3,300
Zaire	3,000
Zimbabwe (Rhodesia)	2,800
Ruanda-Burundi	1,600
Cote d'Ivoire	1,095
Gabon	900
Zambia	900
Tanzania	667
Morocco	625
Ghana	602
Congo (Brazza)	600
Namibia	556
Togo	550
Maurice-Reunion	505
Egypt	500
Angola	499
ex-Ethiopia	460
Burkina Fasso	400
Tunisia	400
Mozambique	372
Algeria	321
Uganda	247
Madagascar	236
Central African Republic	222
Senegal	150
Chad	110
Liberia	50
Others	1,982
Total Africa	58,500

Source: UGBF

Asian Beer Production—1991

(In 000 hectolitres) One hectolitre = 26.42 US gallons

China	80,000
Japan	67,990
South Korea	16,400
Philippines	15,400
Taiwan	4,501
Turkey	3,000
Thailand	2,880
India	2,010
Hong Kong	1,378
Malaisia & Singapore	1,342
Indonesia	1,195
Vietnam	1,000
North Korea	1,000
Israel	533
Cyprus	340
Iran	200
Iraq	100
Syria	90
Sri Lanka	68
Jordan	60
Lybia	40
Others	194
Asian Total	199,721

Source: UGBF

European Beer Production—1991
(In ,000 hectolitres) One hectolitre = 26.42 US gallons

Deutschland (Germany)	118,000
Great Britain	60.843
CEI (Russia)	50.000
España (Spain)	26,447
ex-Czechoslovakia	23,855
France	22.880
The Netherlands	19.893
Belgium	13.799
Poland	12,000
Italy	10,699
Österreich (Austria)	10.188
ex-Yugoslavia	10.000
Romania	9,727
Hungary	9,352
Denmark	8.700
Portugal	6.882
Bulgaria	5,500
Sweden	5.240
Ireland	4.870
Suomi-Finland	4.275
Switzerland	4,183
Greece	3.500
Norway	2,236
Lituania	1.715
Luxembourg	542
Malta	170
Albania	100
Iceland	61
Total Europe	445,687

New World Beer Production—1991

(In 000 hectolitres) One hectolitre = 26.42 US gallons

The United States	237,283
Brazil	65,000
Mexico	40,753
Colomia	24,000
Canada	22,135
Venezuela	12,900
Argentina	8,300
Peru	6,400
Cuba	3,000
Chile	3,000
Equador	1,750
Bolivia	1,450
Dominican Republic	1,400
Guatemala	1,300
Paraguay	1,280
Panama	1,100
Jamaica	850
El Slavador	760
Honduras	758
Costa Rica	740
Uruguay	710
Puerto Rico	690
Trinidad	600
Nicaragua	400
Guyanas	130
Martinique	65
Guadaloupe	30
Others	669
American Total	437,453

Oceana Beer Production—1991
(In OOO hectolitres) One hectolitre = 26.42 US gallons

Australia	19,000
New Zealand	3,700
Others	945
Total Oceana	23,645

Source: UGBF

International Beer Industry Figures

(First four columns are in 1,000s Hl: Consumption per capita is in litres)

Country	Production	Consumption	Exports	Imports	Cnsmptn/capita
Australia	19,155	18,619	812.6	104.3	108.20
Osterreich (Austria)	10,184		807.0	290.0	123.70
Belgium	13,799	11,113	3,145.0	458.0	112.00
Canada	22,135	20,353	2,446.9	663.9	72.00
ex-Czechoslovakia	20,579	18,834	1,752.9	8.4	120.80
Denmark	9,672	6,490	2,560.0	16.2	125.90
Suomi-Finland	4,408	4,276	142.6	63.4	85.50
France	20,991		1,017.0	2,906.0	40.50
Deutschland (Germany)	117,993	113,871	6,755.0	2,809.0	142.70
Hong Kong	1,368	1,647	201.0	493.0	29.00
Hungary	9,302	10,649		1,120.0	
Italy	10,699	13,010	164.6	2,476.0	22.49
Japan	68,583	68,944	315.0	1,003.0	55.60
Korea	15,830	15,693	177.1	3.6	36.30
Mexico	41,279	38,703	2,050.6	171.5	47.00
The Netherlands	19,893	13,639	7,024.6	770.6	90.50
New Zealand	3,626	3,720	137.0	145.9	110.77
Norway	2,269	2,253	17.8	2.3	52.80
Portugal	6,882	6,632	376.7	130.7	67.30
South Afrika	23,000	22,465	525.0	10.0	57.80
Sweden	4,738	5,244	30.8	506.4	61.00
Espana (Spain)	26,447	27,590	265.0	408.0	70.70
Taiwan	4,544	4,731	1.7	178.5	22.82
United Kingdom	57,359	60,845	1,842.4	5,328.5	105.70
The United States	237,283	221,043	2,776.0	9,300.9	87.80
Venezuela	15,179	15,105	110.0	35.6	74.50

Per capita beer consumption
1986–1989–1990
(in litres)

Country	1986	1989	1990
Deutschland (Germany)	146.0	142.9	143.1
GDR (ex- East Germany)	142.0	145.7	141.3
ex-Czechoslovakia	133.0	131.8	135.0
Denmark	126.0	123.4	126.2
Luxembourg	119.0	119.3	121.4
Österreich (Austria)	119.0	119.3	121.3
Belgium	120.0	115.0	121.0
Ireland	105.0	115.6	117.0
New Zealand	121.0	116.8	110.8
United Kingdom	108.0	110.4	110.2
Australia	111.0	111.6	108.2
Hungary	99.0	103.0	107.0
The United States	91.0	88.6	90.8
The Netherlands	86.0	87.5	90.0
Suomi-Finland	65.0	79.4	83.5
Canada	82.0	80.6	
España (Spain)	60.0	71.7	71.8
Switzerland	69.0	69.3	69.8
Bulgaria	64.0	70.3	66.8
Portugal	38.8	63.8	65.1

Source: Wolrd Drink Trends

Per person annual consumption

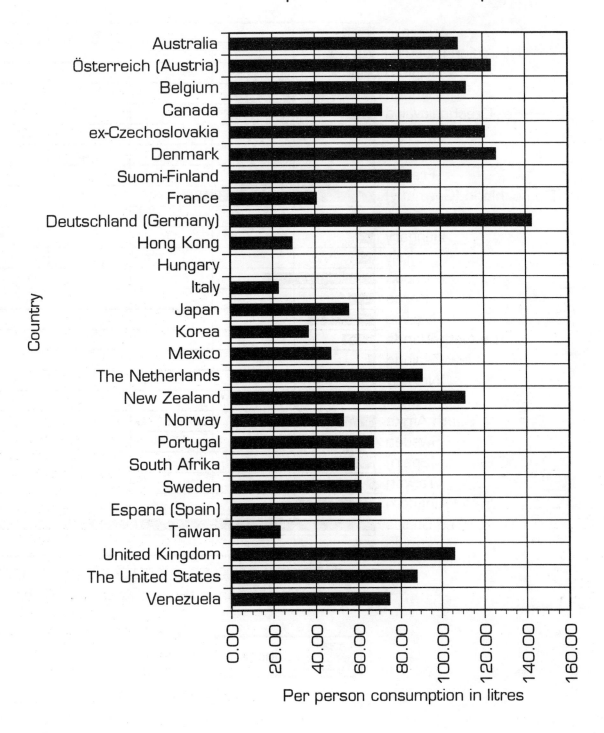

Per person consumption in litres

Country

| | Cnsmptn/capita |

Production of largest beer-producing countries

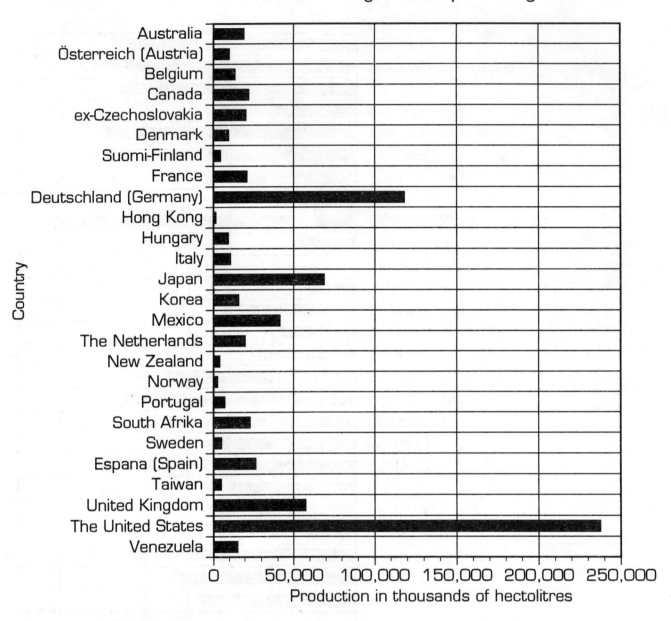

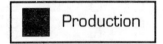
Production

Aa

Abbaye..............................117, *See also* Abbey
Abbaye de Notre-Dame-de-Scourmont...........116
Abbey and Holyrood breweries.....................101
Abbey beers.......................................122
Abbey St Denis......................................39
Abbey St Germain des Prés...........................39
Abbeye de St Sixte.................................116
Abbeye Notre Dame de St Rémy......................116
Abdij........................117, *See also* Abbey
Abdij Koningshoeven.........................116, 118
Abtei........................117, *See also* Abbey
Accra Brewery.......................................67
Achaemenid Persians................................23
Adelscott...153
Adelscott Noir....................................153
Adelshoffen.......................................153
Adirondack Lager...................................46
adjuncts.....................................1, 3, 12
Aecht Schlenkeria Rauchbier Märzen.............152
Affligem.....................................116, 117
African brewers.....................................2
Akershus Bryggeri..................................93
Akkad...104
Al-Chark Brewery (Syria)..........................106
Alaska..140
Albra (Heineken)...................................87
Albra Group..99
alcohol...2
alcohol content....................................13
Ale...144
Ale Boks..151
ale-conner...37
Alexander the Great................................23
Alfa...99
Alkoholfrei.......................................145
Allah..30
Allied Breweries...............................68, 99
Allied-Tetley..................................83, 88
Alloa...101
Allsopp...120
alpha acids...7
Alsace..153
Altbier......................................117, 139
America......................................119, 120
American Can Company...............................17
American Homebrewers Association...................10
American Lager....................................126
American Steam Beers..............................118
Amstel.....................................98, 99, 105
Amstel Lager.......................................73
Anchor Brewery.....................................94
Anchor Porter.....................................124
Anchor Steam Beer.................................139

Anchor Steam Beer Brewery.........................140
ancient peoples of the Mediterranean..............24
Anglican Church....................................38
Anheuser-Busch.....................42, 45, 88, 110
Ann Street Brewery................................102
Anniversary Beers.................................130
Antarctica Paulista................................48
Antwerp..81
Antwerp Province..................................116
Arcen...153
Arcen Brewery.....................................129
Arcen's Oerbock...................................128
Arcener Stout.....................................153
Arcener Winterbier................................129
Archbishop Laud....................................38
Argentina..38
Arkells..96
Arnulf, Bishop of Metz.............................86
aroma characteristics...............................2
aromas, skunky......................................6
Artrois (Motte-Cordonnier).........................87
Asahi Breweries Ltd................................55
Asahi Brewing Company.............................142
Assyria...104
Assyrians..23
Augustin..117
Augustiner-Bräu Wagner.............................88
Augustus Ceasar....................................31
Austin, Texas.....................................134
Australia...........................4, 107, 108
Australian national brewers........................12
Austria-Hungary....................................93
Austrian brewers...................................90
Austro-Hungarian Empire.......................33, 80
autumn harvest....................................130
Aying, Bayern.....................................133
Azores...94

Bb

Babylonia...104
Babylonians..30
Bacterial infection.................................1
Bad Köstritz......................................148
Baden-Württemberg.................................133
Baleares Islands, the..............................95
Ballantines Old India Pale Ale....................121
Bamberg...152
Barley..2
barley..1
barley malt...................................1, 134
barley, roasted..................................2, 4
Barleywine..126
Bass....................................82, 102, 120
Bass Ale...11

Bass Brewery 41
Bass Brewery Museums 121
Bass, William 11
Batemans Brewery 96
Battin Brewery 98
Bavarian 147
Bavarian Weizenbier 1
Bayerisch Wheats 132
Bayern 36, 93, 133, 147
Beamish 126
Beamish and Crawfords 91
Beamish Irish Stout 126
Becks 2, 88
Beechwood chips 152
beer engines 17
Beer Line 35, 79
beer purity law .... 2, See also Reinheitsbegot
Beer Purity Laws 140
beer styles, hybrids 113
beer, clarification 13
beer, premium .... 147, See also Export
Beer, Smoked 153
Belgian 122
Belgian beer styles 115
Belgian beers, boiling time 7
Belgian Bière de table 141
Belgian Christmas beer 129
Belgian fruit beers 1
Belgian monastic orders 116
Belgian speciality beers 154
Belgian styles 117
Belgian Tripple 140
Belgian wheat beers 3
Belgian Wit (white) Bier 1
Belgian Wit beers 2
Belgian Wits 132
Belgium... 2, 4, 6, 14, 24, 32, 33, 40, 88, 92, 107, 114, 115, 116, 117, 125, 129, 130, 131, 132, 138, 154
Belhaven 125
Berlin 132, 133
Berliner Weisse 1, 132, 133
Best Bitter 119
Bière blanche 135
Bière de Garde 87, 126
Bière de Table 138
Bière Régab 67
Big Lamp Brewery 118
Bios Brewery 126
Birthday Beers 130
Bishopric of Freising 39
Bitburger 148
Bitter 118, 119, 139
Bitter, English .... 140, See also Pale Ale

black malt 143
Bligh, Captain 4
Blue Nile Brewery 74
Bock 97, 143
Bock, blond 152
Bockbier 36, 90, 134, 143, 149
Bockbier, German 150
Bockbiere 149
Böckling of Neudenau 89
Bocks 128
Bohemia 33, 79, 80
Boise Valley 39
Bok Ale 140
Bok Ales 128
Bokbiers 151
Bonn 118
Bornem 117
Borsod 90
Brabant 81
Brahma group 48
Brand 98
Brand Duppelbock 151
Brassee a Dakar par Sibras 72
Brasserie Nationale 98
Brasserie Cantillon 130, 136, 137
Brasserie Diekirch 98
Brasserie du Bocq 130
Brasserie Dupont 130
Brasserie Nouvelle de Lutéce 146
Brasserie Simon 98
Brasseries du Logone 65
Brasseries du Pêcheur 87
Brauerei Ayinger 133
Brauhaase 73
Braunschweig 36
Bremen 33, 36
Breslau 93
brewers' guilds 32
Britain 17, 24, 40, 88, 94, 108
British Ale 34
British Barley Wines 129
British Museum 19
British Oak Brewery 127
Brooklyn Lager 46
Brouwerij Huyghe 132
Brouwerij Lindemans 136
Brown Ale 120
Brown Ales 128
Brugse Tripel 117
brune de Paris 145
Brussels 1, 33, 130, 136, 137
bsn Bières 87
Budapest 80
Budwar Brewery 82

Budweiser 46, 58, 142
Budweiser Budvar 96
Burton Abbey 11
Burton IPA 120
Burton Porter 124
Burton upon Trent 11, 12
Burton upon Trent 11
Burton-style ale 13

Cc

Cacador brewery 48
California Common Beer..................... 140
California Common Beer............... 140, 141, 144
Canary Islands 95
Canstatt 88
Canstatter Wasen.............................. 88
Captain Cook Brewery........................ 109
Caramelized malt 3
Carling 44, 99
Carling Black Label 73
Carlsberg 59, 69, 83, 88
Carlsberg Brewery 15
Carlsberg Foundation 83
Carlsberg Laboratories........................ 83
Carlsberg, the new brewery.................. 83
Carlsberg, tho old brewery 83
Carlsberg-Tetley 102
Carlton and United........................... 107
Carlton Brewery 107
Carthage... 23
Cascade Brewery 108
Cascade Hops .... **142**, *See also* **Hops**
cask.. 118
Cask-conditioned beer......................... 17
cassava flour 2
Castle Lager 73
Castle Milk Stout 73
Castletown Brewery........................... 102
Catamount...................................... 124
Catherine (The Great) 95
ccc 95
Ceasar, Julius................................... 86
Celis Brewery 134
Celtic tribesmen 30
Celts... 24
Centennial events 130
Central Europe............................. 39, 42
Ceres, Roman Goddess of Agriculture 8
Ceylon Breweries 59
Challenger Hops........ 127, *See also* Hops, English
Champagne du Nord 132
Champagne of the Spree 132
Champion Beer of Britain 120
Charlemagne.................................... 86

Charles I 38
chemical fertilizers 2
Cherry Stouts................................... 131
Chevalier barley 2
Chihuahua 47
Chimay.. 116
China 38, 55, 56
Christian Crusaders........................... 105
Christian Church 31
Christmas 128, 130
Christmas Ales................................. 129
Church was England 31
Cluster Hops.................... **142**, *See also* Hops
Coburg 139
Code of Botanical Nomenclature (icbn)............. 8
Codex Alimentarius............................ 80
Collins, Nat 14
Columbus 1492................................ 46
Commonwealth Brewery...................... 17
Companhia União Fabril Portuense 94
Confederation of Belgian Brewers (CBB)........... 33
Constantinople................................ 103
Continental Dark 124
Cook, Captain rn 108
Coor... 99
Coors.................................. 42, 45, 46
Coors Brewery 41
Coors Light 140
Corn/maize...................................... 3
Corona 47
Corsendonk Agnus 117
Corvey Abbey sur le Wesser 39
Courage's Imperial Stout...................... 94
Crimea 35
Crombé Brouwerij 138
Crombé's Oud Kriekenbier 6
Crown Brewery 58
crystal malt...................................... 3
Cuauhtétemoc 47
cuneiform....................................... 19
cuneiform tablets.............................. 19
Cuvée de l'Ermitage........................... 117
Czech Republic 4, 33, 96, 107
Czech Republic 39
Czechoslovakia, the ex-....... 6, 81, *See also* Czech Republic

Dd

Damm brewery group (Spain) 95
Dampfbier 139
Danube River Basin 25
Darby, Dr Peter 4
Dark Ages 31
Dark beer 40
Davis, Moss 109
De Arsense Bierbrouwerij 153
De Dolle Brouwers 129
De Kluis Brouwerij 134
De Kluis Brouwerij van Hoegaarden 132
De Kroon's Bierbrouwerij 151
Delirium Tremens 132
Denmark 83, 84, 92, 100
Die Biere Deutschlands 113, 145
Dietrich Höllhuber 145
Dinant 116
Dock Street 46
Doemans Schule 33
Dominion Breweries 109
Don, Ken 110
Doppelbocks 150
Dorber, Mark 121
Dortmund 11, 12, 33, 147
Dortmund Export 12
Dortmund-style 147
Dos Equis 47, 149
Douai 146
Double Diamond 11
Dreher brewing concern 99
Dreher, Anton 80, 83, 91
Dry hops 6
Dubbelbok 151
Dudley 127
Duke William IV of Bavaria 36
Dunkelweizen 133
Dunkles 150
Dunkles (Darks) 147
Düsseldorf 117, 139
Dutch 60, 150
Dutch breweries 118
Dutch gin distillers 93
Duvel 122
Duyck Brewery 126
Duyck, Felix .... 126, *See also* Jenlain

Ee

East African Breweries 68
East African Breweries Ltd 68, 74
East Anglia 33
East Block 33
Easter 130
Eastern Balts 84

Eastern Brewery Company 104
Eckhardt, Fred 113
Edinburgh 101, 125
Egypt 28
Egypt of the Pharaohs 29
Egyptians 6, 34, 105
Einbeck 36, 149
Einbecker Ur-Bock 149
Einfachbier 145
Eis 150
EKU Kulminator 150
EKU–28 97
Eldridge Pope Brewery 13
Emperor Sigismund 36
England 4, 6, 7, 11, 36, 37, 41, 118, 123, 125
English Ales 154
English Bullion 123
English Mild 141
Erding, Bayern 134
Erdinger Weissbräu 134
Erste Kulmbacher Union (EKU) 97
Esen-Duiksmuide 129
Estonians 84
Euphrates River Valley 27
Europe 144
Export 147
Extra Special Bitter 119
Extra Strong Dark Ales 122

Ff

Falken brewery 96
Far East 31
Faro 136, 137
Fäßer 149
Feldschlössen brewing group 97
Filtration systems 12
Fining agents 13
Finland, Suomi 3, 4, 35, 92, 96, 97
Finnish Peninsular 35
Fischer Brewery 153
Flanders 6, 126, 129
Foreign Export Stout 73
Foreign Extra Stout 59
Forschungsbrauerei München 88
Fosters 99
Fosters Lager 107
Fountain Brewery 101
Framboise 130
France 24, 32, 100, 116, 125, 129, 145
Franks 86
Fraser & Neave 59
Fred Eckhardt 130
French beers 126
French brewers 12

Friedrich the Great 89
Frobes Ales 122
Fruit Beers 81, 137
Fruit Lambics 136
Frydenlund Brewery 93
Fuggles 6, 7, 123
Fuggles Hops .... 127, *See also* Hops, English
Fuller's ESB 119
FX Matt Brewing Company 46

Gg
Gabriel Sedlmayr 147
Gabriel Sedlmyer Spaten-Franziskaner-Bräu 88
Galena 7
Galena Hops 120
Galicia 93
Gambrinus .... 81, *See also* Primus, Jan
Gambrinus Brewery 107
Gauls 86
General Investment Company 105
George Bateman & Son Ltd 129
German 144
German beer 36
German brewers 2, 7, 33, 131
German brewing methods 38
German Export beer 147
German immigrant brewers 42
German immigrants 144
Germanic tribes 35
Germans, North 147
Germany .2, 6, 11, 12, 13, 14, 24, 32, 33, 35, 36, 37, 42, 81, 92, 93, 107, 118, 125, 132, 141, 147, 148, 152
Germany, East .... 140, *See also* Germany
Glasgow 101
gods of the Babylonians and Egyptians 30
Gold Rush 140
Goldings 6
Goldings hops 123, 126
Good Beer Guide to Belgium and Holland 128, 138
Goodhead, Job 120
Gordon's Highland Scotch 125
Gösser Bräu 80
Gottfried Krueger Brewing Company 17
Graetzerbier 133
grains 1, 2
grains, torrefied 12
Grand Cru 134
Grand Place/Grote Markt 33
Great Britain 120, 123, 127, 128, 139, 144
Great British Beer Festival 120
Great Depression 30
Greece 97

Greek cultural influences 103
Greeks 30, 34
Grimbergen 117
Grimbergen Dubbel 117
Grolsch 15
Grolsch Brewery 118
Grolsche 99
Grolsche Brewery 99
Guernsey Brewing Company (1920) Ltd 102
Gueux 137
Gueuze 130, 137
Gueuze Museum 137
Guilds 33
Guinness 59, 73, 126
Guinness Book of Records 1
Guinness Extra Stout 7
Guinness Foreign Export Stout 70
Guinness Stout 126
Gulder International 67
Gulph, Ontario 44
Guney Biracilik Malt Sanayii 106
Gutherie, Gus 121

Hh
Hacker-Pschoor-Bräu 88
Hacker-Pschorr Bräu GmbH 148
Hainaut Province 130
Hainout 116
Halcyon barley 2
Halifax 44
Hallertauer 7, 139, 146, 147, 150
Hallertauer Hops .... 130, **142**, *See also* **Hops**
Hamburg 33, 36
Hammurabi of Babylon 22
Hansa Brewery 70
Hansa Lager 73
Hanseatic beer merchants 36
Hanseatic trading centres 33
Hanseatic trading city 149
Hanseatische Pilsenertyp 146
Hansen, Emil Christian 84
Harp Lager 91
Harpoon Lager and Ale 46
Hartney, Harold E, Lieutenant Colonel, dsc 8
Hartwall 85
Hawaii 55
Heileman 45
Heineken ... 59, 63, 71, 72, 76, 80, 90, 91, 98, 99, 101, 109
Heineken Tarwebok 99
Heller Bräu 152
Helles (Lights) 81, 147, 150
Henry the Eighth 31
Herbs & spices .... 6, *See also* Beer ingredients

Hersbruker Hops .... 133, *See also* Hops
Hilden Brewery 102
Hodgson, Mark 120
Hoegaarden 132, 134
Hoegaarden Gran Cru 138
Hoegaarden Witbier 134, 135
Höllhuber, Dietrich 113
Holy Roman Empire 79
home-brewers 3, 4
Hop bittering units 113
hop gardens 39
Hop oils 7
hop plants, male 4
Hop producers 32
hops 1, 4
hops, "pre-isomerized" extract 6
hops, Brewer's Gold 6
hops, Bullion 6
hops, Cascade 6
hops, Challenger (Wye) 6
hops, Cluster 6
hops, Comet 7
hops, copper 6
hops, Copper 6
hops, dry 6
hops, English cultivation of 6
hops, Eroica 7
hops, extract (syrup) 6
hops, Fuggles 7
hops, Galena 7
hops, German cultivation of 6
hops, Hallertauer 7
hops, high-alpha acid 6
hops, Kent Goldings 7
hops, late 6
hops, loose leaf 6
hops, New York 4, 6
hops, Northdown (Wye) 7
hops, Northern Brewer 7
hops, Nugget 7
hops, pellets 6
hops, Perle 7
hops, Saaz 7
hops, Styrian Goldings 7
hops, Target (Wye) 7
hops, Tettnanger 7
hops, Willamette 7
hops, Yeoman (Wye) 7
hops, Zenith (Wye) 7
Horticulture Research International 4
Hungary 79
Hunter, Captain John, rn 107
Hürlimann 97
Hussongs 47

Huzzey, Clem 5
hybrid 142
hybrid beer 140

Ii
Idaho 140
Idaho, hops of 7
Imperial Stout 84, 126
Ind Coope 11
India 31
Industrial Revolution 32, 39
Interbrew 132
Intercontinental 73
International Bittering Units (ibus) 113
Ireland 6, 24, 100, 125
Irish missionary monks 97
Iron Age 24
Iron City .... 46, *See also* Pittsburgh Brewing
Islam 28
Islamic armies 29
Isle of Mann Breweries Ltd 102

Jj
Jackson, Michael 65, 89, 107, 113, 147, 148, 153
Jackson, Michael 148
Jacobsen, Christian 83
Jacobson, Jacob Christian 83
Jan Primus (corrupted to Gambrinus) 154
Jansen, John Henri 94
Japan 38
Japan Brewing Company 55
Japanese brewers 15
Japanese-style Dry Beer 140
Jenlain 126
JJ Wainwright's Select Lager 46
Joseph Schlitz Brewing Company 17
Jugoslavia, the ex- 6
Julian, a Roman emperor 34

Kk
Kaiserdom Rauchbier 152
Kalevala 35, 37, 84
Karl i der Grosse 86
Katherine the Great 42
Kaul 145
Kaul, Wolfgang 113
Keil 33
Kent Goldings 7, 130
Kindl 133
King Christopher 84
King Clotaire ii 86
King Ludwig 88
King of Beers 81
King Pèpin le Bref 39

King Wencelas of Bohemia 37
King, Marcia 85
King, Philip Gridley 107
Kingston 153
Kirin 142
Köbánya brewery 89
Köln 118
Köln's 118
Kölsch 118
König Pilsener 146
Koninklijke Brand Bierbrouwerij 150
Korea 38
Krakus 93
Kriek 130
Kulmbach 35, 147, 150
Kumasi Brewery 67
Küppers 118

Ll

La Glacière 145
La Guillotine 132
Labatt 44
Labatts 124
lactobacillus 132
lactose 12
Lager 97, 106, 125, 144
Lager is king 139
Lager Stouts 153
Lager yeast 140
Lager, liquor-flavoured 153
Lagers 128, 140
Lagers, American, hop rate 8
Lagers, German 140
lambic 130
Lambic Vieux 136
Lambics 137
Le Micro Brasserie 87
Leffe Brune 117
Leffe Radieuse 117
Lent 130
Leopard Brewery 109
Lesse 116
Leuwenhoek, Antoine van 9
Levant 23
Liefmans Frambozen 6, 130
Lindeman's Framboise Lambic 10
Lindemans Framboise 130
Lion Lager 73
Louvain 81
Louwaege Stout 126
Löwenbräu 58, 88, 106
Löwenbräu (of Switzerland) 97
Lowestoft 122
Lubeck 33

Lueven 1
Luitpold of Bavaria 88
Luther, Martin 149
Luxembourg 100, 107
Luxembourg Province 116

Mm

Macardles 91
Mackeson Stout 126
Madeira 94
Maibocks 128
Maisel 139
Maisel Bräu 139
Malayan Breweries Ltd 59
Mallasjuoma 85
malt 4
malt, black 3
malt, caramel 3
malt, chocolate 3
malt, roasted 4
malt, Vienna 4
Mamba 65
Maredsou 116
Maredsous 117
Maris Otter-barley 2
Marktoberdorf 139
Martel, Charles 86
Matt, Nicholas 46
Mauritius Breweries Ltd 70
Mautner-Markhof 80
McEwan, William 101
McEwen's Scotch Ale 125
Mediterranean 23
Meiboks 151
Melbourne 107
Melle 132
Melotti Brewery 66
Mesopotamia 19, 25, 28, 104
Meta Brewery 66
Mexico 38
Michelob 80, 142
Middle Ages 81, 97, 117
Middle East 31
Middle Euphrates 22
Mikkro Bryggeri 93
Mild 119, 123, 127, 138, 139
Miller Brewing Company 15, 42, 45, 46, 130
Miller Genuine Draft 56
Miller Lite 140
millet 2
Minty 132
Moctezuma 47
Modelo 47
Modern Porter 124

Mohammedan conquests.................................. 22
Molson 44
Molson Brewery 44
Monasteries 32
monasteries, French and German .... 6, *See also* Klosters
Mönchshof Brauerei 147
Monrovia Breweries Inc................................... 69
Montreal 45
Moortgat Brewery 122
Moretti 91
Mousel et Clausen 98
München 12, 33, 40, 80, 88, 147, 148, 149
Münchener... 147
Münchener Lager 147
Munich 147
Murphy's Stout 126
Murphys 91, 126
Muslims... 28

Nn

NABLABS 1, 92, 98, 138,140, 141, 145
Nagykanizsa... 90
Namur Province 116
Napoleonic Wars 132
National brewers 140
Near East 29
Nebuchadnezzar 22
Negra Modelo 47
Neo-Babylonians.. 23
neo-prohibitionists 112
Netherlands................... 4, 6, 118, 145, 150, 151
New American Wheats....................................... 132
New Amsterdam Beer.. 46
New Brunswick... 44
New England.. 39
New England Brewing Company 85
New York state.. 39
New Zealand..................................... 4, 107, 108
New Zealand Breweries 108
Newcastle Breweries 101
Newcastle Brown Ale.. 123
Newcastle upon Tyne.. 118
Newman's Albany Amber.................................. 14
Newman's Saratoga Lager 14
Newman, Bill 14
Niedersachsen.. 149
Nigerian Breweries Ltd 71
Nile Breweries... 75
No Alcohol Beers-Low Alcohol Beers.............. 138
No alcohol/low alcohol beers 1
Nochebuena 47
Nordik Wolf 96
North America... 4, 33, 38, 39, 59, 125, 127, 141,

142, 143, 144
North American beer....................................... 143
North American Bock beers 143
North American brewers 12
North American Malt Liquors 140
North American Porters 124
North American Premium.................................. 140
North American Standard................................. 140
North Brabant.. 99
North Europeans... 30
North German style Pilsener **147**, *See also Pilsener*
North German Weissebier 133
North German Wheats 132
North Germans.. 147
North Trabant Provence 116
Northern Brewer..................................... 146, 147
Northern English Brown 123
Northern Europ 39
Northern Europe 24, 30
Norway 4, 84, 95
Norwegians 3
Norwich 33
Notre Dame du Sacré-Coeur 116
Nova Scotia... 44
Nugget 7

Oo

oats 1, 3
Oetker 95
Oirschot 151
Okells Brewery.. 102
Oktoberfest 88
Old Ale 127
Old Ales 138
Old Peculiar 127
Old Red Ale 138
Olde Heurich 46
Ontario.. 44
Oranjeboom 98
Ordre du Houblon 6
Oregon, hops of 7
Oriental Brewing 57
Orval 116
Österreichische Bräu 80
Ottowa Valley 45
Oud Bruin 114
Oud Bruins 115
Oudenarde 81
Oulton Broad Brewery...................................... 122

Pp

Pabst 42, 45
Pabst Brewing Company 17
Pacific Northwest 4, 6
Pacifica 47
Pale Ale 118, 121, 125
Pale Ales 118
Pale Bock 134
Pales Ales 126
Paris 145
Paris Brown 145
Pasteur, Louis 9, 83, 87
Paulaner-Salvator 88
Peche 130
Pécs 90
Pelforth 87
Perle hops 126
Peroni Group 91
Pharaohs 19
Pharonic Egypt 62
Philippines 55
Phoenicia 22, 23
Phoenician influence 103
Pierre Celis 134
Pils Ale 140
Pilsen 80, 82
Pilsener 81, 118, 122, 139, 146, 147, 154
Pilsener beer 33
Pilsener Urquell 7, 146
Pilsener, American 13
Pilseners 126, 147
Pilsner 94
Pilsner Urquell 82
Pilsner, Pilsener, Pils .... **146**, *See also Lager*
Pimlico Porter 124
Pinkus Alt 118
Pipkin barley 2
Pippin I (The Old) 86
Pippin II 86
Pitfield London Porter 124
Pittsburgh Brewing 46
plantains 2
Plzn (Pilsen) 33
Pocket Guide to Beer 113
Poland 79
Porett 91
Porter 94, 102, 120, 124, 125, 134
Porters 126
Portuguese 60
Prague Breweries 82
Premium Beer .... 142, *See also* Standard American Lager
Premium Lagers 142
Primus 63, 72, 76

Primus, Jan 81
Prinz Bräu 91
Prior Double Dark 46
Pripps 96
Profile: Adnams Mild 123
Profile: Arcener Stout 153
Profile: Beamish Stout 126
Profile: Big Lamp Bitter 118
Profile: Brand Imperator 151
Profile: Bräu Weisse 133
Profile: Bridport IPA 121
Profile: Carlsberg Elephant Beer 152
Profile: Celis Grand Cru 139
Profile: Celis White 135
Profile: DAB Original 147
Profile: De Ferboden Frucht 132
Profile: Double Diamond 120
Profile: Duvel 122
Profile: Frambozenbier 131
Profile: Fuller's ESB 120
Profile: Goudenband 115
Profile: Grolsch Premium Lager 145
Profile: Hoegaarden Wit 135
Profile: Hudson Lager 144
Profile: Jenlain 127
Profile: Kindl Weisse 133
Profile: König Ludwig 148
Profile: Larkin Best Bitter 119
Profile: Larkin Porter Ale 125
Profile: Lindemans Faro 136
Profile: Lutèce 146
Profile: Merrie Monarch 122
Profile: Münchener Hell 148
Profile: Oktoberfest Märzen 149
Profile: Old Jones 127
Profile: Paulaner Salvator 150
Profile: Pilsner Urquell 146
Profile: Pinkantus Weizenbock 134
Profile: Rodenbach Red Ale 116
Profile: Rosé de Gambinus 137
Profile: Sam Adams Wheat 136
Profile: Samuel Adams Boston Lager 143
Profile: Samuel Adams Double Bock 152
Profile: Sarah Hughes Mild 127
Profile: Thomas Hardy's Ale 123
Profile: Traquair House Ale 125
Profile: White Horse IPA 121
Profile: Winter Warmer 129
Prohibition 85, 143
Prohibition in America 30
Prohibitionists 108
prohibitionists 33
Prophet Mohammed 28
Protestants 108

Protz, Roger ....113, *See also* camra
Prussia 93
Prussians 79
Purnode 130

Qq
Quebec 44, 45
Queen Theresia 88

Rr
Raaf Bierbrouwerij 118
Ramses III 29
Rancé 32
Rastal 89
Rauchbier 139
Rauchbiers 153
Real Ale revolution 91
Real Ales 118
"Record of Darius" 19
refrigeration 148
Reinheitsgebot 2, 4, 12, 13, 36, 38, 80, 81, 87,
88, 92, 93, 97, 101, 102, 131, 140, 144
Rhenania Alt 118
Rhodesian Breweries Ltd 77
Rice, (Oryza sativa) 3
Ringnes 93
Rochefort 116
Rodenbach 138
Roman and Greek kings 31
Roman Empire 24, 31, 79, 103
Roman Empire 31
Romans 30, 34, 35
Rome (64bc) 23
Rosé de Gambinus 130
Rushton, Thomas 107
Russia 35, 36
Russian Empire 85
Russian Imperial Stout 94, 126
Rwanda 72
rye 1, 3

Ss
Saaz 122
Sahm 89
Sahti 3, 85
Sailer-Bräu 139
Saison 130
Saison Regal 130
Sake 3
Salmon, Professor Ernst 5
Samiclaus Bier 1, 97
Samuel Adams 46
Samuel Smith Imperial Stout 126
Samuel Smith Nut Brown Ale 123

Samuel Smith Oatmeal Stout 126
Samuel Smith Taddy Porter 124
Samuel Smith Winter Warmer 129
Samuel Smiths Oatmeal Stout 3
San Diego, California 82
San Francisco 140
San Miguel beer 95
San Miguel brewery 61
Sangster, Andrew 96
Sans Peur, Jean 6
Sapporo 55, 142
Sapporo Brewing Company Ltd 55
Saranac 46
Sauerländer Pilstypus 146
Saxons 24
Scandinavia 24, 35, 36
Schaffer 42
Scharl, Benno (German monk) 9
Schlitz 42
Schou Brewery 93
Schultheiss 133
Schultheiss group 73
schwartzes Pils (Black Pils) 147
Schwarzbier (Black Beer) 147
Scotch Ales 81
Scotland 125, 129
Scottish & Newcastle 102
Scottish Brewers 101
Scottish malt whisky 153
Seasonal Beers 132
Secularization Act 36
Sedlmyer, Gabriel 80, 83
Sheaf Stout 126
Shepherd Neame 96
Siberia 55
Sibra brewing group 97
Sierra Nevada Porter 124
Sierra Nevada Stou 126
Sierra Nevada's Celebration Ale 129
Sierra Nevada's Porter 130
Silesia 93
Sinebrychoff 85
Singha (Boon Rawd Brewery Co Ltd) 60
Sint-Pieters-Leeuw 136
Six-rowed barley 2
Skol 98, 99
Skol Pils 80
Slovenia 92
Small Beer 24
Smoked Beer 152
Sociedade Central de Cervejas 94
Société des Brasseries de Haut Ogooué 67
Sopron 90
South African Breweries Ltd 73

South African Brweries (sab) 90

South German style Lager ....**147** , *See also Münchener Lager*

South Germans 147

South-West Breweries Ltd 70

Southern English Brown 123

Spain 23, 97

Spalt hops 133, 146, 147

Spaten Brauerei 147

Speciality beers 153

Spice Ale 135

Spiced Beers 131

Spices **131-132**

spices 135

Spring barley 2

St Arnou de Lorrain 86

St Benedict 31

St George Brewery 66

St Idesbald Abdij 117

St Petersburg 94

St Sixtus 116

Staatlisches Hofbräuhaus 88

Starkbier 97, 149

Staropramen 82

Steam Beer 139

Steffl Export 80

Steinbier 139

Stella Artois 132

Stiftsbräu 80

Stille Nacht 129

Stockholm Brewing Company 96

Stout 13, 124

Stout 2, 94, 120, 124, 125

Stout Porter 124

Stout, Dry 126

Stout, English Milk .... 126, *See also* Stout, Sweet

Stout, Extra 125

Stout, Oatmeal .... 126, *See also* Stout, Sweet

Stout, Sweet .... 126, *See also* Oatmeal Stout

Stout, Sweet .... 126, *See also* Stout, English Milk

Stouts 126

Stouts 153

Strasbourg 153

Strohs 42, 45

Strong Ales 138

Stropken Grand Cru 138

Styrian 122

Styrian Goldings 126

Süddeutschen Pilsener 146

Suffolk 122

Sun Lik 61

Suntory 55, 142

Super Premium beer 142

Superior 47

Sweden 84, 92

Swiss Brewers Society 97

Switzerland 1, 24

Syria 22

Tt

't IJ Brouwerij 118

'T IJ's IJ Bockbier 128

t&r Theakston Ltd 127

Table beer 24, 145

Tacitus 35

Tafelbier 138, 145

Tangerloo 116

Tanzania Breweries 68

Tanzania Breweries Ltd 74

Target 7

Target hops 120

Tasmania .... 6, 108, *See also* Hops

Tecate 47

Tekal Brewery 106

Tempo Brewing Industries 105

Tennants 109

Tetley-Carlsberg 11

Tettnang 147

Tettnanger 146

Thai Amarit Brewery 60

The 1914–18 war 44

The Arab Breweries Company 105

The Dutch 129

The Economic Union (eu) 36

The Essentials of Beer Style 113

The European Beer Almanac 113

The Netherlands 24, 36, 98, 100, 116

The White Horse 121

Thebes 29

Thomas Hardy's Ale 13

Thomas-Bräu 88

Thuringia 148

Tiger Stout 59

Tigris and the Euphrates 25

Tilburg 116

Tim Web 128

Toohey's Standard Brewery 107

Tourpes-Leuze 130

Trappist brewery at Tilburg 98

Trappist style 117

Trappiste 116

Trappistenbierbrouwerij De Schaapskooi 116

Trappists monasteries 32

Traquair House Ale 125

Trieste 40, 80, 91

Trippels 117

Tropical 95

Tuborg 83

Tuborg Brewery 106
Turkish Export 106
two-rowed barley 2

Uu
Union de Brasseries 87
United States 2, 3, 6, 118
Ur-Bock 149
Us Heit Bierbrou-werij 118
Utica Club 46

Vv
Valhalla 24
Valley of the Kings 29
Vander Linden's Frambozen 6
Vanha Apteekki (Old Drug Store) 85
Vaux Double Maxim 123
Velten, Eugene 83
Victoria 47
Vielle Provision Saison Dupont 130
Vienna 80
Vieux Lambic 136
Vikings 24, 92
Villiers-devant-Orval 116
Vlezenbeek 136
vollbiere 146

Ww
Washington, hops of 7
water 1
water, brewing 10
Weihenstephen Alt 118
Weisse 97
Weissebie 133
Weissebier 133
Weizen-Doppelbock 134
Weizenbier 3
Weizenbock 133, 134
Weizenbockbier 134
Werner Brombach GmbH 134
West Flanders Province 116
West Midlands 5, 127
West-Central Asia 39
Westmalle 116
Westmalle Abbey 117
Westmalle Dubbel 117
Westvleteren 116
Wheat 1, 2
Wheat Beer 13, 135, 136
wheat malt 3
wheat, hard (Triticum durum) 2
wheat, soft (Triticum vulgare) 2
wheat-malt 134
Whitbread 80, 91, 99, 101, 109

White 134
White Beer 135
Widmer Alt 118
Wiegand & Copeland brewery 55
Wien 33, 40
Wien (Vienna) 149
Wiener-style beer 149
Wienerbier 149
Willamette Hops .... **142**, *See also* **Hops**
Willamette Valley 39
Wilson Mild Stout 126
Wine Line 35
winter barley 2
Wisconsin 39, 140
Witbier 135
Witbier's 135
Witte van Hoegaarden 135
Woodstock Brewery 14, 110
World Guide to Beer 113
Wrexham in Wales 102
Wuhrer Group 91
Wye College 7

Xx
Xingu 48

Yy
Yakima Valley 39
yeast 1
Yeast, ale (Saccharomyces cerevisiæ) 8
Yeast, lager (Saccharomyces carlbergensis) 8
Yeast, lager (Saccharomyces uvarum) 8
Yeast, wild (Saccharomyces candida) 9
Yorkshire 127
Younger, William 101
Youngs Brewery 109, 110
Yuenglings Pottsville Porter 124

Zz
Zaire 63
Zottegem 138
Zottegemse Grand Cru 138
Zywiek 93